T5-CRR-571

Women's Collections

Libraries, Archives, and Consciousness

The *Special Collections* series, Lee Ash, Editor:

- *Theatre & Performing Arts Collections,* edited by Louis A. Rachow
- *Biochemistry Collections,* edited by Bernard S. Schlessinger
- *Gerontology & Geriatrics Collections,* edited by Prisca von Dorotka Bagnell
- *Science/Fiction Collections: Fantasy, Supernatural & Weird Tales,* edited by Hal W. Hall
- *Banking and Finance Collections,* edited by Jean Deuss
- *Aeronautics and Space Flight Collections,* edited by Catherine D. Scott
- *Women's Collections: Libraries, Archives, and Consciousness,* edited by Suzanne Hildenbrand

Women's Collections

Libraries, Archives, and Consciousness

Suzanne Hildenbrand
Editor

The Haworth Press
New York • London

Women's Collections: Libraries, Archives, and Consciousness has also been published as *Special Collections,* Volume 3, Numbers 3/4, Spring/Summer 1986.

The Haworth Press, Inc., 28 East 22 Street, New York, NY 10010-6194
EUROSPAN/Haworth, 3 Henrietta Street, London WC2E 8LU England

Library of Congress Cataloging in Publication Data

Main entry under title:

Women's collections.

Also published as Special collections, v.3, no. 3/4, spring/summer, 1986.
Includes bibliographical references.
1. Libraries—Special collections—Women's studies—History. 2. Libraries—Special collections—Women—History. 3. Women's studies—Library resources—North America. 4. Women—Library resources—North America. 5. Women's studies—Archival resources—North America. 6. Women—Archival resources—North America. I. Hildenbrand, Suzanne. II. Special collections.
Z688.W65W64 1986 026.3054'0973 84-22529
ISBN 0-86656-273-7

Women's Collections

Libraries, Archives, and Consciousness

Special Collections
Volume 3, Numbers 3/4

CONTENTS

ACCESS

Representative Women's Collections

Compiled by Suzanne Hildenbrand

List of Authors

Susan Bellingham, Head of Special Collections, University of Waterloo Library

Bettye Collier-Thomas, Director of the Bethune Museum Archives

Ellen Gay Detlefsen, Library and Information Science and Women's Studies, University of Pittsburgh

Suzanne Hildenbrand, School of Information and Library Studies, State University of New York at Buffalo

Patricia Miller King, Director of the Arthur and Elizabeth Schlesinger Library, Radcliffe College

Mary-Elizabeth Murdock, Director of the College Archives and the Sophia Smith Collection, Smith College

Sarah Pritchard, Reference Specialist in Women's Studies, Library of Congress

Susan E. Searing, Women's Studies Librarian-at-Large, University of Wisconsin System.

Elizabeth Snapp, Director of Libraries, The Texas Woman's University

Beth Stafford, Women's Studies/Women in International Development Librarian, University of Illinois at Urbana

Edyth Wynner, Consultant to the Schwimmer-Lloyd Collection of the New York Public Library

Foreword

Had this journal existed twenty years ago, or even a few years ago, an issue devoted exclusively to ''Women's Collections'' might have seemed absurd. As we complete the editorial work on this issue, however, American women have marched 'round a corner of history.

There is a diminishing controversy over the place of women in our American past, in the present, and in the distinctly clouded future. Women's Collections, separately or as part of university or other institutional holdings, are still seeking definition, objectives, and variously projected goals, even as their use by researchers and students increases at a phenomenal rate.

Professor Hildenbrand has managed to get a fine variety of papers from her expert contributors. I believe that there emerges a point of view that will help everyone in this field to better define the intentions of women's collections and the purposes of their future growth, particularly with regard to the problems of acquisitions and bibliographical controls.

A noticeable exclusion from this issue is specifically lesbian collections, except for some passing references. Our first reason for this exclusion is that *Special Collections* is planning an important issue devoted to lesbian and gay collections within the next two to three years. Our second reason is that these collections still have too meager support, generally lack permanent quarters, and are not sufficiently managed professionally to warrant comparison with one another. I am, myself, sure that at least some of the lesbian and gay collections now in existence—and some that are being planned—will become much stronger in the next few years, their resources adequately controlled bibliographically, and that they will take their place among other gender-type libraries in short time.

Once again I want to thank our Guest Editor and her contributors—all women, it may be noticed—for their time and their devotion to the scholarship of their field. As the sole male contributor to this issue, I feel a justifiable pride of place among them as a very profeminist editor, the issue having been my own idea!

Lee Ash

Bethany, CT
August 1984

INTRODUCTION

Women's Collections Today

Suzanne Hildenbrand

Women's collections today owe their number, size and vigor to feminism, with its dual commitments to activism and scholarship on behalf of women. While libraries and archives have long collected materials by, for, and about women, they have traditionally done so for male-defined goals, such as building a male-centered history or training women for traditional roles. But feminism forces a shift to woman-centeredness, with the objective of expanding woman's public role. Recognizing feminism as the dynamic force behind women's collections provides a framework for understanding the history of these collections.

The development of contemporary American women's collections can be linked to the development of feminism in modern America. After the suffrage victory in 1920 feminism is generally held to have gone into a long decline, only to emerge again in the 60s. The 1963 publication of Betty Friedan's *The Feminine Mystique* is often credited with stimulating the feminist revival that has since flourished and matured. American women's collections, looked at against this backdrop of a feminist peak followed by a long decline and resurgence, show three distinct, if sometimes overlapping, phases. Each phase is characterized by a different activity. Only a minority of library collections takes part in each phase but it is a cutting-edge minority that sets a pace that others will follow.

The first phase is characterized by preservation, the second by growth and development, and the third by the building of consciousness. When feminism is weak, seemingly the vision of a few eccentrics or theoreticians, women's collections are few in number and have a limited agenda. Preservation of even a portion of the record is a major goal in such times. Paradoxically, many major women's collections of today can trace their origins to periods of low interest in feminism. With a mature feminist movement now some twenty years old, women's collections are numerous and have a varied agenda that includes active building of consciousness among different constituencies. It is interesting to note that in library history, as in general history, periodization devised with male activities in mind is inadequate for understanding women's experience. To many, the '50s seem to have been a Golden Age for libraries, while today seems a desolate period. It is quite the opposite for women's collections.

PRESERVATION

Writing in 1946, the aging suffragist Alma Lutz despaired of the antifeminist attitudes prevalent among young women of the day. Yet she found consolation in the establishment of so many women's collections in recent years. For Lutz this development meant that although the contemporary outlook was bleak, a record was being preserved that would serve as the foundation for a better history for women in the future, and therefore, for a better place for those women in their own society. Indeed, the 1930s and 1940s saw a remarkable trend towards the establishment of women's collections, as veterans of the feminist campaigns of the early Twentieth century anxiously sought institutional homes for their private papers, and other materials they had collected, in a world suddenly disinterested in, or hostile to, the cause to which they had devoted their lives.

Most influential among these activists was Rosika Schwimmer, Hungarian born but stateless feminist and peace activist. Schwimmer persuaded historian Mary Beard of the need for a center in which to preserve women's records. Accordingly, Beard launched the drive for a World Center for Women's Archives in 1935. As conceived by Beard, the archives was to be highly active in the promotion of what we would today call Women's Studies. Seminars, teaching, public lectures, sharing of research on women, and the task of linking scholarship and activism were to be features of the archives. The feminist consciousness of the day, weakened by the poor economy and the impending war, was unable to support the WCWA and the movement collapsed. It was not a total failure however, for it encouraged many individuals and institutions to preserve materials that might otherwise have been lost; and it contributed to the establishment of two of the most important women's collections.

The opening of the Sophia Smith Collection in 1942 and the opening of the Women's Rights Collection at Radcliffe College in 1943, both including materials from the WCWA, represent a major step. (In 1965 the Radcliffe collection was renamed for two major supporters, The Arthur and Elizabeth Schlesinger Library on the History of Women in America.) Both colleges went beyond the traditional commitment to institutional history by collecting the papers of their graduates and faculty, and moved toward building collections that would form the basis of a larger women's history.

Even earlier, in a separate movement, reflecting the segregated nature of the society, a small group of black women, including activist and educator Mary McLeod Bethune, had been working on their own. Their goal was to collect and preserve the sources for a specifically women's history within the larger framework of black history. Willing to cooperate with the WCWA, despite the racism of some white WCWA women, they continued on their own after it collapsed.

The collection of Dr. Aletta Jacobs and Carl Gerritsen, a Dutch activist couple of the late 19th century, although begun in another time and place, became Americanized and shows today the same relationship to American feminism as other American women's collections. After Gerritsen's death in 1903 the collection was sold and came to the United States, during an early period of concern with women's issues.

The preservation phase is dominated by charismatic and colorful activists—Schwimmer, Bethune, Jacobs and Gerritsen—and the scholars—Beard, Schlesinger—who appreciated the importance of their records to history. Most of the important action in this early phase was concentrated in the northeast. This region was not only the population center but also had been the center of organized agitation over the "woman question." Furthermore, it was the site of the major cultural institutions, including public libraries and women's colleges. These latter played a role of inestimable value in the movement for women's collections.

GROWTH AND DEVELOPMENT

Many of these collections languished for decades, poorly supported and understaffed. The upsurge of feminist consciousness, however, stimulated enormous growth and development of women's collections. Paradoxically, this very positive phase also stimulated dissatisfaction with the ability of traditional library practice to accommodate women's materials. Growth manifested itself in three major ways. First there was the creation of many new collections. Many were action-oriented, reflecting the demands of contemporary women. Among these is the library at Catalyst, a non-profit organization designed to further women's entry into executive positions; and still others, such as the Lesbian Herstory Archives, were formed to serve the interests of a particular community of women. Secondly, the old collections expanded enormously in size and scope. One marked trend that reflected the evolution of women's history was toward the collection of materials on non-elite women. The Bethune Archive contains not only the papers of the National Council of Negro Women, but also those of household workers. A striking transformation was that at Texas Woman's University where one of the earliest separate women's collections, of books by standard authors, grew to a major research collection. In Canada the collection of the National Council of Women grew so large that it was necessary to seek a new home for it and the University of Waterloo, eager to develop its holdings for the Women's Studies program, provided one. A third relevant type of growth occurred in the general collections where women's holdings became more important. One result of this rapid growth was the competition for major collections that were privately held. Since the transfer of the Miriam Y. Holden Collection to Princeton University in 1979 there are no major women's collections held privately.

Development activities, largely designed to expedite access and share resources, included the publication of catalogs, bibliographies and newsletters, the development of special personnel to assist users, and the microfilming of many collections. The catalogs of both the Smith and Radcliffe collections have been published, as has that of the Lady Aberdeen Collection, at the University of Waterloo. The catalog of the holdings at Catalyst is available online. Numerous local guides to holdings or bibliographies have been published such as the *Checklist of Holdings of the Woman's Collection at the University of North Carolina at Greensboro. The Women's Collection Newsletter* from Northwestern University, and *Nursing Archives News* from Boston University are typical of newsletters issued by women's collections; one describes the ongoing activities of a large general collection and the other, those of a small, specialized collection. Women's Studies bibliographers have appeared on the staffs of universities such as the University of Pittsburgh, Ohio State University and San Jose State University and the Library of Congress has added a Reference Specialist in Women's Studies to the staff of the General Reading Rooms. Microfilming has made the Gerritsen Collection, among others, more accessible; it has also created a new collection, the History of Women, consisting of material from different collections, that is widely available.

During this period there was a growing awareness that traditional library and archival tools were not always adequate to the needs of women's collections and their users. Subject headings were a frequent target of criticism, along with other cataloging and classification practices.

This period of growth and development, fueled by a growing feminist consciousness, was clearly a positive phase for both feminism and the women's collections movement. Women's collections began to serve constituencies that were more varied socially and geographically than previously. Not surprisingly, the role of the large public university grew. In addition numerous small special interest collections sprang up. Librarians, archivists and scholars play major roles in this phase. Greater experience with women's materials, and heightened consciousness have both shown traditional library practices to be frequently inappropriate to the needs of women's collections.

BUILDING CONSCIOUSNESS

In this last phase some women's collections pioneer a new role that actively promotes feminist consciousness and scholarship. While these collections draw on traditional practices such as outreach and networking, they set new standards for the whole profession. Probably best known among the consciousness-building activities was the Women in the Community project conducted by the Schlesinger. This project developed a consciousness of women's history in many localities, and also helped to create women's history materials in the form of oral history tapes and transcripts. The women's Information and Referral service of the Montclair (N.J.) Public Library, and programs such as those offered to high schools and colleges on women in medical history by the Women in Medicine Collection of The Medical College of Pennsylvania and travelling exhibits such as those of the Bethune are further examples of this kind of consciousness-building activity.

The office of Women's Studies Librarian-at-Large at the University of Wisconsin takes the traditional subject bibliographer role beyond its usual scope and involves advising and teaching many different groups in research centers and in the community around the state. The inadequacy of published guides and reference tools has led to the publication of the monumental *Guide to Women's History Sources,* compiled by Andrea Hinding (N.Y., Bowker, 1978). Several collections publish guides to Women's Studies. The office of the Librarian-at-Large for Women's Studies at Wisconsin will be updating the major scholarly bibliography of published materials in the field, Esther Stineman's *Women's Studies: A Recommended Core Bibliography* (Littleton, Colorado, Libraries Unlimited, 1979). The *Women's Studies Review* was begun by the WS bibliographer at Ohio State University. Many of the collections hold public talks, seminars and conferences such as "Preserving Women's History: Archivists and Historians Working Together, An International Conference" sponsored by the Schlesinger Library and the Sophia Smith Collection held at Smith College in 1984. Increasing attention is given to technical aspects of access, especially as collections automate. The Rawalt Resource Center of the Business and Professional Women's Foundation is developing new cataloging and classification strategies and Catalyst has developed its own thesaurus. Both of these collections collaborate with the Thesaurus Task Force sponsored by the National Council for Research on Women.

The leaders in the consciousness building phase include the great historic collections in the women's colleges, some major public universities and a few specialized collections. Librarians, archivists, scholars and activists all participate. They are actively engaged in seeking out materials, users and promoting research on women. They appear to be closer than ever to achieving Mary Beard's vision of a half century ago, of a new kind of "woman's college," where women can pursue the truth about their past and present.

CONCLUSION

The success of women's collections today should not obscure the limited and fragile nature of that success. There are numerous women for whom there are no adequate research collections and whose past and present suffer accordingly. These include, the Hispanic women of the US, Francophone women of Canada, Native American women of both nations, the poor and others. Many action oriented women's organizations lack adequate information services to support their efforts on behalf of women. Access services remain inadequate.

The link between feminism and women's collections is a source of potential danger, as well as a source of strength. As women's history shows, commitment to feminism has been cyclical. More difficult times may be ahead for even those collections that are flourishing today, while those that are marginal today may face extinction. It may well be necessary to remind another generation, as a WCWA brochure did many years ago, that "During the past fifty years women have fought for the right to work and achieve in every field of endeavor. But without the records there will be no history of this achievement."

* * * * *

The definition, classification and selection of women's collections pose numerous problems. Some of these collections stand alone in separate buildings, others are the contents of a file cabinet or two in rooms used primarily for other purposes. Some consist of books that circulate with the general collection, distinguished only by a bookplate. The only guide to whether or not a collection is a women's collection is if the sponsoring institution describes it as such. Most women's materials, of course, are in general collections.

Women's collections might be classified or analyzed from a variety of perspectives such as size, purpose, coverage, sponsorship and so on. The collections selected for inclusion in this issue are representative of various types, and are meant to illustrate the origins, breadth and depth of women's collections today rather than any one criterion. Exhaustive coverage is neither intended nor claimed.

The long effort to collect the records for black women's history is described in essay by Dr. Bettye Collier-Thomas, Director of the Bethune-Museum Archive.

Background on the modern American movement to establish women's collections—as well as information on women and peace work in Europe and America—is to be found in the Schwimmer-Lloyd Collection of the New York Public Library. It is here described by Dr. Suzanne Hildenbrand, with the assistance of Ms. Edyth Wynner, consultant to the Collection.

The two major women's research collections of today are described by their directors. Dr. Mary-Elizabeth Murdock, of the Sophia Smith Collection and Dr. Patricia King of the Schlesinger Library on the History of Women in America present overviews of the wealth of material in their collections.

Texas Woman's University, which awards more doctorates to women than any other American institution, has developed an extensive research collection on women and it is presented here by the Director of Libraries at TWU, Ms. Elizabeth Snapp.

In Canada, The University of Waterloo has developed a major women's collection around the library of Lady Ishbel Aberdeen. The collection is described by the Head of Special Collections at the library, Ms. Susan Bellingham.

An introduction to the great wealth of holdings on women at the Library of Congress is provided by Ms. Sarah Pritchard, Reference Specialist in Women's Studies at LC.

Turning from the traditional research collection to smaller, generally more action-oriented collections that reflect important new trends, Dr. Hildenbrand describes a handful that are influential.

Access to women's materials can be expedited by librarians, technical access tools and traditional bibliographies. Ms. Susan E. Searing of the University of Wisconsin system explains the role of the Women's Studies Librarian-at-Large in that system. Dr. Ellen Gay Detlefsen of Library and Information Science and Women's Studies at the University of Pittsburgh explores the problems of access in Women's Studies and some innovative methods of handling them. Finally, Ms. Beth Stafford, Women's Studies/Women in Development Librarian at the University of Illinois at Urbana presents important bibliographic guides to literature on women whose lives are particularly difficult to research, minority and third world women.

BACKGROUND READING

Bell, Martha S. "Special Women's Collections in United States Libraries." *College and Research Libraries* 20 (May 1959):235-241.

Lutz, Alma. "Women's History—Background for Citizenship." *AAUW Journal* 40 (Fall 1946):6-9.

National Council for Research on Women. *Directory.* Old Westbury, Feminist Press, 1982?

Ten Houten, Elizabeth S. "Some Collections of Special Use for Women's History Resources in the United States." *AAUW Journal* 67 (April 1974):35-36.

Thoreen, Bonnie. "Women's Reference Collections." *Booklegger* 1 (January-February 1974):18-21.

Turner, Maryann. *Biblioteca Femina: A Herstory of Book Collections Concerning Women.* New York City(?): Celebrating Women Productions, 1978.

Turoff, Barbara K. *Mary Beard As Force In History.* Dayton, Ohio: Wright State Univ., c1979.

Zavitz, Carol and Hans Kleipool, "International Guide to Women's Periodicals and Resources, 1981/2: Guide International sur les Ressources et Periodiques de Femmes, 1981/2." *Resources for Feminist Research/Documentation sur la Recherche Feministe,* X (1981/2).

COLLECTIONS

Library of Congress Resources for the Study of Women

Sarah Pritchard

Now estimated at almost 80 million items, the collections of the Library of Congress provide an incomparable wealth of material for the study of women. Books, journals, music, photographs, manuscripts and works in all formats are produced by women, treat the history and status of women, and furnish the general context necessary to an analysis of women's roles in society. Some previous articles have described certain holdings related to women, notably manuscripts and rare books;[1] however there have been no general surveys. This essay will attempt to demonstrate the breadth of the Library's resources for women's studies: print and non-print materials in the general and special collections, exhibits, events, services to special groups, and the place of women as staff and users.

THE INSTITUTION

In 1801, the Congress of the United States decided to establish a central collection of books to aid legislators in their work. According to the shipping invoice from the British supplier, not one of these first 728 volumes was written by a woman nor dealt primarily with the legal or social status of women. However, from this nucleus the Library of Congress grew steadily, and shortly before it was destroyed by fire in the War of 1812, the Library included Mercy Otis Warren's history of the American Revolution, essays by Madame de Stael and Ann Radcliffe, dramatic works by Elizabeth Inchbald and Stephanie de Saint-Aubin, and several titles edited or translated by women. The Library was rebuilt in 1815 with the purchase of Thomas Jefferson's personal book collection, establishing the broad intellectual scope of the institution and increasing the holding of women's literary works.

The history of the Library of Congress (LC) as an institution involves not only books, but people. Women have been active in many roles: as librarians, as patrons, and as library users. It seems that women have been using the Library for study since its early years; members of the public were admitted at the discretion of the Librarian, and Congressmen and Senators introduced their family and friends. By 1835, local society papers carried sarcastic observations on the use of the Library as "a sort of public boudoir, for belles and their favorites."[2] There is also evidence for more serious use of the Library by learned women; Harriet Martineau's 1838 writings on her American travels describe her visit to the Library.

The staff of the Library was fairly small until the opening of the Library's own building in 1897. Early personnel records have not been completely analyzed, but by 1896 the staff numbered 42 including at least two women. The following year, of 66 new positions granted, 26 were filled by women and ten more women were appointed in 1898. Details about some women appear in the 1910 annual report of the Librarian of Congress; of 359 staff members, 149 were women. Most were clustered in processing and copyright functions, a few in managerial and specialist positions. Many women catalogers had prior library training, notably from Melvil Dewey's New York State Library School. Anna Kelton was a professional librarian who worked at LC from 1900 to 1910 and became Chief of the Index Division of the Copyright Office. She left the Library after her marriage and, as Anna Kelton Wiley, became prominent as a suffragist, member of the National Woman's Party and the National Council of Women, and activist in many social and political groups. Her papers, as well as the historical archives of the Library, are housed in the Manuscript Division. The current status of women staff at LC is monitored by the Women's Program Office, discussed later in this paper.

The Library's public programs in music and poetry are almost entirely a result of the generosity of women, notably Elizabeth Sprague Coolidge, Gertrude Clarke Whittal, Katie Loucheim, and Leonora McKim. Recent annual reports show seventy per cent of the $5.5 million held in trust with the U.S. Treasury donated by women; $3.3 million alone from Mrs. Whittall and Mrs. Coolidge. Large gifts have been made by Mary Pickford, Lillian Gish, and other women.

BOOKS AND PRINTED DOCUMENTS

It is hard to know how best to proceed through the holdings of the Library. Administratively, some divisions work on a particular subject, others work with particular formats or languages, still others provide service to particular groups. Books and printed documents are, of course, found in every room but will be examined here in five groupings: the general collections, including the main stacks, government documents, and serials; the Rare Book and Special Collections Division; resources in children's literature; the Area Studies divisions (European, Asian, Hispanic, African and Middle Eastern); and the Law Library.

1. The General Collections

This enormous base of books, journals, and documents in all subjects and languages supports the bulk of day-to-day research at LC. The number of bound volumes is fast approaching 20 million; since works relevant to women's studies are found in every classification from A to Z, it is impossible to estimate their number as a separate category. Catalogs from second-hand and antiquarian book dealers rarely list books not already in the collection in some form. A sampling includes: hundreds of collective biographies; long runs of reports from such organizations as the National Council of Women, the Association for the Advancement of Women, and the various Female Anti-Slavery Societies; many accounts of travels and war experiences; 19th century religious tracts on the role of women. Again, the holdings of literature by women authors, academic and popular works about women, and supporting social, historical, and technical documentation in all languages are immeasurable. The reference collection in the Main Reading Room has over 350 works devoted to aspects of women's studies, and similar reference books are located in the Library's twenty other reading rooms.

Through its exchange and depository programs, the Library has extensive holdings of U.S. and foreign government publications, and those of international organizations like the United Nations. As with other materials, these are integrated in the general stacks, so works related to the status of women are not set apart; however, the documents contain a wealth of demographic and economic data concerning women. Covering all countries and dates, the newspaper collection is a highly-used source of contemporary accounts of individual women and of occurrences important to women's history, but comparatively few of the 33,000 titles are indexed. The collection of serials includes reports from women's societies, obscure 19th century literary periodicals, modern scholarly and political journals, conference proceedings, foreign language serials, and pieces from ephemeral organizations. Some are held only in microform, but a large number are still in bound volumes.

2. *The Rare Book and Special Collections Division*

Where the general collections represent an all-encompassing mass of knowledge for women's studies, the "special collections" by definition are usually segmented by language, subject, format, donor, or other category. Significant "named" collections have been described in Annette Melville's 464-page guide, *Special Collections in the Library of Congress* (Washington, 1980). The Rare Book and Special Collections Division has custody of the Library's most precious books and has the largest collection of incunabula in the Western hemisphere.

Among the personal libraries housed in that division (for example those of Woodrow Wilson, Thomas Jefferson, and Harry Houdini), the library of Susan B. Anthony ranks as one of the most interesting, not only for the history of the suffrage movement, but also for the social and intellectual history of the second half of the 19th century. The 400 volumes were boxed and donated to the Library by Anthony herself in 1903. The books themselves are not particularly rare but have become so because of the care with which Anthony annotated them in preparation for their deposit at the "Congressional Library." In her 1792 American edition of Mary Wollstonecraft's *Vindication of the Rights of Women,* Anthony wrote:

> Presented to the Library of Congress by a great admirer of this earliest work for woman's right to equality of rights ever penned by a woman. As Ralph Waldo Emerson said "A wholesome discontent is the first step towards progress," and here in 1892 [sic], we have the first step—so thinks
>
> Susan B. Anthony
>
> Jan. 1904 Rochester, NY

Anthony's library includes works by the most noted American authors of the 19th century and documents the often conflicting aims of suffrage, abolitionist, and other reform movements. Even more indicative of her life and philosophy are the thirty-three scrapbooks in which she methodically pasted newspaper clippings, flyers, programs, and the like. Following Susan B. Anthony's example, suffrage leader Carrie Chapman Catt donated in 1938 what she called her "feminist library," in the name of the National American Woman Suffrage Association. The library was the official book collection of the NAWSA and includes gifts from Anthony, Julia Ward Howe, Elizabeth Cady Stanton, Lucy Stone, and others active in the suffrage movement. Among the 912 items also are scrapbooks kept by Catt and the NAWSA. The papers of Catt, Anthony, and the NAWSA are held in the Manuscript Division.

Within the Rare Book Division are several other collections which, although not explicitly related to women, provide rich insight into the social and cultural life of women. The history of taste and the relationship of women to food preparation and household technology can be examined through the Katherine Bitting gastronomical collection. Vast amounts of popular literature are represented by collections of dime novels, pulp fiction, and playbills, which include both works written by women and those which exemplify social roles and images of women. The division's collections in spiritualism, the occult, and the Shakers support research in the area of women and religion.

The overriding strength of the Rare Book and Special Collections Division is in American history. The resources needed to study the history of American women are found throughout the comprehensive holdings in colonial and early American imprints, almanacs, and broadsides; the Confederate States Collection; the Wagner-Camp collection of western Americana, and several collections of anarchist, extremist, and radical movement literature. In the general stock of rare books are countless first editions by women authors, for example Phillis Wheatley, Margaret Sanger, Mary Edwards Walker, Sarah Orne Jewett, Mary Baker Eddy, and many obscure women writers of the 1850's.

Women have played a constant role in the history of fine printing and bookbinding. Not only do our colonial imprints demonstrate the work of women printers, but the 20th century fine printing collection has works produced by women like Clare Van Vliet, Carol

Blinn, Jane Grabhorn, and Natalie D'Arboloff. Artistic bindings by 19th and 20th century women are also in the collection.

3. Children's Literature

The Library of Congress has the finest juvenile collection in the United States and supports research, cataloging, seminars, and publications in children's literature. These resources afford many opportunities to study the childhood experiences of girls, their education and recreation, images of girls and women in children's books, and the work of women authors, illustrators, and editors in this field.

There are 18,000 children's books in the Rare Book and Special Collections Division, stretching from the 18th century to the present. These include "Big Little Books," pop-up books, and other items of unusual format. The history of the education and socialization of girls is furthered by a wide variety of schoolbooks: a full set of McGuffey readers, Confederate texts, 19th century Hawaiian texts, early Bulgarian schoolbooks, and more. Excellent primary sources in 18th and 19th century didactic literature include advice books, gift and poetry books, and biographies. Supporting these holdings are the vast general collections, with large numbers of books for children acquired through copyright. Novels from the Stratemeyer series and other girls' adventure and romance series are well-represented, as are popular and scholarly writings reflecting the history of childhood and the particular images with which girls grow up. The Comic Book Collection held in the Serial and Government Publications Division is strongest for the post-1950 period, and includes westerns, super-heroes, and romance comics.

Service to libraries, librarians, publishers and scholars of children's literature is provided by the Children's Literature Center of the Library of Congress. The Center's vertical files and card catalogs pinpoint such areas as "sexism" and "girls," and direct users to bibliographies on non-sexist book selection and similar topics related to women's studies. Biographical files aid in locating scarce information on women editors, authors, and illustrators, supplementing the reference collection in the Center's office. Staff of the Center have worked on exhibits, colloquia, and publications, many of which draw on works by or about women, for example an exhibit commemorating the centennial of Louisa May Alcott's *Little*

Women,[3] and a lecture given by author Eleanor Cameron in honor of National Children's Book Week.[4]

4. Area Studies

Research in a particular language group, geographical area, or socio-political connection is facilitated by the acquisitions, publishing, and reference functions of the four area studies division: African and Middle Eastern, Asian, European, and Hispanic. Because the scope of these divisions cuts across all subjects, essential works for the study of women are found in each.

The African and Middle Eastern Division has custody of all works in Hebraic and Near Eastern Languages and maintains reference collections in those areas and in African studies. The African Section has pamphlet files with materials about women and through its bibliographies of government and international documents has access to much statistical data on women's health and economic and political status in Africa. Among rare editions in the Hebraic Section are 16th century printings of the Tehinot and other early prayerbooks and liturgical works for Jewish women, complementing many other works for studying the traditions of women in Jewish religion and law. The section has works from Jewish women printers, bibliographies on Jewish women and on women in the Kibbutz movement, issues of *Lilith,* a radical Jewish feminist magazine, and the writings of contemporary Israeli women.

The Near East Section holds a variety of items on women and feminist movements in the Near East. Two significant items are the periodical *Fatat al-Sharq* [The Young Woman of the East], published in Egypt from 1906 to 1936, and the works of Qasim Amin (1865-1908) who was a prominent voice for the emancipation of women in the Arab world. Poets like Farugh Farrukhzad (1935-1967) and other Persian women writers are well-represented. From Turkey, the section holds writings of Afetinan, a noted woman historian, and Khalide Edib Adivar, a leader in the war of independence, both of whom were collaborators of Ataturk. In 1965 the section made special note of two new bibliographies of books by and about Turkish women.[5]

The countries of southern and eastern Asia are split among three sections in the Asian Division: Chinese and Korean, Japanese, and South Asian. The Chinese and Korean Section has extensive holdings from pre-revolutionary China and the People's Republic, with many works on women's history and status published in the 1920's to 1940's. A beautiful example of traditional binding cased in fascicles with block prints is an 1825 edition of Liu Xiang's *Lie nu zhuan* [Biographies of Model Women], a didactic classic extolling the heroic deeds and virtues of chaste widows. Other illustrated folios contain portraits of Chinese empresses and of ethnic women in native costume. The section has an up-to-date run of the main women's periodical of the post-revolutionary era, *Zhongguo Funu* [Chinese Women], documents from the national women's congresses held in similar official publications tracing the role of women in the development of the new republic. Also in these stacks are several shelves of books and journals by and about women from North and South Korea.

The Japanese Section holds books demonstrating the long historical traditions of women in that country; the most rare item may be the 1654 woodblock printed edition of Lady Murasaki's *Genji monogatari* [Tale of Genji], of which no other library is known to have a complete set. *Seito,* an early feminist magazine published from 1911 to 1916, is held in a reprint edition, and scattered issues of the modern magazine *Feminist* are available. Recently acquired are a ten-volume set of laws, regulations, and documents relating to women over the past century *(Nihon fujin mondai shiryo shusei)* and an eight-volume collection of representative works by contemporary women authors. Bibliographic studies are enhanced by the section's copies of library catalogs from the National Women's Education Center in Saitama Prefecture and the Ochanomizu Women's University in Tokyo.

The South Asian Section's specially-created card files represent items in the general stacks as well as in the Asian Division itself, and enable the user to locate information on the economic, social, and political status of women in particular countries of this region.

The European Division's strongest resources reflect its origin as the former Slavic and Central European Division. The division has custody of a large collection of uncataloged Russian brochures and pamphlets including works by 19th century revolutionist women. Specialists in the division draw on the comprehensive general collections of books, serials, and official documents from the East and West European countries. Interesting items identified in this category are articles about American farm women in Soviet agricultural journals; early 20th century commentary by Russian women on their travels in the United States; documents on radical social change attempted by the Communist Party in Soviet Central Asia; and numerous studies of the work patterns and education of modern Soviet women. The division is also able to acquire miscellaneous "samizdat" material, possibly including recent feminist works.

Through its publication of the *Handbook of Latin American Studies,* the Hispanic Division has an active network of contributing scholars, several of whom have done research in women's issues. Another of its major activities is the production of the Archive of Hispanic Literature, a collection of tape recordings of noted authors reading from their works. As of 1980, at least sixty women were represented, for example Nobel prize-winner Gabriela Mistral, Victoria Ocampo, and Elena Poniatowska. Vertical files contain biographical information for the authors included in the Archive. In the division's reference collection are the catalog of the Ibero-American Institute in Berlin, with considerable listings about women, and a card file providing access to a microfilmed collection of over 8,000 plays in pamphlets, many written by 19th century women and never published elsewhere.

5. *The Law Library*

Established as a separate department in 1832, the Law Library of the Library of Congress now comprises the world's most comprehensive collection in foreign, international, and comparative law. Although there are no separate collections explicitly addressing the legal status of women, the wealth of the general holdings is such that this subject can be pursued across diverse topical and geographical boundaries using a full range of codes, constitutions, official gazettes, treaties, and periodicals. Perhaps the first work specifically on women's legal position was the 1632 English imprint, *The Lawes Resolution of Women's Rights,* originally acquired with the library of Thomas Jefferson. In honor of International Women's Year in 1975, the Law Library mounted an exhibit entitled "The Status of Women: International and Comparative Law," displaying items dating from 1538 to 1975 and representing the major research division of the department: American-British Law, European Law, Far Eastern Law, Hispanic Law, Near Eastern and African Law. Of the research produced for Congress by these divisions, some studies relevant to women have been done on German abortion law, Egyptian divorce law, and marital property laws in Czechoslovakia.[6] Specialists in foreign law assist library users with such valuable resources as handwritten decrees of Empress Elizabeth and Empress Anne of 18th century Russia, and extensive documentation on the legal status of women in 20th century China. American women's legal history can be traced from recent Supreme Court decisions back to the earliest colonial records.

ARCHIVAL RESOURCES

For the historian and biographer, the crucial sources are primary documents such as personal manuscripts, organizational archives, and legal records. The Library of Congress has two major repositories of archival material, the Copyright Office and the Manuscript Division.

1. Copyright

Often thought of solely as a current processing center, the Copyright Office in fact has original records dating back to 1870 and the first federal copyright law. It is impossible to say how many unknown women are entered in the vast copyright catalog, the largest single card catalog in the world. The entries are indexed by authors, titles, and other claimants (publishers, editors, photographers, etc.) and represent books and textual items, graphic arts, video tapes, unpublished plays and music, fabrics, game boards, advertising copy, and an endless assortment of creative accomplishments. While the cards and original applications can provide dates, names, addresses and other data about individual women, the Copyright Deposit Collection retains many of the actual copyrighted items, especially for unpublished materials. These artifacts represent the total spectrum of images of women in American culture. No complete analysis has been done of the possibilities for the study of women inherent in this collection, but one example surfaced several years ago when 53 unpublished lectures given by Maria Montessori in the U.S. between 1913 and 1918 were discovered. A prominent Montessori scholar who has studied at LC for many years is preparing the heretofore unknown printed notes for publication.

2. Manuscripts

The Manuscript Division of the Library of Congress is one of the world's greatest treasuries for the history of America and of individual Americans. Comprising 34.6 million pieces, the collections gather together the papers of presidents and pioneers, writers and artists, organizations and families covering the entire scope of public and private life. Women's papers at LC were first highlighted as a group by Anita Nolen (see note 1) and were systematically incorporated into Andrea Hinding's *Women's History Sources: A Guide to Archives and Manuscript Collections in the United States* (New York: Bowker, 1979). A book-length guide to all of the division's collections is in preparation, and will include a separate essay on women's manuscripts. Several of the collections owned by LC have been microfilmed and can be purchased from the Library or commercial publishers, for example the National Women's Party papers and the Blackwell Family papers. Sources cited above and the *National Union Catalog of Manuscript Collections* identify the full range of dates, correspondents, and associations represented by each collection and document many smaller collections not noted here.

Manuscripts chronicling the history of woman suffrage are the most unified portion of women's papers. Complete records of the National American Woman Suffrage Association and the National Woman's Party span from 1890 to the present and are joined by personal papers, diaries, and scrapbooks of movement leaders: Susan B. Anthony, Carrie Chapman Catt, Lucy Stone, Elizabeth Cady Stanton, and Harriet Stanton Blatch. Also relevant are the papers of Julia Ward Howe, Anna E. Dickinson, Anna Kelton Wiley, and Cornelia Bryce Pinchot. Tracing women's movements after the 1920's leads one into the papers of the League of Women Voters, the National Women's Trade Union League, and the recently acquired records of ERAmerica.

Women's work in social and political reform movements interweaves many other collections of individual and organizational records: the National Consumers' League, the NAACP, the Leadership Conference on Civil Rights, and the National Council of Jewish Women; personal papers of Margaret Sanger (birth control movement), Mary Church Terrell (educator, civil rights activist), Sophonisba Breckinridge (social worker, peace movement), Belle Case LaFollette (suffrage, labor, and peace movements), and Maud Wood Park (writer, president of LWV). Many women active in public life also served in the Federal government and held national political posts. Further notable collections are those of Bess Furman, Agnes Meyer, Katie Loucheim, Clare Boothe Luce, Judge

Florence Allen, Florence Harriman, and Oveta Culp Hobby. The letters and institutional affiliations of these women bring the entire range of modern social, political, and cultural life into focus.

In addition to the exceptional collections of the NAACP, LCCR, and Mary Church Terrell (above), other resources for the study of Black women include the records of the Ladies' Auxiliary of the Brotherhood of Sleeping Car Porters, the family correspondence of Frederick Douglass, and personal papers of educator Nannie Helen Burroughs and Ruth Anna Fisher. Fisher, a 1905 graduate of Oberlin College, was connected with the Library of Congress from 1927 to 1956 and was the first American woman engaged in researching and copying foreign documents for the Library.

The Terrell and Burroughs papers extend to a discussion of women educators and philanthropists. Myrtilla Miner's correspondence reveals her work in establishing a school for free Black girls in Washington in 1851; Harriet W. F. Hawley and Anna L. Dawes were both involved with Indian missions; Maria Kraus-Boelte was a pioneer in kindergarten education; and Fidelia Coan served as missionary in Hawaii from 1834 to 1872.

The division's collections also portray the work of women in health, anthropology, and sociology. Again, the Margaret Sanger collection is extensive, as are the papers of Clara Barton and Elizabeth Blackwell. The Civil War drew upon the expertise of physician Esther Hawks, surgeon Anita McGee, and nurses Sara Fleetwood, Carrie Cutter, and Mary Ann Ball Bickerdyke. McGee was one of the founders of the Women's Anthropological Society of America, but in this field the classic records are those of Margaret Mead, recently opened to researchers. The papers of Helen Lynd include drafts of the sociological study *Middletown,* cowritten with her husband. Child psychologist Louise Ames wrote widely and cofounded the Gesell Institute with Frances Ilg, whose papers are combined with those of Ames.

Without knowing the future importance of their endeavors, many women travelers and pioneers kept diaries and letters that are now remarkable documents of women's experiences. Further Civil War observations were made by Issa Breckinridge, Mary Custis Lee, Josephine Roedel, Flora McCabe, and Antonia Ford who operated as a Confederate spy. Frontier life is described by Minerva M. Peters, Elizabeth S. Wright, and Elizabeth J. R. Burt; even earlier hardships are recounted in the 18th century diaries of Charlotte Browne and Emily Donelson. Travels abroad are narrated by Harriet Low, who visited China in the 1830's, and Mary French Sheldon, whose collection documents her writings and field trips in Africa from the 1890's to the 1930's. Many other collections record women's travels independently and with their families.

Professional authors, editors, and journalists leave papers tracing the very development of their art. Clare Boothe Luce, Bess Furman, and Agnes Meyers, mentioned for their political careers, also were prolific writers. Mary S. Logan, Gertrude Lane, and Helen Reid served as newspaper and magazine editors and publishers. Autograph manuscripts of Mercy Otis Warren's history of the American Revolution and of the works of 19th century Southern writer Constance Cary Harrison are in their respective collections. The galleys, typescripts, and correspondence of Shirley Jackson and Marcia Davenport are valuable for studying literary method, as are the collections of poets Edna St. Vincent Millay and Louise Chandler Moulton. Just announced is the acquisition of the papers of Muriel Rukeyser.

The work of artists is documented by the personal papers of photographers, sculptors, actresses, and musicians. The Manuscript Division has the correspondence of photographer Frances Benjamin Johnston, sculptors Vinnie Ream Hoxie and Adelaide Johnson, and musician Marian MacDowell, although their final creations may be elsewhere in the Library. The history of women on the stage is reflected in the papers of Frances Kemble, Charlotte Cushman, Jean Davenport Lander, Minnie Maddern Fiske, Margaret Webster, Lillian Gish, Ruth Gordon, and Jessica Tandy.

Because of its preeminent official role, the Library of Congress is a repository for the personal papers of senators, presidents, and civic leaders. The wives of these men participated in society at its most refined levels and have left a rich archive of first-hand accounts. The largest collection of a First Lady is that of Lucretia Garfield, but equally interesting are those of Abigail Adams, Dolley Madison and Edith Bolling Wilson. The Roosevelt years are depicted by the papers of Alice Roosevelt Longworth, White House social secretary Edith Helm, and housekeeper Victoria Nesbitt. Life in Washington, D.C. is chronicled by Anna Thornton, Margaret Bayard Smith, May McClellan, and Laura Crawford, daughter of the mayor of Georgetown. Significant for 20th century social history are the papers of Evalyn Walsh McLean and Belle Willard Roosevelt.

Manuscripts constitute the single largest body of unique resources at the Library, for the study of American history in general and of women in particular. Each researcher will bring a new perspective to the collections and will undoubtedly discover angles and directions not even considered in this survey.

NON-BOOK RESOURCES

In this section, those formats other than the written page will be discussed in the context of women's studies: microforms, prints and photographs, film and video, audio recordings, music, and maps.

1. Microforms

Microforms are generally a secondary format for the reproduction of information that was first issued as a book, journal, technical report, manuscript, photograph, musical score, or even a computer printout. As a subset of the entire library, LC's 4.2 million microforms address every subject and are housed in almost every division. Materials filmed from the general collections are serviced by the Microform Reading Room; these include several hundred 19th century works in women's history and long runs of classic women's rights periodicals.

Recently LC has acquired a number of major collected sets in women's history: *The Gerritsen Collection of Women's History,* with 3331 monographs and 260 periodicals; Research Publication's *History of Women,* comprising over two million pages and their new *Witchcraft in Europe and America;* and the archives of the Women's International League for Peace and Freedom. Smaller sets include Cornell University's *Women's Rights Pamphlets,* the *Herstory* collection of contemporary women's magazines, Greenwood Press' *Periodicals on Women and Women's Rights,* and oral histories of *Twentieth Century Trade Union Women.* Conference reports are collected for the World Conference of the International Women's Year in 1975 and the International Socialist Congress of 1910 when International Women's Day was declared.

The Microform Reading Room holds educational and historical filmstrips, although LC does not collect comprehensively in this area. Representative items are a 1922 filmstrip on "Personal Hygiene for Girls," a 1959 reel on "The Frontier Woman," and from 1954 "Through the Years: Jewish Women in American History.'' Newer titles are ''Ain't I a Woman?,'' six reels from 1975, and ''Women in Literature,'' four strips from 1976. Materials about women are also found in microfilmed dissertations, news and radio transcripts, historical documents from the U.S. and abroad, collections in labor history, slavery, and the Holocaust, reprints of plays and pamphlets, and archive inventories.

In the Manuscript, Law, and Newspaper Reading Rooms are microforms pertinent to their collecting areas. Government documents are increasingly distributed in microform and include many statistical and historical reports on women from the United Nations, the Agency for International Development, and the Joint Publications Research Service. Reports from the National Technical Information Service are serviced by the Science and Technology Division although their scope extends from women's health to their status in the workplace and economic characteristics.

2. *Prints, Drawings, and Photographs*

The Prints and Photographs Division estimates holdings of 200,000 prints, 50,000 posters, and 8.6 million photographic negatives and prints, with additional collections of architectural drawings, stereoscopic views, artists' catalogs, and political cartoons. Like the Manuscript Division, this division is so rich in resources for the study of women that one is limited to broad generalizations and selected highlights.

The divisional catalog and the specific subject index provide subject and name entries for a vast amount of individual and collected material including political cartoons, popular and applied graphic arts, lithographs, and photographs. These two files contain numerous headings with ''women'' as the main category or as a subdivision of another category such as World War II or Indians of North America. Cartoons satirizing women's social and political activities, photographs of suffrage parades and conventions, pictures of women's educational institutions, and countless images of women doing every kind of work can be located through these files. Both traditional and non-traditional representations from the 18th to the 20th century provide a first-hand view of the public and private experiences of women in America and in other countries. Black women, Korean women, Albanian women, women athletes, women miners, labor union members, women pioneers, nuns, and advertising models are but a few in these collections.

Women artists are well-represented in files of fine prints, illustrations, and exhibit catalogs. Some of the names in the 20th Century Fine Print Collection are Louise Nevelson, Mary Corita Kent, Minnetta Good, Peggy Bacon, Vera Berdich, and others listed in reference works on American printmakers. Exhibit catalogs are held for both famous and lesser-known contemporary artists: Kathe Kollwitz, Ruth Abrams, Isabell Siegel, Doris Caesar, Brazilian Myra Landau and Frenchwoman Paulette Helleu. The Cabinet of American Illustration from the 19th and 20th centuries includes the works of Charlotte Harding, Alice Barber Stephens, Anne Harriet Fish, Ethel Rundquist, Helen Dryden, and of course the idealized females of Charles Dana Gibson.

Women are also both creators and subjects of the pieces in the poster collections. Theatrical posters, political posters, advertisements, and items for other events and purposes are held by the division. Concert promoter Bill Graham donated 24 posters designed by Bonnie MacLean exemplifying the San Francisco music scene of the 1960's, while copyright deposits have brought in such material as motion picture and exhibit posters, ads for the suffrage history series "Shoulder to Shoulder," and travel posters.

The architectural resources include drawings and blueprints, photographs, records of the Historic American Buildings Survey (HABS) and other documentary projects. Although several new studies have appeared on the history of women in architecture, fewer of these women are represented in LC's collections. Some examples are Julia Morgan, architect of the Hearst mansion in San Simeon, and Maude Meagher who have buildings in the HABS, and Frances Benjamin Johnston who documented the architecture of the South.

The mention of Johnston leads into the photography collections, an ever-growing archive particularly valuable for the study of women. The Johnston holdings are among the most notable, including many donations of her own photos and those by other women photographers. There are extensive holdings of works by Gertrude Kasebier, Toni Frissell, and Dorothea Lange, and folios from Diane Arbus, Julia Margaret Cameron, Imogen Cunningham, Berenice Abbott, and Doris Ulmann. Acquired through copyright and gifts, the Master Photographs Collection also preserves the work of a large number of less famous women photographers. Some of these same photographers were involved in the government-sponsored projects of the 1930's and 40's, the Farm Security Administration-Office of War Information photographs. Classic images of American life were created by this corps of photographers and demonstrate a breadth of cultural documentation that has not been equalled. Lange's pictures of rural and migrant women are among the more famous in the FSA-OWI files, which are arranged geographically and then by categories of people, homes, types of work, community life, and so forth. Women are not classified separately but are integrated, and prominently visible, throughout the files which are open for browsing. The Library's American Folklife Center has recorded with photographs its various field projects, furnishing more recent views of American traditions and ethnic groups. Another open file of photographs is an alphabetically-arranged biographical collection, with portraits of all the noted women leaders, activists, scientists, writers, and social pacesetters; some are of women forgotten to history or have never been identified.

3. Motion Pictures and Television

Closely related to the visual imagery represented in the Prints and Photographs Division are the film and video holdings of the Motion Picture, Broadcasting, and Recorded Sound Division (MP/B/RS). Strongest in the history of American film, the division also has good collections of German and Japanese films and is building its resources for video broadcasting history. The newest program of the division centers around Mary Pickford, who gave copies of her films dating back to 1910 and in whose name generous grants have been given to the Library to support film screenings, seminars, and publications in film history. Recent commemorative events included the dedication of the Mary Pickford Theater in the Library's James Madison Memorial Building, a special series of Pickford's films, and an exhibit on her life and times. Lillian Gish has also contributed heavily in support of the Library's film resources.

The division's reference collection amply documents women as actresses, directors, and screenwriters, whose feature films and obscure shorts are in the collections for scholarly consultation. Two special card indexes to film and television periodicals have been prepared, both with entries under "women." Bulging vertical file folders yield articles on women and film, programs from women's film festivals, catalogs from feminist producers, course syllabi, and further ephemera of value to women's film studies.

Some of the earliest films in the collection are a reel from 1904 showing the "Parade of Women Delegates" at the St. Louis World's Fair, and a 1913 Kinetophone by Thomas Edison called "Votes for Women." Suffrage parades were a popular topic for early filmmakers, and news films about women are a good portion of the Theodore Roosevelt Association Collection. Card files by director allow the researcher to locate films by Leni Riefenstahl, Ida Lupino, Elaine May, Alice Guy Blache, and Lina Wertmuller. Still photographs and film reviews are also cataloged by the division. Television broadcasting is a newer area in which women are succeeding as reporters, actresses, producers, and writers. The image of women in television programs and the role of women as newscasters can be traced in the developing collection of videotapes.

4. Sound Recordings

The Library collects sound recordings on cylinders, tapes, and discs that play back radio shows, music, government war propaganda, literary lectures, and oral histories. Although listening facilities are provided by the Music Division, the recordings may come not only from that area but from the programs of the Hispanic Division, Poetry Office, American Folklife Center, and MP/B/RS.

Non-musical recordings include poetry readings and literary lectures presented at the Library by noted women poets such as Adrienne Rich, Audre Lorde, Margaret Atwood, Gwendolyn Brooks, Toni Morrison, Joyce Carol Oates, and Anne Sexton; writers Ursula LeGuin, Anais Nin, and Katherine Anne Porter; actresses Ruth Gordon, Peggy Cowles, and Jessica Tandy. Radio broadcasts bring out the voices of Betty Comden, Claudette Colbert, Clare Boothe Luce, Jessica Dragonette, Loretta Young, and stars of radio's "golden age" performing music, sketches, and interviews. Recent acquisitions make available debates and proceedings from the U.S. House of Representatives.

In the field of folk culture and ethnomusicology, the Library holds recordings made by scholars Laura Bolton, Frances Densmore, Helen H. Roberts, and Ruth Rubin, as well as those of folksingers and blues artists like Aunt Molly Jackson and Sarah Ogan Cunning. Special projects preserved songs of suffragists, mill workers, women prisoners, and women in the armed forces. Documentation on these recordings is provided by the Archive of Folk

Culture, which has available a 12-page bibliography by Holly Cormier entitled *Women and Folk Music* (Washington, 1978).

Standard disc and tape recordings are owned for all forms of serious and popular music as described below in the collections of the Music Division. Women recording artists whose private libraries have been donated include Rosa Ponselle, Geraldine Farrar, Alma Gluck, and Helen Traubel. Works from the growing domain of "women's music" are collected and demonstrate the involvement of women as recording engineers and producers.

5. *Music*

Sheet music, songbooks, historical treatises, recordings, instruments, and the ephemera gathered by performers are some of the formats used for the study of women and music. Women's studies in the Music Division can focus on women as composers, instrumentalists, vocalists, musicologists, teachers, conductors, and patrons. The reference collections in the division's Performing Arts Reading Room include several new works on women and music, providing biographies, bibliographies, and discographies. The division also prepared a card index to periodicals in music from 1900 to 1940, predating the *Music Index* and citing numerous early articles about women.

Through copyright deposit and special gifts, the division has an excellent collection of sheet music and scores from women composers. Unpublished music is retained by the Copyright Office. Works are held by 20th century composers Thea Musgrave, Lili Boulanger, Louise Talma, Amy Cheney (Mrs. A. J. J.) Beach, Margaret Ruthven Lang, and countless others. Ruth Crawford Seeger gave not only autograph scores but correspondence and materials documenting her life as a composer and folklorist. The Arthur P. Schmidt Collection is named for a music publisher who produced many works written by women, scores for which are in his collection. Scores from Ellen Taaffe Zwilich, in 1983 the first woman to win the Pulitzer Prize for music, can be compared with recordings made during performances given at the Library. Songwriters, popular composers like Carole King, and writers of religious music are very well represented in the collections.

The careers of women musicians and performers can be followed using recordings, music, manuscripts, concert programs, libretti, and the like. Opera star Geraldine Farrar left a large group of materials including papers, photographs, scrapbooks, and props. Singer Helen Traubel, pianist-composer Helen Hopekirk, and jazz singer Ethel Waters are examples of other women whose personal records may be studied in the Music Division. Many Black women's lives are connected with the archives of the National Negro Opera Company. The Performing Arts Reading Room also encompasses the world of dance, for example, photographs and papers from Martha Graham's original choreography for Aaron Copland's *Appalachian Spring,* which was commissioned by the Library with funds from Elizabeth Coolidge.

Published texts and typescripts are sometimes the only sources for studying women musicologists and educators, however, popular lecturer Rebecca Crawford donated her collection of iconography including photos, programs, letters and memorabilia about musicians. Rose and Ottilie Sutro gave documents tracing their attempt to found a national conservatory of music in Washington. The papers of Clara Steuerman, president of the Music Library Association, also come under this category.

Most of the women cited earlier as patrons of the Library gave money specifically for music programs. Gertrude Clarke Whittall donated major collections of musical scores and instruments, and funded the construction of a pavilion to exhibit them. Elizabeth Sprague Coolidge provided for the construction of a concert auditorium and the commission of new musical works, Katie Loucheim and her husband funded the public broadcasting of concerts, and Leonora Jackson McKim established a concert fund.

6. Maps

Cartographic resources can be applied in women's studies to look at women in cartography, to map demographic trends, to trace explorers' routes, and in analyzing land ownership and migratory patterns. The Library's Geography and Map Division has the books, journals, maps, and atlases necessary for such studies.

As early as the 17th century, American women were drawing maps. The division owns what may be one of the oldest maps of America produced in the country itself, a 1667 drawing of the colony of Virginia by Virginia Farrer, daughter of a cartographer. A recent article in *The Map Collector* used unique holdings of the division to describe the work of Eliza Colles (1776-1799), probably the first American woman to make copper plate map engravings.[7] Geographical journals in the collection are filled with new examinations of women explorers, scholars of geography, and cartographers.

Women's place as property owners is recorded in the extensive collections of county atlases, the Sanborn Collection of fire insurance maps, and land ownership maps. Frequently, women's names or pictures of their homes are inscribed on more ornate maps. Few of these items are separately cataloged, and those that are rarely have subject headings. One interesting map that is cataloged under "women" is a map of Israel produced by the Women's International Zionist Organization showing the location of child care centers, women's centers, and so forth. Much demographic and economic data about women has been interpreted in the form of national atlases and census maps. Maps have also been used to study urban work patterns, migration, and spatial aspects of women's lives.

PUBLIC EVENTS

The Library supports a variety of public activities such as exhibits, concerts, literary programs, and colloquia. Many of these have developed themes in women's history and literature or have drawn on the talents of women artists, performers, and scholars.

From 1965 on, the annual reports of the Library list the major and minor exhibits held each year. Often the occasion is the anniversary of a person or an event as in exhibits staged for the centennial of Anne Sullivan's birth (1966), the 150th anniversaries of Charlotte Cushman (1966) and Elizabeth Blackwell (1971), and the fiftieth anniversary of woman suffrage (1970). Manuscripts and photographs owned by the Library have been used to illustrate the lives and works of Edna St. Vincent Millay (1968), Gabriela Mistral (1971), and the ladies of the White House (1965). In 1975, a major traveling exhibit was prepared entitled *Women Look at Women,* displaying 150 photographs from 1890 to 1975. Several outside exhibits of women photographers have borrowed works from the Library.

The Poetry Office coordinates poetry readings, literary lectures, dramatic presentations, and the work of resident poets. Five women have served as consultants in poetry: Louise Bogan, Leonie Adams, Elizabeth Bishop, Josephine Jacobsen, and Maxine Kumin. In addition to those poets named earlier in the section on recordings, the Office has also presented readings by Alicia Ostriker, Marge Piercy, Lucille Clifton, June Jordan, Denise Levertov, Marianne Moore, Muriel Rukeyser, May Sarton, Alice Walker, and Eudora Welty. Joan Aiken, Catherine Drinker Bowen, and Agnes de Mille are among the women who have lectured at LC, and Kumin lectured specifically on women poets during her tenure as consultant. Recordings or transcripts are available for these programs. Dramatic presentations have been given using the works of Emily Dickinson, Hester Thrale, Lorraine Hansberry, and Anna E. Dickinson.

The American Folklife Center and its reference arm, the Archive of Folk Culture, make the results of folklore projects public through exhibits, recordings, and concerts. In 1977 the Center embarked on seven regional field research projects which almost always look at women's cultural roles and folklife activities, for example quilt-making, crafts, food preparation, and community relations. Field notes contain interviews and biographical data about the women in the studies. Narrative traditions, ethnic schools, folk music, and social ceremonies are other areas in which women play an important part and which are documented by the AFC.

Within the corridors of the Library, researchers and invited scholars have opportunities to meet at both casual and formal seminars. Those who use LC regularly, with assigned study desks, may join the Scholars' Committee and attend their colloquia; in 1979, so many were interested in women's issues that a separate Women's Studies Discussion Group was formed. The WSDG has informal meetings every month or two, where researchers can exchange ideas, scan new books, and hear short talks.

SPECIAL SERVICES

All of the resources described so far have been those available at the Library to the public and to scholars in general. The Library provides additional services to meet the needs of special groups and to distribute information through wider networks. These include computerized cataloging and referral services, braille books and tapes for the blind and physically handicapped, research and analysis for members of Congress, and support services for LC personnel. There are other areas of special attention; however, each of those listed here has some bearing on women's studies.

Cataloging data has been distributed by LC in card form since 1901 and on computer tapes since the late 1960's. Librarians and researchers may purchase cards or computer runs through the Catalog Distribution Service or may use in-house computer terminals to tailor complicated search requests in women's studies. One may use access points such as call number, author, and key words from the titles and subject headings. Because women's studies is so interdisciplinary, carefully designed searches can generate lengthy lists of citations; for example, a run done for this author covering 1968 to early 1982 produced over 10,000 entries excluding fiction. The Library's computer system also maintains a database compiled by the National Referral Center listing organizations from the U.S. and abroad that provide information resources in the sciences, social sciences, and humanities. The NRCM file has categories like "women," "women in—," "women's history," "women's rights," "sex role" and "education of women." The center has just issued a 40-page directory of the organizations dealing with women's health issues, *Who Knows? Selected Information Resources on Women's Health* (Washington, D.C.: Library of Congress, National Referral Center, 1983), edited by Monica Bowen.

Through a network of regional libraries around the country, the National Library Service for the Blind and Physically Handicapped produces and distributes books, magazines, and music on tapes, discs, and in braille. Titles available tend to be from mainstream literature and do include a few hundred on women's issues as well as many works of women writers. In 1979, two women compared the catalog of NLS/BPH to listings from major lesbian and feminist bookstores, identifying needs for further collection development.

The Congressional Research Service provides reference, research, and consultative services for senators, representatives, their staffs and committees. In each subject division are analysts who monitor women's policy issues in law, economics, science, education, defense, foreign affairs, and natural resources. Coordinating their efforts through an interdivisional team, women's issues specialists have produced seminars for Congressional staff on the "gender gap," women in the military, and women's employment prospects. Briefing papers and literature packets have covered the ERA, abortion, child care, women in the armed forces, and domestic violence. Internal publications distributed to Congressional offices present factual and background data on women presidential appointees, non-traditional jobs for women, and other topics as requested. CRS uses computer technology to index and monitor legislation, government documents, and journal articles on public policy concerns and has entered a wide range of citations on women's achievements, economic status, education, health, and legal rights.

Equal opportunity and support services for women employees are provided through the Women's Program Office, part of the Federal Women's Program. The Office contributes to policy development in affirmative action, non-sexist language, part-time employment, sexual harassment, and maternity benefits. The Women's Program Advisory Committee has members from each LC department and undertakes statistical analyses of sex ratios in job series, staff programs on employment, health, and similar areas, management training seminars, and preparation of informational resources such as a directory of local child care centers.

The Library's collections in all formats, its staff, patrons, and very history as an institution can all be considered resources for the study of women. Whether historical or contemporary information is needed, explicitly feminist or broad female experiences sought, the riches of this great library await.

NOTES

1. *The Quarterly Journal of the Library of Congress (QJLC)*, volume 32 number 4 (October 1975) is almost entirely devoted to "The Life and Age of Woman" with articles on sex differences by Margaret Mead and Rhoda Metraux; poetry by Gwendolyn Brooks and Josephine Jacobsen; "Women in the Era of the American Revolution" by James H. Hutson; "Afro-American Women" by Sylvia Lyons Render; "The Library of Susan B. Anthony" by Leonard N. Beck; a legal history of women in prison by Marlene C. McGuirl; representative images of women selected from the Prints and Photographs Division; and a major survey of women's manuscripts by Anita Lonnes Nolen.

Other issues of the *QJLC* contain scattered reports on new acquisitions of works by and about women, for example *QJLC* v. 31, October 1974, with an update on the Manuscript Division noting the papers of Katie Loucheim and Agnes Meyer (p. 250-254); *QJLC* v. 21, April 1964, citing some titles by women authors in the Near and Middle East sections (p. 152, 153); *QJLC* v. 34, January 1977, "The First Feminist Bible" by Madeleine B. Stern.

2. *Champagne Club* (Washington), v. 1, January 3, 1835:55.

3. Ullom, Judith C. *Louisa May Alcott: A Centennial for Little Women; An Annotated, Selected Bibliography.* (Washington: Library of Congress, 1969).

4. Cameron, Eleanor. "Into Something Rich and Strange: Of Dreams, Art, and the Unconscious," *QJLC*, v. 35, April 1978: 92-107.

5. "Reports on Acquisitions: Near and Middle East," *QJLC* v. 22, July 1965: 278.

6. *The Abortion Decision of February 25, 1975 of the Federal Constitutional Court, Federal Republic of Germany*, translation and introduction by Edmund C. Jann (Washington: Library of Congress, Law Library, 1975); Jwaideh, Zuhair E. *Nature and Scope of Marriage and Divorce Laws in Egypt and Iraq* (Washington: Library of Congress, Law Library, 1976); Glos, George Ernest. *The Law of Marital Property in Czechoslovakia and the Soviet Union* (Washington: Library of Congress, Law Library, 1981).

7. Ristow, Walter. "Eliza Colles, America's First Female Map Engraver," *The Map Collector*, no. 10, March 1980:14-17.

Women for Peace: The Schwimmer-Lloyd Collection of the New York Public Library

Suzanne Hildenbrand
with the assistance
of Edyth Wynner

The Schwimmer-Lloyd Collection at the New York Public Library is important not only for what it contains on the lives of Rosika Schwimmer (1877-1948) and Lola Maverick Lloyd (1875-1944), but also for its holdings on women's work for peace and feminism and on the origins of the World Center for Women's Archives movement. The importance of this collection has grown since World War II and the consequent loss of many European women's records. Furthermore, the renewed interest in peace work among many American women heightens its potential importance. Both Schwimmer and Lloyd were founders of the Women's International League for Peace and Freedom.

THE LIVES

Schwimmer's years of experience at the center of both the international peace and feminist struggles are reflected in her personal collection. She was born into a Hungarian Jewish family of comfortable means whose fortunes suffered reverses as she grew up. Forced to work to support herself and her family she became a journalist and soon allied herself with varied reforms including child welfare, labor organization and birth control. However, feminism and peace activism quickly came to consume her energies almost exclusively. Her pre-World War I activities on behalf of women included helping to found the Hungarian National Council of Women, and attendance at the 1904 Berlin Congress of the International Council of Women where she met Carrie Chapman Catt and was present at the founding of the International Woman Suffrage Alliance. Having promised Catt that she would found a suffrage organization in Hungary, she did so and insisted, (to Catt's displeasure) that men as well as women be eligible for membership. She translated Charlotte Perkins Gilman's *Women and Economics* and edited a feminist magazine. Her most memorable work for suffrage was her organization of the 1913 meeting of the International Woman Suffrage Alliance in Budapest. Thereafter her feminist activities were increasingly linked to peace action. For Schwimmer peace was the peculiar responsibility of women. In the last months of her life, in 1948, she sent a message to women gathered at Seneca Falls (NY) to celebrate the hundredth anniversary of feminist struggle in the United States, reminding them to fulfill the promise made so long ago, to "abolish war if granted political power."

In the spring and summer of 1914 Schwimmer worked in London as the press secretary of the IWSA and correspondent for several continental papers. She was anxious over the events in Europe and the lack of concern they elicited in Britain. She made a personal appeal to the British Prime Minister, Lloyd George, and came to the United States where she conferred with both Secretary of State William Jennings Bryan and President Woodrow Wilson about her plan for a neutral conference to mediate the war. Receiving sympathy but no encouragement from Wilson, she determined to stump the U.S. for her plan. She was a brilliant speaker and among those who heard her in Chicago was Lola Maverick Lloyd, Texas born and Smith College educated daughter-in-law of Henry Demarest Lloyd, the reformer and writer. Lloyd, convinced that, "I must do something for peace!" came to devote her life to peace work. She became a friend and supporter of Schwimmer and remained so until her death. Social reformer Jane Addams, too, responded to the pressure generated by this tour and launched the Woman's Peace Party, with Addams President and Rosika Schwimmer International Secretary. In April 1915 some 1200 women, from neutral and belligerent countries attended the International Congress of Women at the Hague in neutral Holland. At this Congress the Women's International League for Peace and Freedom, destined to draw the ire of red-baiters in the 1920s and McCarthyites in the 1950s, was founded with Addams President, and Dr. Aletta Jacobs and Rosika Schwimmer vice presidents. Disappointed by the lack of response from President Wilson, Schwimmer found a more responsive listener in Henry Ford. She collaborated with him on the Peace Ship venture which carried delegates, including Schwimmer, Lloyd and three of Lloyd's children, to a peace conference in Europe.

The closing days of World War I found Schwimmer back in Budapest where the new government of pacifist and liberal Count Michael Karolyi invited her to serve first on the National Council and then as Minister to Switzerland. When the Karolyi government was replaced by a communist government, she was invited to serve but declined. She was denied the vote and refused permission to travel abroad. When a right-wing government replaced the red regime, she went into hiding since as feminist, pacifist and a member of the Karolyi government, she was in danger of reprisal. Aided by influential foreign friends and with the help of a forged passport (which described her as a housewife) she made her way to Vienna.

Schwimmer arrived in the United States in 1921. She had numerous friends, and hoped to earn her living once again as a lecturer and writer. But she soon fell victim to the anti-red hysteria of the 20s. Accused variously of being a Bolshevik agent, a German spy and an adventuress who had bilked Ford out of a fortune, she found it impossible to support herself as planned and had to rely upon the generosity of her family and friends. In a celebrated case, hotly debated in the press, she was denied United States citizenship by the United States Supreme Court in May 1929. Fifty years later the New York Public Library marked the decision with an exhibit that drew upon materials in the collection, and that was attended by many leading feminists and peace advocates. Schwimmer had been denied citizenship for refusal to promise to bear arms in defense of the Constitution. (Pacifism is no longer a barrier to naturalization.) Although Justice Oliver Wendell Holmes argued brilliantly for her in a dissent in which he was joined by Justices Brandeis and Sanford, Schwimmer found herself not only without employment but without citizenship. Undeterred, she continued to speak and work for peace.

The 1930s was a bad time for women and especially for feminists as the poor economy and the darkening clouds of war eroded women's earlier gains. But Schwimmer's situation was worse. Without U.S. citizenship she could be declared an enemy alien if war broke out between the U.S. and Hungary. Her papers would be liable to seizure and possible loss. She had managed to retrieve her archives and books from Hungary after World War I, and had continued to add not only her personal papers, but also other relevant materials. Also, she feared that a general war in Europe would destroy the record of what women had done for peace and to secure their own rights; and she knew that this would make it harder to renew the struggle in the future. Schwimmer came, therefore, to advocate the creation of a center in the United States, safe from the ravages of war, for feminist and pacifist materials.

Mary Beard, to whom she presented the idea, was enthusiastic. However, Beard modified the original idea, and Schwimmer agreed. They decided that the archives holdings were to include the record of all of women's accomplishments, not only those in feminism and pacifism. Beard also favored a kind of women's institute or college where scholars would present their research on women. Beard aggressively pursued this plan for several years while Schwimmer's role was played down. Her lack of citizenship and the rumors that had circulated about her were a heavy liability. Beard was able to enlist the help and sponsorship of Eleanor Roosevelt, something Schwimmer could probably not have done. While many outstanding contemporary women, such as Amelia Earhart, agreed to contribute their papers to the World Center for Women's Archives, the Center was never realized. The approaching war which turned attention and contributions to other causes, as well as the numerous disagreements among the sponsors themselves, all helped speed the collapse of the movement. Schwimmer placed her papers on deposit in the New York Public Library in 1940; then she and Lola Maverick Lloyd gave their papers as a gift in 1942. In 1974 the collection, cataloged and arranged, and its printed material microfilmed, was opened to the public.

THE COLLECTION

As Schwimmer foresaw, World War II had a disastrous impact on women's collections in Europe. Hence the Schwimmer-Lloyd Collection is a major repository of European women's records for the late 19th and early 20th centuries. There is, of course, material from the days of Schwimmer's activity in Europe: papers relating to the Budapest Suffrage Congress, a complete set of the feminist periodical that Schwimmer had edited, copies of the original law (1901) to protect children's rights that Schwimmer influenced, a collection of children's books, and papers relating to the Hungarian Neo-Malthusian or birth control movement before World War I. There is also material smuggled out of Hungary in 1922 by Rosika's sister Franciska and their mother, illuminating the turbulent postwar years in Hungary. Much of this material is unique, as such items in Budapest were destroyed during World War II. In the late 1930s the papers of Schwimmer's maternal uncle, Leopold Katscher, were crated to be sent to her in New York. World War II broke out before most of the material was shipped but almost all of it was retrieved after the War. This material includes five hundred letters from Baroness Bertha von Suttner, written to Katscher during 1886-1914. Suttner was the first woman to win the Nobel Peace Prize. Full documentation exists on Schwimmer's role in the Ford peace mission and on the citizenship case. Three containers have material on the proposed World Center for Women's Archives. The collection includes press clippings, correspondence, newspapers and periodicals, handbills and pamphlets, books and photographs of family members and of persons active in the various movements in which Schwimmer and Lloyd participated. There are letters from Jane Addams, Emily G. Balch, Mary R. Beard, Carrie Chapman Catt, Zona Gale, Alice Paul, Anna Howard Shaw, Baroness Bertha von Suttner, Albert Einstein and Count Michael Karolyi. Organizational correspondence files include those of the Ford Peace Expedition, the International Committee for Immediate Mediation and the Campaign for World Government. There is also much on the suffrage struggle, feminism and disarmament, as well as an extensive collection of German and Hungarian newspapers from the World War I era.

The children of Lola Maverick Lloyd have carried on their mother's interest in peace, and their papers are added to the collection, as are the papers of various Schwimmer relatives. Also included are the papers of Edyth Wynner, longtime secretary to Rosika Schwimmer and now consultant to the collection.

Although one of the largest personal collections in the Rare Books and Manuscripts Division of the New York Public Library, measuring almost 1700 linear feet, the Collection is not yet well known. This may be due to the fact that so much of the material in the collection—approximately half—is either in German or Hungarian. European scholars have used the collection in recent years for studies of the German Protestant churches and the peace movement and for a life and collection of letters of Count Michael Karolyi. Edyth Wynner and Georgia Lloyd, daughter of Lola Maverick Lloyd, drew upon the collection for their book *Searchlight on Peace Plans: Choose Your Road to World Government* (NY, Dutton, 1944,

1949). Of greater interest to historians of women are the studies by Barbara J. Steinson on "The Mother Half of Humanity: American Women in the Peace and Preparedness Movements in World War I" (in *Women, War and Revolution* edited by Carol Berkin and Clara Lovett, Holmes and Meier, NY 1980) and *American Women's Activism in World War I* (NY, Garland, 1982) and the chapter entitled "Educating Women to a 'New History': The History of Humankind" in Barbara Turoff's *Mary Beard as Force in History* (Dayton, Wright State Univ., 1979); all were based on material in the Collection. Correspondence between Schwimmer and Addams has been microfilmed. Access to the holdings is expedited by a detailed inventory.

The Rare Books and Manuscripts Division is open to the public from 10:00 AM to 6:00 PM Monday through Wednesday and Friday through Saturday. It is closed on Thursdays, Sundays and legal holidays. Access to materials in the divisional Annex and storage area is subject to the following delay: materials requested on any weekday are available on the following day, except for materials requested on Friday or Saturday, which become available on the following Monday and Tuesday, respectively. Readers are encouraged to make selections in advance of their arrival, to insure their availability. Inquiries may be addressed to Ms. Susan Davis, Curator, Manuscripts and Archives Division, Room 319, New York Public Library, Fifth Avenue and 42nd Street, New York, NY 10018.

Towards Black Feminism: The Creation of the Bethune Museum-Archives

Bettye Collier-Thomas

On October 15, 1982, President Ronald Reagan signed into law a bill designating the Mary McLeod Bethune Memorial Museum and the National Archives for Black Women's History a National Historic Site. Located in the nation's capital at 1318 Vermont Avenue and known throughout the United States as "Council House," this site served as the first national headquarters of the National Council of Negro Women (NCNW) and the last official Washington, D.C. residence of Mary McLeod Bethune. Currently the site houses a museum and archives whose focus is black women's history.[1]

Black women's history and the Bethune Museum-Archives owe a special debt to the foresight and dedication of Mary McLeod Bethune. Although women's history and black history have recently come of age, the thrust to legitimate, define and document developments in these areas, has roots in the 19th century. Early efforts to preserve black women's records and to interpret their life and history was part of a larger movement to document black history which occurred in the early 20th century.[2]

This essay will trace the history of the Bethune Museum-Archives, an institution which developed as a result of Mary McLeod Bethune's interest in black and women's history and the National Council of Negro Women's collaboration with Mary Beard and the World Center for Women's Archives. These two elements combined to birth an idea which was sustained for over forty years. The NCNW's promotion of black women's history and their efforts to develop an institution to collect, preserve, exhibit and interpret that history was part of the larger feminist thrust of Bethune and the organization.

In their quest for data regarding the genesis of women's history, historians frequently cite Mary Beard as one of the earliest proponents of the research and writing of women's history and as the moving force for the organizing of the World Center for Women's Archives (WCWA). Until recently little recognition was given to the efforts of black women to collect and preserve the history of their individual and collective achievements as well as those of the race. Almost a decade before Rosika Schwimmer's proposal for a "feminist pacifist archive" became the basis for organizing a World Center for Women's Archives, Mary McLeod Bethune and the National Association for Colored Women (NACW) were concerned about the collection of materials pertaining to black women of achievement and their organizational efforts. Encouraged by Carter G. Woodson, who founded the Association for the Study of Negro Life and History (ASNLH) in 1916, the NACW focused upon the additional need for black women's history.[3]

The National Council of Negro Women has been the major advocate for black women and black women's history for over 40 years. Mary McLeod Bethune understood the importance of history and was determined to see that black women and black men received recognition for their contributions to American life and history. In 1936, one year after she founded the NCNW, Bethune was elected president of the Association for the Study of Negro Life and History, a position she held for fourteen years. As president of the major national black history organization, she was a key advocate of black history.[4] Prior to that date, and as early as 1927, Bethune as the president of the National Association of Colored Women, argued forcefully for the collection and preservation of "anything of historical value pertaining to colored women in general and especially of the National Association of Colored Women."[5] Bethune's promotion of the NACW's history, association with Carter G. Woodson and the ASNLH, and efforts to unify black women under the aegis of the NCNW are key elements that informed her later involvement with Mary Beard and the World Center for Women's Archives.

The WCWA was organized in 1935. In an initial letter, signed by Mary Beard and five other prominent women, individuals were invited to become Sponsors of WCWA. The WCWA organizational structure included a Board of Directors, which was the key decision-making body, and an extensive list of Sponsors, who served in an advisory capacity. Sponsors attended the annual meetings, however, it is not clear that they participated in the deliberations of the Board of Directors.[6]

Although Beard contacted a few black women to discuss their achievements and to ascertain the nature and availability of their papers, until late 1938 little effort was made by either Beard or the WCWA to involve black women and their organizations in the development of the WCWA. During the WCWA's first two years, its board concentrated on developing financial support and recruiting prominent white women to be Sponsors. Economic stringency and a lack of enthusiasm for women's history hampered the WCWA's fund raising and recruitment efforts. It took three years for the WCWA to attract 100 Sponsors, all white. After the first annual meeting, held on November 14, 1938, black women were invited to serve as Sponsors.[7]

The WCWA lasted for five years. During its existence it maintained an all-white Board of Directors. Mary McLeod Bethune and Mrs. James Weldon Johnson were the only black women to serve as Sponsors.[8] WCWA's first contact with Bethune and the NCNW was in November 1938, when Marjorie White, a WCWA representative attended the NCNW convention held in New York and circulated among the delegates to enlist NCNW support for WCWA. It appears that through conversation with several key NCNW board members, White indicated the need for a "Negro Women's Archives Committee of the World Center for Women's Archives" and suggested that Mrs. Bethune serve as the chair.[9]

Mrs. Bethune learned of White's presence at the NCNW Convention and of the WCWA's invitation after the Convention's close. In December, 1938, Bethune pledged the support of NCNW and informed White that she would work with the proposed committee, but preferred that Mrs. Juanita Jackson Mitchell serve as committee chairperson. Finding it difficult to travel from St. Paul, Minnesota to the WCWA offices in New York city, Mitchell resigned within months. For a short time, until Bethune could identify "the finest representative available" from the standpoint of experience in library collections, Sue Bailey Thurman filled the position. It was on Thurman's recommendation that Bethune invited Mrs. Dorothy Porter to serve as chair of the committee. Bethune instructed Porter to develop a "representative exhibition" of materials pertaining to black women, to be displayed within one week at a dinner sponsored by the all white Washington, D.C., WCWA unit, which initially was seen as the group which would coordinate with the Negro Committee.[10]

Mary Beard and other WCWA administrators were concerned

that the records of women of all races, creeds and political persuasion in America and in the world be represented in the proposed Archives. Recognizing that "the American Negro woman has played important roles in the social history of America," WCWA officials stressed that "far less is known about her public interests by and large than should be the case." They sought records and documents "referring to her participation in every field and period of our history." Marjorie White suggested that the membership of the Negro Women's Committee include women representative of all geographical areas, women who were authorities on black women's history and women who were leaders in fields in "education, business, engineering, science, exploration, theatre, social work, art, nursing, banking, etc."[11]

The choice of the NCNW as the conduit for collecting materials relating to black women's history raises several questions. Did WCWA consider the NACW for involvement in this project? Does the choice of the NCNW indicate a decline in the significance of the NACW and/or the escalation of Bethune's personal power? Although Beard had consulted with Mary Church Terrell about the project several years prior to the NCNW involvement, why wasn't Terrell, the first president of the NACW and a woman of considerable influence, invited to membership on the board and to broker an invitation to the NACW? Why was the NCNW the only national black woman's organization invited to work with the WCWA project? Why did Mary Beard and the WCWA choose to include only two black women as Sponsors and no black women on the Executive Board? It will not be possible to answer all of these questions in this essay, however, historians must begin to explore in greater depth the historical relationships between black and white women, particularly their efforts at interracial cooperation.

The NCNW, like the WCWA, was founded in 1935. While the organization was certainly favored by having Mary McLeod Bethune as founder and first president, it did not have the record of achievement or level of membership reflected in the NACW. Founded in 1896, the NACW was the oldest and most distinguished organization of black women. The creme de la creme of black female leadership had dominated the organization's administrative positions as well as the membership. This was certainly known to Mary Beard and many other white women who served as Directors and Sponsors of the WCWA. Admittedly, the founding of other national organizations of black women affected and in some ways eroded the once all powerful position the NACW held, but in 1938, it was still one of the most revered and highly respected organizations of black women. The key to understanding the WCWA's selection of the NCNW as the organization to identify and collect the historical papers of black women appears to lie more in the perception than the reality of NCNW's power and in the charismatic leadership and influence of Mary McLeod Bethune. Of additional importance was the close relationship of Mary McLeod Bethune and Eleanor Roosevelt, a WCWA Sponsor.[12]

By 1935 Mary McLeod Bethune had achieved national recognition as a leader in black educational, political, and social circles. Her success as the founder and first president of Bethune Cookman College, her visibility as the president of NACW, her recognition by key white political and economic figures provided a foundation for the launching of the final and most important phase of her career. The last 20 years of Bethune's life saw her rise to a level of fame and recognition in America, and throughout the world, unknown to most black women and men in America. The years 1935 to 1955 include the second greatest accomplishment of her life, the founding of the National Council of Negro Women, a new and unfettered vehicle that could be structured to achieve most of her personal and professional goals.[13]

After a careful assessment of the American society, black organizations and the problems of race and gender in America, Bethune concluded that there was a need for an organization that would unify and solidify black women into a powerful, active force that could effectively alter the way Afro-Americans were perceived and dealt with. She concluded that she could maximize the power of black women by creating an organization similar to that of the white-controlled National Council of Women. The NCNW was the first black "organization of organizations" and the first national coalition of national black women's organizations. While the NACW had succeeded in building a network of local clubs into state and regional federations, the NCNW proposed to unify national organizations of black women. In fact through the structure of the NCNW, Bethune proposed nothing less than the cooptation of the membership and influence of even the NACW. Initially, Mary Church Terrell and Charlotte Hawkins Brown were fearful that the new organization would eventually eclipse the NACW. Their fears were justified.

At its founding the NCNW included representatives of 29 black women's organizations, 14 of which became affiliates. Through these organizations' collective memberships, Bethune could easily claim an "outreach" to 500,000 black women. Thus the NCNW and Bethune had in effect created a new power base from which black women could articulate their concerns and act as a unit. By 1938, using Washington, D.C., as her base of operations, and proceeding under several official titles, Bethune was one of the most highly recognized and sought after speakers in America. She travelled extensively, lecturing to diverse groups of black and white Americans and meeting with philanthropists and other influential whites who could aid her in the identification of financial and other support for her many projects. In all of these contacts she stressed that the NCNW represented 500,000 black women.[14]

Bethune was accurate in her projection of the number of black women represented through the membership of affiliate organizations, however, the public, particularly white Americans, perceived the NCNW and Bethune as more powerful than they actually were. This perception of NCNW's power was particularly attractive to predominantly white organizations like the WCWA that sought to alleviate the problem of working with multiple black organizations by identifying one representative of a diverse constituency. However, had the WCWA made a close analysis of the NCNW's affiliates, it would have discovered that while Bethune had carefully worked to include key NACW women on the NCNW board and frequently structured committees to include women highly recognized in the NACW, the reality was that the NACW gave tacit recognition and practically no support to the programs and activities of NCNW. Even if the NACW and the NCNW were noncompetitive organizations, there was little likelihood that the NACW would have considered donating their records to the WCWA. Following Bethune's earlier admonition, the NACW continued to collect and assemble its records at the national headquarters and in 1933 published *Lifting As We Climb,* a history of the organization.[15]

The failure of Beard and the WCWA's board to identify and involve diverse national associations of Afro-American women in the organization precluded any full and complete documentation of black women's history. Considering the prevailing attitudes regarding race and the continuing problems and tensions in the women's movement, especially when the question of including more than token black women was broached, it is likely that Beard and the WCWA board chose to include only two black women as Sponsors and the NCNW as an organization, to avoid the conflict of race. Citing prominent WCWA sponsors and board members such as Mrs. Vincent Astor, Mrs. Franklin D. Roosevelt, Pearl Buck, Dorothy Canfield Fisher, Fala La Follette, Mary Beard and others including Dorothy Porter, chair of the Negro Women's Archives Committee, felt that "these women had been democratic enough to include Negro women in their organization." Many of the women's organizations represented on the lists of sponsors and board of directors had chosen to exclude black women from membership in their organizations. Old wounds engendered by issues of politics and race had not healed.[16]

Dorothy Porter worked with the NCNW from December 1939 to 1942 serving first as the chair of the "Negro Women's Committee of the World Center for Women's Archives," and later as the National Chairman of the NCNW's Committee on Archives. As the chair of the WCWA's Negro Women's Committee she successfully organized two exhibitions that included documents and artifacts relating to black women. The first exhibition, held in December 1939 under the auspices of the Washington unit of the WCWA, consisted "of original music compositions, manuscript diaries, manuscript letters and printed books," materials on loan from the Howard University Moorland Foundation, of which Mrs. Porter was the Supervisor. The second exhibition, displayed at the American Negro Exposition held in Chicago from July to September, 1940, received considerable attention.[17]

Mrs. Bethune identified four women, Mary Church Terrell, Elizabeth Carter Brooks, Sue Bailey Thurman and Juanita Mitchell, who were invited by Dorothy Porter to serve on the WCWA's Negro Women's Committee. Terrell and Brooks were very prominent women. Like Bethune, both had served as president of the NACW.[18] Thurman and Mitchell were young women affiliated with the NCNW. Thurman, the first editor of the *Aframerican Woman's Journal,* a publication launched in conjunction with the project, was a key figure in the articulation of the need to document black women's history.

Mitchell, an attorney from a prominent Maryland family, was introduced to the work of the NAACP and other civil rights organizations through her mother, Lillie Carrol Jackson, who was one of the first women to serve in a major administrative position in the National Association for the Advancement of Colored People (NAACP) at the state level. Terrell and Brooks were important historical figures who owned extensive collections of manuscripts, photographs and artifacts. Even though Terrell and Brooks served on the Committee and were invited to submit materials for the Women's exhibit at the Negro Exposition in Chicago, there is no indication that they were interested in placing their collections in the WCWA. Accepting Mrs. Porter's invitation to participate on the WCWA Negro Women's Committee, Terrell stated that her papers were so voluminous that she was "bewildered and confused." She requested a meeting with Mrs. Porter at the Moorland Foundation to discuss the value of her collection.[19]

As originally conceived, Porter and her committee were to work with the Washington unit of the WCWA, however, within two months of her appointment, Porter wrote Mary Beard about the "confusion" in the Washington unit. There were questions about the leadership provided by the president, Mrs. Emil Hurja. After the resignation of Mrs. Hurja and the collapse of the Washington WCWA unit, Beard informed Porter that the "Negro women" would work directly with her. Beard suggested that the problems of the Washington unit were related to the dissatisfaction of some of the members who wanted the WCWA to be located "at the capital" instead of New York city.

Mary Beard not only informed Dorothy Porter that she would work directly with her but offered her "an independent position as a direct member of my committee on Archives with your fine committee as the group which you will represent on my committee." Several questions are suggested by this statement. Was Bethune informed or consulted about this change in Porter's status? Was Beard suggesting that Porter represent the committee as an official group, not the NCNW? Was Beard trying to remove the Negro Women's Committee from the NCNW? Was there a conflict rooted in the committee's title, Negro Women's Committee of the World Center for Women's Archives, which did not communicate a direct relationship with the NCNW? Was there discussion among NCNW members and others about the need to develop an archives for black women?[20]

There is no indication that Bethune knew about Beard's efforts to change the locus of control for the Negro Women's Committee from the NCNW to the WCWA. However, she was concerned that the public know of the committee's relationship to the NCNW and on one occasion informed Dorothy Porter that she should state that she was the chair of the NCNW's Negro Women's Committee on Archives. However, failure of the WCWA by September, 1940 forestalled a power struggle for control of the committee.[21]

Prior to that time, Beard was aware of the suggestion that black women should develop their own archives, but there is little written evidence of the attitudes and discussions of NCNW members and other black women about the need to develop a national archives for black women. Beard was sensitive to any suggestion that the records of any group of women be placed in any repository other than that of the WCWA. One indication of the concern about the papers of black women being placed in a center that black people controlled was the response of Arden H. Duane to Mary Beard's suggestion that the Chicago black press covering the Negro Exposition give recognition to the black women's exhibit and mention that these and other materials were being collected for the WCWA. Duane, a member of the Associated Negro Press of Chicago asked Beard what kind of work could she suggest for him that "would be of greater help than work he has done in promoting the recognition of negro (sic) women's qualities and spurring their ambition to develop further." In relating this incident to Dorothy Porter, Beard stated "He thinks that perhaps he should try to organize a World Center for Negro Women." Beard's response was "evidently he did not know that our WCWA is reaching out for archives of negro (sic) women as for archives of all other women."[22]

Dorothy Porter accepted Mary Beard's invitation to serve as an independent on the WCWA's headquarters committee. Overjoyed by the acceptance, Beard began to define Porter's role with the WCWA committee. She suggested that membership on the Negro Women's Committee should be enlarged to include more than 10 persons since Porter would be covering the "whole country," and that she should begin to solicit direct memberships from black women for the WCWA. Clarifying her position, Beard told Porter, "I feel sure that by drawing Negro women, interested in the proposed great women's archive, directly into relation with headquarters, all sorts of irritations and delays which might otherwise arise through other procedures can be avoided—and avoided to the best and most permanent interests of Negro women."[23]

Although the correspondence between Porter and Beard does not specifically state problems which Porter encountered in her work with the NCNW and black women at large, Beard appeared to be well aware of the likelihood of an ensuing struggle. She encouraged Porter to write to her about the archives collecting as problems appeared. Without providing a context, Beard admonished Porter that:

> Thus the women of your race, by this decision to avoid lesser intentions, reveal their full understanding of the intention underlying this movement for a great Woman's Archive. It is too magnificent an ideal to be wrecked on silly rocks.[24]

As the chair of the Negro Women's Committee of the WCWA, for which position she was selected by Mrs. Bethune to represent the NCNW, and as the Supervisor of the Moorland Foundation, a position she had held for 10 years, Porter found herself in a most difficult position. Since her "first loyalty" was to the collection and development of Afro-American materials for the Moorland Foundation, it was difficult for her to be totally committed to either the WCWA or the development of the NCNW's Negro Women's Archives. Porter viewed her involvement in the WCWA's project as a way "to publicize black women." This was in fact her "main interest." After the failure of the WCWA, Mrs. Bethune appointed Mrs. Porter as National Chairman of the NCNW's Archives Committee for the period 1941-1942.[25]

It is difficult to assess the work of the Negro Women's Committee of WCWA since its formal existence covers a period of less than a year. Black women were invited to participate when the project was beginning to fail. Even though the committee was composed of a chair and four members, Dorothy Porter, as chair, and Sue Bailey Thurman, as the editor of the *Aframerican Woman's Journal,* a publication launched in conjunction with the project, were the only functioning members. As Supervisor of the Moorland Foundation, Dorothy Porter was able to assemble two exhibitions which included documents on loan from the Moorland and other materials from private collections. Sue Bailey Thurman accompanied the black women's exhibit to Chicago for the Negro Exposition and supervised its installation. In addition to these efforts, Mrs. Porter identified and contacted over 25 black women, inviting them to exhibit their materials in the Chicago Exposition and informing them of the WCWA project. Many of these women failed to respond to her requests. Lacking funds to travel, she was unable to make the personal contacts necessary for developing a collection. Women who placed materials on loan for the Chicago exhibit were not willing to donate them to WCWA. Thus, the Negro Women's Committee collected no records for deposit in WCWA.[26]

The success of the Negro Women's Committee of the WCWA was limited by its composition and inability to do extensive field work. The WCWA's need to have one black woman's organization as the facilitator, instead of establishing state committees among black, women, similar to those for white women, or integrating black women into the existing state committees was a serious impediment to its collection efforts. WCWA's decision to invite only two black women, Mrs. Mary McLeod Bethune and Mrs. James Weldon Johnson, to be WCWA Sponsors indicated an unwillingness to confront racial issues, which the presence of a diverse representation of black women at the WCWA meetings might engender.[27]

The importance of the WCWA Negro Women's Committee must be determined by the long term results of its promotion and its advocacy for black women's history and the collection and preservation of black women's records. After the failure of WCWA, the NCNW committee continued to function for over 20 years under various titles. The NCNW, stressing black women's history and black history, sought materials for exhibit at its national headquarters, developed lectures, radio programs, black history kits and a variety of other materials. Its role in the promotion of the broader field of Afro-American history and black women's history has not received the attention of scholars searching for the genesis of black and women's history. The efforts of the NCNW, beginning in 1940, to promote the establishment of a "National Archives for Negro Women's History" have been overlooked by scholars seeking the roots of women's history. The realization of that goal took 39 years. The 1979 dedication of the National Archives for Black Women's History and the Mary McLeod Bethune Memorial Museum as well as the sponsorship of the "First National Scholarly Research Conference on Black Women" represent major milestones in black and in women's history and the realization of a dream Mary McLeod Bethune had articulated over 50 years earlier.

Following the failure of the WCWA the NCNW sharpened its programmatic focus of black history and women's history. Dorothy Porter continued to serve as chair of the Archives Committee until December, 1942. Assessing the work of the Archives Committee with the WCWA, in 1941, the Committee defined its function and purpose, suggested collecting priorities and made recommendations for developing the program. Citing the types of documents and materials to be preserved, the Committee suggested as sources "women of many different vocations and walks of life" including teachers, physicians, artists, housewives, authors and domestic employees.'' In identifying as donors, elite and non-elite black women the Committee echoed the NCNW's founding theme, that the organization would reflect the interest and concerns of all black women. In 1941, few historians or archivists were concerned about ordinary black women. It is only recently that the historical profession has begun to explore documentation of ''the people's history.''[28]

In a serious effort to direct the collecting activities and to institutionalize the function of the Archives Committee, a series of recommendations were presented to the NCNW Executive Board, which included requests for the NCNW to designate a permanent center to receive and preserve documents and materials donated to the Archives; identify funds for clerical service; provide authority for the Committee to continue to locate and collect materials; sanction the development and circulation of a small loan exhibition to colleges, universities and others; and encourage the active support of the NCNW membership in the location and collection of materials.[29]

On the surface the recommendations of the Archives Committee were very reasonable, however, considering the NCNW's organizational development needs, the requests for financial and human resources to buttress this effort were far reaching and in some ways almost impossible to insure in 1941. The NCNW was functioning on a very limited budget, with Bethune and members of the Executive Board frequently volunteering their time and money for travel and other expenses to insure the success of the organization's program. Until 1943, the organization was headquartered in Bethune's NYA office during the day and in her living room by night. With a concern for maintaining the integrity of NCNW programs, there was little willingness to designate an existing repository such as the Moorland Foundation, for collection and preservation purposes. Thus, while the recommendations were well received and accepted, there was no board action.[30]

Dorothy Porter's appointment as national chair of the Archives Committee was continued until November, 1942, however, the Committee engaged in very little program activity during that year. After 1940, a steady stream of archival defined projects emanated from Sue Bailey Thurman, the editor of the *Aframerican Woman's Journal.* Thurman became the guiding force for the NCNW's promotion of black women's history. For Thurman, the archives was and is the ''single most inspiring idea of the NCNW. The dream that brought us all together was a sense of history.'' Thurman served as the chair of the Archives Committee for a brief period in 1939, however, her appointment as editor of the *Aframerican Woman's Journal* and other commitments precluded her continuance in that position. She relinquished the slot, but not her interest.[31]

The *Aframerican Woman's Journal* was formally launched in the Spring of 1940 as the official organ of the NCNW and as a part of the NCNW's overall Museum-Archives program. Mary Beard was the featured speaker at the ``christening'' dinner which was held at Howard University. Sue Bailey Thurman, like Bethune and many of the women on the NCNW Executive Board, had a strong feminist bent. While black history was frequently advocated, her specific focus was the neglected achievements of black women. Serving as the *Journal's* editor from 1939 to the Spring of 1944, she utilized a variety of techniques to underscore the importance of black women's history. The *Aframerican Woman's Journal* was a perfect vehicle for stressing the contributions of black women, while arguing for social change. The *Journal* with Harriet Tubman as its patron saint, included articles and special features such as ``The History of the Club Women's Movement;'' ``Cuban Social Life and the Negro Women;'' ``Cameos of Heritage;'' and ``A Course in Progressions with Dates of Achievements.'' Book reviews, ink drawings, poetry, short stories and plays highlighting black history were indicative of the NCNW's efforts to promote an ``historical consciousness'' among its readers. The focus of the *Journal* was national and international. The NCNW stressed the plight of third world women and called upon women to unite against racism and sexism. Digesting legislation and targeting specific issues for collective action by black women's organizations, the *Aframerican Woman's Journal* was a powerful instrument for communicating the NCNW program.[32]

Throughout the 1940s the NCNW strongly emphasized the documentation of black women's history. In 1940 the Executive Council endorsed Bethune's recommendation that ``the NCNW acquire national headquarters which shall be a memorial and shrine in honor of these pioneer women leaders who hewed a pathway for us to follow.'' The recommendation stressed that ``these headquarters shall be used to house and preserve historical archives depicting the history of Negro women.'' In 1943 the NCNW purchased a building which served as its national headquarters for 23 years. It was at this site, that the NCNW initiated community and national programs designed to enhance the Archives program.[33] After 1945, the NCNW developed structured programs which emphasized black and women's history and which aimed at the institutionalization of the archival program. These changes were directly related to personnel changes which occurred in 1943 and 1944. In 1944, Sue Bailey Thurman moved to Boston with her husband, the eminent theologian, Howard Thurman, who was appointed Dean of Boston University's School of Theology. She resigned as editor of the *Aframerican Woman's Journal* and was appointed chair of the Archives Committee.[34]

In 1945, the NCNW sponsored a "Visual Information Series" on "Negro Women in History." Beginning in February, monthly programs were held which were billed as "interracial" during which books written by black women were reviewed and exhibitions featuring photographs, documents and art work of living black women who had made significant contributions in journalism, medicine, education, business, the visual and performing arts were displayed. A key feature of these programs was the administration of a test on "The Contribution of the Negro to the Culture Patterns of American Life." Citing one hundred black men and women who had "attained national and international acclaim" the NCNW stressed that the individuals listed warranted public "research and study," and that because they were affiliated with diverse organizations, institutions and programs, a study of their achievements would provide "greater insight into the history of the American Negro." The list included 19th and 20th century figures. In conjunction with the test, the NCNW distributed a bibliography of newspapers, magazines, books and a listing of key research centers such as the Moorland Foundation, the Schomburg Collection on Negro Life and History, Hampton Institute, Fisk University and the Library of Congress.[35]

The success of the 1945 "Negro Women in History" programs demonstrated that there was strong public support for black women's history and an archives program. Bethune and Thurman were convinced that it was time to make a major national bid for support of this effort. To achieve this purpose, in 1946 they designed strategy to widely publicize the NCNW archival program. Strategies included the holding of a mass meeting at Madison Square Garden; the sponsorship of "National Archives Day" programs, the initiation of radio interviews; the promotion in schools and colleges of a prize winning essay contest on Negro Women in America; the development and promotion of "On This We Stand," a scripted radio program describing the history of black women in America; the formal location of the Museum-Archives in a building situated in the rear of the national headquarters and the identification of several highly visible prospective donors who had in their possession original materials which could form the basis of a major archival collection.[36]

Mary McLeod Bethune's vision for herself, the NCNW and the celebration of black women through history was expansive. Never one to think and plan at a level less than spectacular, she always identified persons and places of national significance for program activities associated with her diverse projects. "National Archives Day" was projected as having a two fold purpose to instill "courage and pride" and to give impetus to the efforts of black women's organizations through the dissemination of information about black women's achievements. Commentators, Walter Winchell, Orson Wells, Constance Bennett and Kate Smith were identified as key media persons to help publicize the Archives Day program. Archivists, anthropologists and historians such as Dr. Margaret Mead, Dr. Carter G. Woodson, Dr. Lawrence Reddick, Dr. Charles Johnson, Dr. E. Franklin Frazier, Dorothy Porter and Mary Church Terrell were suggested as participants on the National Archives Board.

The plans for launching the National Archives project were defined in great detail, some parts of which were implemented, however the main goal, to establish a functioning archives, was not achieved. The NCNW paid staff was very small and extremely burdened with numerous tasks. Lacking staff and funds the NCNW was not able to establish an archives. The owners of Madison Square Garden never responded to Mrs. Bethune's request to use that facility. Mrs. Bethuen was interviewed by mainly local radio stations in Washington, D.C. "On This We Stand" was presented by Station WWDC in Washington, D.C. and a few NCNW Sections sponsored National Archives Day programs. Sue Bailey Thurman's mother donated $1,000 for refurbishing the Museum-Archives building, however, the money by necessity was diverted to other purposes.[37]

The failure of the NCNW to establish a functioning Museum-Archives in 1946 did not deter Bethune from her purpose. Mrs. Bethune continued to stress the importance of the project and in 1948, one year before her retirement as NCNW President, she called a meeting to discuss long range plans for operation of a Museum-Archives Department. Plans for this department included the enlargement of the Archives Committee to include female librarians in black colleges, editors of women's pages of the black press and NCNW representation from each state. Apart from sporadic meetings and occasional representations about the need for an archives, there was little activity on the project during Mrs. Bethune's last three years as NCNW president.[38]

From 1949 to 1957 the NCNW was involved in the development of its national stature and in the extension of its collaborative work with black and white organizations, focused upon issues of civil and human rights. Bethune's immediate predecessors, Dr. Dorothy Boulding Ferebee and Mrs. Vivian Carter Mason, particularly Mrs. Mason, were engulfed by the escalating civil rights movement. Although the Museum-Archives Department continued to be listed as a program focus, there was little activity during the years 1947-1952. Distance and personal considerations prevented Mrs. Thurman, the chairman of this department, from developing and initiating major program activities. From 1952 to 1960 the NCNW continued to promote Afro-American and women's history and began to develop outreach projects which could insure "interpretation and action on a local level."[39] In 1952, NCNW President Dr. Ferebee requested that Mrs. Thurman suggest ways to achieve this purpose. Mrs. Thurman's report included a seven point program which among other things called for the NCNW to develop the small brick structure located in the rear of the headquarters, "as a permanent place in which to house the historical archives and museum of NCNW."[40]

Thurman's recommendations were comprehensive and similar to the 1941 and 1946 archival program plans, required a reordering of the NCNW's priorities and resources, which the organization was not prepared to support. Focusing her attention on the development of outreach programs, Thurman implemented several projects during the period 1955 to 1958. In 1955 and 1957 respectively, the NCNW purchased the Harriet Tubman quilt, and a set of eight "Historical Negro Dolls." In 1958 with Thurman as editor, the NCNW published the *Historical Negro Cookbook of the American Negro.* All of these projects were widely advertised as productions of the Museum Archives Department.[41]

By 1956 the NCNW administrative structure had changed. The National Departments and Committee Chairmen with the exception of the Museum Archives Department were replaced by Regional Directors. From 1940 to 1963, several persons were appointed to serve as the NCNW National Historian. Mary Church Terrell,

Mabel Robinson, Dr. Nancy Woolridge, Gertrude Robinson, Dr. Lorraine A. Williams and Juanita Dandridge represented the NCNW at conferences, workshops and a variety of gatherings. Lacking a clear cut definition of their responsibilities, each historian imprinted the office with her style and particular interests. Mary Church Terrell wrote and spoke on the history of the club movement; Sue Bailey Thurman emphasized collection, preservation and exhibition of black women's history; Mabel Robinson focused upon the integration of Afro-American history into textbooks and the development of Negro history courses in public schools; Gertrude A. Robinson promoted the documentation of NCNW's history; and Lorraine A. Williams worked to establish the Educational Foundation which included publication of the *Historical Cookbook* and reproduction of the Historical Negro Doll collection.[42]

NCNW's National Historians engaged in and promoted a variety of projects, however, the promotion of black women's history prior to 1960 was a function of the Archives Committee and the Museum Archives Department. With the exception of Sue Bailey Thurman, only one national historian played a visible role in defining the records collecting priorities of NCNW. The 1956 "Report of Plans for Preserving Historical Data of the Council," indicated that some of the functions earlier discharged by Thurman were being assumed by Gertrude Robinson and that there was a distinct shift in focus, from documenting black women's history in general to the collection and preservation of NCNW history. This change was precipitated by the response to the 1955 death of Mary McLeod Bethune, who was being acclaimed as a major historical figure. There was a recognition that the NCNW had matured as a civil rights and woman's organization. NCNW President, Vivian Carter Mason argued that there was a need to educate the public about the work of the organization. Taking her lead from Mason, Robinson stressed that documentation of NCNW programs and personnel from the local to the national level would keep the Council informed of the work of NCNW women throughout the nation; gain friends for the organization; increase the membership, and demonstrate the NCNW's "far reaching effects."[43]

In December, 1957, Dorothy I. Height became the NCNW's fourth president. During her administration many program ideas which were defined by previous administrations would be realized. During her tenure, which extends from 1957 to the present, the NCNW continued to emphasize the importance of the Museum Archives program. Miss Height, assuming the reins of leadership on the eve of the civil rights revolution of the 1960s, was in a most fortuitous position. Under her leadership the NCNW with its impeccable credentials was among the first black organizations to receive federal and foundation funding for a variety of social and heritage programs. During her tenure, NCNW's promotion and implementation of Afro-American and women's history projects gained national and international recognition.[44]

The Heritage Educational Program proposed in 1968 grew out of local community Institutes and Vanguard Training Sessions which were organized by the NCNW's Project Womanpower, a Ford Foundation funded project. The "Heritage presentations," including lectures and discussions of African and Afro-American history were so successful that the NCNW was literally bombarded with requests from persons throughout the United States for materials which could be utilized to initiate heritage programs and curriculum guides for introducing black history into public school curricula. In arguing for the need to establish the Heritage Educational Program, the NCNW concluded that "textbooks and other teaching materials are white oriented."[45]

In 1969, the NCNW introduced plans to produce an African and Afro-American Heritage Kit, which included a bibliography of books, curriculum guides and a series of pamphlets focused upon African and Afro-American history. In initiating the Heritage Educational Program, the NCNW for the first time in its history employed professional historians to develop scholarly materials and to make presentations on Afro-American history. These historians, primarily male, wrote materials which did not include a feminist perspective, but were comprehensive surveys of African and Afro-American history. This was in keeping with the larger societal emphasis on black history. The program lasted until 1969 and was highly successful.[46]

In 1972, the NCNW returned to its traditional focus upon black women's history. Proposing a "Black Woman's Institute" NCNW staffer Frances Beal argued that the early 1970s was an era when many women, young and old, were beginning to question their changing roles in the home and society. Surveying college campuses she concluded that young, educated black women knew little about the historical role of black women "in the struggle for social justice and economic opportunity in the United States." The Black Women's Institute was viewed as a "mechanism" by which the NCNW could "collect, interpret and distribute information about black women." In addition to researching and publishing factual articles on abortion, drug abuse, and legislation affecting black women and their families, the Institute would develop materials on the "history and role of black women in the U.S." The Institute would also provide a center to assist black women with their day to day problems. The Institute was never realized, however, many of the proposed programs were incorporated into the NCNW's Women's Center.[47]

In 1976, the year of the American Bicentennial Celebration, the NCNW received a small grant from the American Revolution Bicentennial Administration. NCNW inaugurated "the Bethune Collection on Black Women's Organizations." Proposing a "Discovering Our Heritage" Bicentennial Collection "of search and discovery of the notes, letters, writings, minutes and other memorabilia of Black women's groups," the NCNW again set out to develop a national archives for black women's history. The project directed by Dr. Ruby Puryear helped to publicize the need for collecting the records of black women's organizations and succeeded in identifying some secondary sources and taping a few noted male and female black leaders.[48]

For 38 years the NCNW listed the Museum Archives as a program focus, and developed a variety of projects which provided continuity for the idea, however, the full realization of Bethune and Thurman's dream came on November 11, 1979 with the dedication of the Mary McLeod Bethune Memorial Museum and National Archives for Black Women's History.

THE MAJOR HOLDINGS

The major collection at the Archives is the records of the National Council of Negro Women. Consisting of 97 boxes, measuring 88 cubic feet the collection contains information on civil rights, women's issues, education, employment, health, housing, consumer issues and international relations. Included are correspondence of founder Mary McLeod Bethune, minutes, reports and financial and membership records, as well as NCNW publications such as *Aframerican Woman's Journal* and *Black Woman's Voice.* Over a thousand photographs are included. The collection covers the period 1935-1978.

The National Committee on Household Employment

Covering the period from the 1960s through the 1980s and measuring 26 cubic feet, this collection includes correspondence, publications, news articles, photographs, reports, financial records and minutes.

The National Association of Fashion and Accessory Designers

Founded in Chicago by Jeanetta Welch Brown, this organization sought greater recognition for Black women in fashion design. It includes correspondence, news articles, convention materials and programs, covers the period 1950-1980 and measures 6 cubic feet.

Polly Cowan Papers

Cowan directed Wednesdays in Mississippi/Workshops in Mississippi, projects of the NCNW that brought interracial teams of women volunteers to the South, during the Civil Rights movement. Her papers, measuring 4 cubic feet, include correspondence, newsletters and minutes, and tapes and transcripts of interviews.

Susie Green Papers

Green was the first Black woman to be licensed as a printer and her papers include samples of her work and the financial records of her company, the Unique Printing Co. in Washington, D.C. The collection is dated from 1935, and 1960-70 and measures 6 cubic feet.

Dovey Johnson Roundtree Papers

Roundtree was one of the first thirty-nine Blacks in the Woman's Army Corps; she later became a minister of the African Methodist Episcopal Church and then an attorney. The collection includes a scrapbook, photographs, newsclippings and a WAC newsletter. The collection measures a cubic foot and covers 1938, and 1942-48.

Other

There are 2500 historical photographs of Black women as well as vertical file material divided into biography, organizational and subject categories and articles published and unpublished. Audio-visual material includes phonograph recordings of the 1963 march on Washington, radio interviews of Mary McLeod Bethune and NCNW filmstrips. Books and other publications relating to Black Women's Studies are also collected.

FOOTNOTES

1. U.S. President, "Weekly Compilation of Presidential Documents" *Federal Register,* 18, No. 41 October 18, 1982, 1320-1321.

2. 19th Century black women writers and lecturers frequently emphasized the role of black women in history. The growth of the black woman's club movement encouraged the development of books, pamphlets, articles, poetry and other materials emphasizing the important contributions of black women to history. The extensive involvement of NACW women in promoting Negro History Week during the 1920s encouraged a greater interest in women's history. For examples of earlier efforts SEE: "Race Gleanings," *Indianapolis Freeman,* October 3, 1896; Ibid, What Part Does Our Womanhood Play," March 2, 1912; "Our Women," *The Washington Bee,* March 16, 1907.

3. Anne Kimbell Relph, "The World Center for Women's Archives, 1934-1940, "Signs: *Journal of Women in Culture and Society* 4 No. 3 (Spring 1979) 597-603; Ann J. Lane, ed., *Mary Ritter Beard: A Sourcebook* (New York: Schocken Books, 1977). 32-41, 210-215; For information pertaining to Bethune's and NACW's efforts to document black women's history SEE: "President's Message," *National Notes* (November, 1927); Ibid (May, 1928); Elizabeth Lindsay Davis, *Lifting As They Climb* (D.C.: National Association of Colored Women, 1933).

4. Bettye Collier-Thomas, *NCNW, 1935-1980,* (D.C.: National Council of Negro Women, 1981 xxi; Mary McLeod Bethune, "The Association for the Study of Negro Life and History: Contribution to Our Modern Life, *Journal of Negro History 20,* (1935) 406-410; *Ibid.,* "The Negro in Retrospect and Prospect," 35, (, 1950) 9-19.

5. Mary McLeod Bethune, "Special Notice" *National Notes,* (June 1928), 12.

6. Relph, "World Center for Women's Archives," 599-600.

7. Several of these sources indicate that during the period 1935 to November 1938, Mary Beard made an effort to collect the papers of prominent black women and black women's organizations without involving any black women in the WCWA project. Letter, Mary Church Terrell to Dorothy Porter, February 6, 1940, National Archives for Black Women's History (NABWH) NCNW Records, Series 4 Box 1, Folder 1; Letter, Lucy D. Slowe to Mary Beard, March 16, 1936, Mary Ritter Beard Collection, Schlesinger Library, A-9, Box 1, Folder 15; Letter Mary Beard to Sadie Daniel St. Clair, December 19, 1939, *Ibid.;* Letter, Marjorie White to Mary White Ovington, October 26, 1938, *Ibid.;* Letter, Mary McLeod Bethune to Marjorie White, December 13, 1938, NABWH, NCNW Records, Series 4 Box 1, Folder 1; Relph, "World Center for Women's Archives, 598. Brochure," World Center for (See footnote 8)

8. Brochure, "World Center for Women's Archives" NABWH, NCNW Records, Series 4, Box 1, Folder 1.

9. Letter, Bethune to White, December 13, 1938, *Ibid.*

10. *Ibid.;* Letter, Mary McLeod Bethune to Dorothy Porter, December 7, 1939, *Ibid.;* In 1939 Dorothy Porter was employed at Howard University as Supervisor of the Moorland Foundation, a repository which assumed national and international significance during the 1950s as one of several major centers for documentation of Afro-American history. In 1967, after Mrs. Porter's retirement, the Foundation's title was changed to the Moorland Spingarn Research Center.

11. Letter, Marjorie White to Juanita Mitchell, January 17, 1939, *Ibid.*

12. Thomas, *NCNW, 1935-1980;* Tullia Brown Hamilton, "The National Association of Colored Women, 1896-1920," (unpublished Ph.D. dissertation, Emory University, 1978); Elaine M. Smith, "Mary McLeod Bethune," in *Notable American Women: The Modern Period* ed. by Barbara Sicherman and Carol Hurd Green (Cambridge, Mass.: Harvard University Press, 1980) 76-80; Bettye Collier-Thomas, "Eleanor Roosevelt and Mary McLeod Bethune: A Collaboration of Greatness," speech given at the NCNW Convention, New York City, November 1983.

13. Rackham Holt, *Mary McLeod Bethune: A Biography* (New York: Doubleday and Company, Inc., 1964), 163-175.

14. Thomas, *NCNW 1935-1980,* 1-7; In 1938, Mrs. Bethune served simultaneously as the Director of the Negro Division of the National Youth Administration, President of the Association for the Study of Afro-American Life and History and President of Bethune Cookman College.

15. The NACW never affiliated with the NCNW. Mary Church Terrell, Charlotte Hawkins Brown and a number of prominent black women were not in favor of Mrs. Bethune founding a new organization, the NCNW. For a more detailed discussion SEE: Thomas, *NCNW 1935-1980;* Davis, *Lifting As We Climb.*

16. Letter, Dorothy Porter to Claude A. Barnett, May 1, 1940; NABWH, NCNW Records, Series 4, Box 1, Folder 1.

17. Letter, Mary McLeod Bethune to Dorothy Porter, December 19, 1939, NABWH, NCNW Records, Series 4, Box 1, Folder 1; "Report of the Archives Committee of the National Council of Negro Women," by Dorothy B. Porter, October 17, 1941, *Ibid.*

18. Mary Church Terrell was the first president of the NACW (1896-). As a nationally known lecturer and a member of the National American Woman's Suffrage Association and numerous other organizations, she was well known among white and black women in the woman's rights movement. Elizabeth Carter Brooks was president of the NACW from 1908 to 1910. Her work with the National YWCA and other social service organizations was well known. Sue Bailey Thurman was the wife of the noted black theologian, Howard Thurman.

19. Letter, Mary Church Terrell to Dorothy Porter, February 6, 1940, NABWH, NCNW Records, Series 4, Box 1 Folder 1; During the 1940s and early 50s, Mrs. Porter acquired some materials from Mrs. Terrell which formed the basis for a small collection, however, the bulk of Terrell's papers were donated to the Library of Congress by Phillis Terrel Langston, the daughter of Mary Church Terrell.

20. Letter, Mary Beard to Dorothy Porter, February 21, 1940, *Ibid.* Also SEE: Mary Ritter Beard, A-9, Box 1, Folder 15, collection, Schlesinger Library Radcliffe College.

21. Letter, Mary McLeod Bethune to Dorothy Porter, June 27, 1940, NABWH, NCNW Records, Series 4, Box 1, Folder 1; Relph, "World Center for Women's Archives," 598, 602-603.

22. Letter, Mary R. Beard to Dorothy Porter, May 26, 1940, *Ibid.;* Letter, Arden M. Duane to Mary Beard, May 20, 1940, Mary Ritter Beard Collection 4, Schlesinger Library, A9, Box 1, Folder 15.

23. Letter, Dorothy Porter to Mary Beard, March 27, 1940. *Ibid.;* Letter, Mary Beard to Dorothy Porter, March 31, 1940, NABWH, NCNW Records, Series 4, Box 1, Folder 1.

24. *Ibid.*

25. Dorothy Porter, telephone interview, Washington, D.C., August 12, 1983. Letter, Mary McLeod Bethune to Dorothy Porter, December 9, 1941, NABWH, NCNW Records, Series 4, Box 1, Folder 1.

26. Letter, Dorothy Porter to Emil Hurja, January 11, 1940, Mary Ritter Beard Collection, Schlesinger Library, A-9, Box 1, Folder 15, "Negro Women's Archives," *Aframerican Woman's Journal,* (Summer and Fall 1940; "Editorial," *Ibid.;* 3 Letter, Dorothy Porter to Emil Hurja, December 15, 1939, NABWH, NCNW Records, Series 4, Box 1, Folder 1; Letter, Claude Barnett to Dorothy Porter, Series 4, Box 1, Folder 1; Letter, Claude Barnett to Dorothy Porter, May 10, 1940, *Ibid.;* Letter, Dorothy Porter to Claude Barnett, June 1, 1940, *Ibid.;* Letter, Dorothy Porter to potential donors to Archives, June 21, 1940, *Ibid.;* Letter Florence B. Price to Dorothy Porter, June 25, 1940, *Ibid.;* Letter,

Dorothy Porter to Florida R. Ridley, July 1, 1940, Ibid.; the NCNW Collection contains a number of other letters soliciting materials for exhibition; Eleanor M. Young, "American Negro Exposition Official Release," September 3, 1940, List of Items for NCNW Women's Archives Exhibit.

27. Letter, Mary Beard to Mrs. Cooper, April 29, 1940, Mary Ritter Beard Collection, Schlesinger Library, A-9, Box 1, Folder 15, Reporting on a meeting with Dorothy Porter and the WCWA Negro Women's Archives Committee, Mary Beard states that they discussed the question of including Negro Women in state branches and that they "seemed" to feel that their interest would be best served by working directly with NCNW in New York.

28. NABWH: NCNW Records, Series 4, Box 1, Folder 1, Report of the Archives Committee of the National Council of Negro Women, October 17, 1941; Bettye Collier-Thomas, "Documenting Women's History," paper presented at Organization of American Historians Conference, meeting in San Francisco, California April, 1980. Linda Henry, "Promoting Historical Consciousness" The Early Archives Committee of the National Council of Negro Women," *Signs: Journal of Women in Culture and Society,* 1981, Vol. 7, no. 1, p. 251.

29. *Ibid.;* Report of Archives Committee.

30. NABWH, NCNW Records, Series 2, Box 1 Folder 8, "Findings of the National Council of Negro Women in Meeting Thursday, October 25, 1940,—Conference Room Department of Labor—Washington, D.C."; *Ibid.;* Folder 7, minutes of the NCNW, Official Secretary's Report, October 25, 1940; Henry, "Promoting Historical Consciousness," 254

31. Sue Bailey Thurman, telephone interview, San Francisco, California, August 12, 1983; NABWH, NCNW Records, Series 2, Box 1, Folder 5, "Minutes of NCNW, Inc." November 4, 1939, p. 5.

32. *Ibid.;* Series 5, Box 1, Folders 13-32; *Aframerican Woman's Journal,* SEE: Issues 1940-1948; Henry, "Promoting Historical Consciousness."

33. NCNW Records, "Findings of the National Council of Negro Women;" *Aframerican Woman's Journal,* Fall, 1944, "The Final Chapter, Dedication of National Headquarters." p. 6.

34. Thurman, telephone interview; *Aframerican Woman's Journal,* Fall 1944, "Our New Editor," p. 2; Mrs. Gertrude Scott Martin was appointed the new editor.

35. NABWH, NCNW Records, Series 5, Box 36, Folder 512, "The Visual Information Series of the National Council of Negro Women."

36. Ibid.; Series 5, Box 4, Folder 63, "Madison Square Garden Unity Celebration" plans for March 12, 1946; "Notes taken during conversation with Sue Bailey Thurman," November 20, 1946; "Interview with Mary McLeod Bethune Monday, June 17th, 1946"; "Proposed National Archives Day," June 2, 1946; Sue Bailey Thurman and Lucy Schulte, "On This We Stand (A radio script)" Presented over Station WWDC in Washington, D.C., June 29, 1946, on the occasion of the initiation of the National Negro Women's Archives and Museum Department, by the National Council of Negro Women of the United States; Letter, Mary McLeod Bethune to "Management" of Madison Square Garden, March 12, 1946, NABWH, NCNW Records, Series 5, Box 4, Folder 63.

37. *Ibid.;* For discussion of Archives' funds SEE: Minutes of Executive Committee Meeting, January 25, 1947, Series 3, Box 1, Folder 20; Letter, Mary McLeod Bethune to Executive Committee February 25, 1946 *Ibid.;* In 1946, the NCNW program called for an expansion of NCNW services. This expansion precipitated a fiscal crisis which was resolved in part by the release of two thirds of the NCNW staff and the utilization of the $1,000 donated by Thurman's mother.

38. Mary McLeod Bethune retired as president of NCNW in November 1949; Memorandum, Mary McLeod Bethune to Members of Permanent Headquarters Committee, October 1, 1948, *Ibid.,* Series 5, Box 4, Folder 63.

39. Letter, Dorothy Boulding Ferebee to Sue Bailey Thurman, September 12, 1952, NABWH, NCNW Records, Series 1, Box 1, Folder 3.

40. "Program Suggestions for National Projects to be Implemented Through Local and Regional Council Units, for the Historical Archives and Museum Department of the National Council of Negro Women," 1953, NABWH, NCNW Records, Series 7, Box 1, Folder 3.

41. Letter, Sue Bailey Thurman to Vivian Carter Mason, February 4, 1955, NABWH, NCNW Records, Series 7, Box 1, Folder 3; *Ibid.;* Regulations for the use of the Harriet Tubman Quilt'' Undated typescript; Memorandum, Arnetta G. Wallace to National Affiliates, December 21, 1957, ''Meta Warrick Fuller Historical Doll Project,'' Letter, Sue Bailey Thurman to Elsie Austin, April 30, 1958, Sue Bailey Thurman, *The Historical Cookbook of the American Negro* Washington, D.C. the National Council of Negro Women, 1958.

42. *Ibid.*, Gertrude A. Robinson, November 14, 1956, ''Report on Plans for Presenting Historical Data of the Council,'' Vivian Carter Mason, ''National Council of Negro Women: Report 1953-1957,'' November 8, 1957; Minutes of the Executive Committee Meeting,'' February 9, 1946, Series 3, Box 1, Folder 20, 12,13, and 14.

43. Robinson, ''Report on Plans for Presenting Historical Data of the Council.''

44. Thomas, *NCNW, 1935-1980.*

45. John Henrik Clark, ''A Curriculum Guide to the Study and Teaching of Afro-American History,'' 1967, NABWH, NCNW Records, Series 10, Box 7; Memorandum, Frances Beal and Merble H. Reagon to Dorothy I. Height, ''Heritage Educational Program,: December 11, 1968, *Ibid;* Prospectus, ''African and Afro-American Heritage Kit,'' 1969, *Ibid.*

46. *Ibid.*

47. ''Black Women's Institute'', and ''Women's Center Statement,'' *Ibid.*, unprocessed collections.

48. Letter, Dorothy I. Height to NCNW Sections and Affiliates, February 10, 1976, *Ibid.*, unprocessed collection; ''Bethune Collection on Black Women's Organizations,'' *Ibid.* unprocessed collection.

Exploring Women's Lives: Historical and Contemporary Resources in the College Archives and The Sophia Smith Collection at Smith College

Mary-Elizabeth Murdock

The legacy of Sophia Smith, a Hatfield, Massachusetts spinster of abundant means, founded Smith College in 1875 to insure that intellectually able young women could secure an education fully comparable to that available, then, to men. More than a century later, Smith College is the largest privately endowed college for women in the world. It is not surprising therefore, that one of its major scholarly commitments has long been to collect and to preserve carefully the records of many thousands of women's lives. Given this objective, two distinguished archives of women's history have gradually evolved. While their mission was identical, their composition clearly differed.

The general focus of the College Archives, the older of the two repositories, is composite Smith College history, but numerous primary source collections clearly do support specific scholarly research projects in women's history. Foremost among these resources are the Class Files, 1879 to the present, that contain *undergraduate* records, "letters home" and related manuscripts of thousands of Smith alumnae. The personal and professional papers of selected Smith female faculty members, governors and administrators also are invaluable indicators of the status and influence of some nineteenth and twentieth century academic women. Moreover, official and student publications, myriad photographs and records of on and off-campus activities, committees and organizations document precisely the progressive intellectual and social maturation of Smith College as a world renowned educational institution for women.

In contrast, the specific objective of The Sophia Smith Collection since its inception in 1942, has been to acquire and to preserve substantive primary sources and selected secondary materials that document the lives of women in the United States and throughout the world. Today, the College Archives and The Sophia Smith Collection form one independent department that is housed in Alumnae Gymnasium, the gift of Alumnae to the College in 1891, a handsome, newly renovated and furnished facility. Its director reports to the President of the College. The ascendance of this distinguished department began decades ago.

THE COLLEGE ARCHIVES

When Nina Eliza Browne graduated from Smith in 1882, she received a cache of materials about Sophia Smith and her "women's College" that her mother had begun in 1875. To please her mother as well as herself, Nina Browne continued to collect and to preserve independently "everything I could lay my hands on"[1] until 1921. In that year, the Trustees finally appointed Miss Browne, one of the nation's first professionally educated librarians,[2] the Archivist of Smith College. Her charge was to expand and to administer the fledgling "Historical Collection" and she did so until 1937. Because Nina Browne quickly established successfully the tradition of "persuading" alumnae to donate to the "Historical Collection" *any* materials that revealed some facet of life at Smith, her "Semi-Centennial Exhibit" in 1925 was a fabled highlight of Smith's fiftieth anniversary—a milestone year. Alumnae donations had indeed created archival files of such surprising scope and depth that the survival of the "Historical Collection" as a department of the College appeared to be assured. But in 1937, failing vision mandated Miss Browne's retirement and her treasured "Historical Collection" languished for three years.

Its renaissance began in 1940 however. In that year, Acting President, Elizabeth Cutter Morrow, always an enthusiastic advocate of the "Historical Collection," revitalized it as the Archives of Smith College, an independent department of the College, and appointed as Archivist, Margaret Storrs Grierson '22, Ph.D., Bryn Mawr. She served in this capacity until her retirement in 1965. Later in 1940, the new president, Herbert J. Davis, also demonstrated his support for the Archives, as well as his desire to broaden greatly the range of its resources, by sending a MEMORANDUM to "Heads of department and administrative offices" that identified eleven specific categories of records that should be "regularly submitted" to the Archives. They were as follows: (1) all college publications (2) office, department and committee manuscript material and memoranda (3) non-current office, department, committee and individuals' files (4) course materials (5) buildings and grounds records (6) faculty and administrative papers (7) files relating to distinguished visitors (8) clubs and activities records (9) personal letters revealing campus life (10) photographs (11) articles about Smith College, women's education or problems confronting women's colleges. While these resources still are not systematically transferred to the College Archives, informal deposits do tend to parallel these guidelines thus determining the basic current content of the College Archives.

In June 1983, approximately 1,100 linear feet of processed and catalogued College Archives' files are housed on stacks in a temperature and humidity controlled, halon protected vault. New, unprocessed materials are kept there as well. Although no materials circulate, any interested person, ranging from junior high school age to advanced scholars, may request permission to use unrestricted resources on site in the College Archives' Reading Room or to secure a limited number of photocopied items for a fee and as regulations allow.

Scholars investigating the history of women should examine these College Archives' holdings: alumnae class files (1879 to the present), papers of some faculty women, Smith College Medalist files (Smith women of distinction), official College and student publications, records of the Institute for Coordination of Women's Interests, the Smith College Relief Unit (volunteer work in France, World War I), WAVES (officer training program at Smith, World War II), the Cambridge School of Architecture, women in Sports (especially basketball, field hockey, volleyball) extensive photograph resources, women in the arts (especially music, theatre), women in science, student clubs and activities, demographic studies, class questionnaires, studies concerning single-sex colleges vs. co-educational institutions.

Hundreds of campus colleagues use annually College Archives' primary resources as do alumnae, students and the general public. A variety of exhibits intrigue our visitors; publishers and other individuals purchase a wide array of photographs for a variety of uses.

Excepting certain holidays, College Archives' hours are Monday through Friday *only,* 9:00 to 5:00 September through May; hours are 8:00 to 4:00, June through August. The staff responds to reasonable mail inquiries and requests for photcopies as time permits.

THE SOPHIA SMITH COLLECTION (WOMEN'S HISTORY ARCHIVE)

Two years after Margaret Grierson became Archivist, Yale librarian, Grace Fuller '03, persuaded President Davis to organize, in 1942, a group soon named the Friends of the Smith College Library. Its mission was to enrich all of Smith's libraries by encouraging individuals to donate books or funds to them. As its first Executive Secretary, Mrs. Grierson worked enthusiastically to launch a new "special project" of the Friends—a "Collection of Works of Women Writers." It is worth noting that President Davis had first proposed such an idea to the Alumnae Association of Commencement in 1941.[4] Five years later, this "Collection" was rechristened The Sophia Smith Collection to honor the founder of the College.[5]

From its inception, the steady influx of primary and secondary donated sources that swelled its files soon identified The Sophia Smith Collection as promising archive whose specialty was documenting "the intellectual and social history of women." The Collection received materials originally intended for the World Center for Women's Archives, that had to be placed elsewhere when the WCWA collapsed. Other new collections arrived from a very wide range of donors and, again, the papers of some Smith alumnae were among them because College Archives' files contained then and now the papers only of Smith women's undergraduate years.

By 1944, it was evident that gifts of rare resources were arriving at Smith "with gratifying liveliness."[6] Yet, it was this rapid growth that soon motivated Margaret Grierson to reassess not only the current and future needs and objectives of the "Women's Collection," but, also, to devise an effective strategy for countering what could surely become a serious threat to its survival—the emergence of a rival women's archive at Radcliffe College, internationally known today as The Arthur and Elizabeth Schlesinger Library on the History of Women. After careful reflection, Mrs. Grierson's recommendations to President Davis were threefold. First, Smith should expand the scope of its "Women's Collection" to include materials *about* as well as *by* women. Second, she urged a new acquisitions philosophy that would emphasize collecting *historical* sources rather than primary literary creations thus rejecting President Davis' earlier focus for the "Women's Collection."[7] An historical focus was critically important in her view, because it would enable scholars to use the "Women's Collection" to learn more about women and their myriad accomplishments throughout history. This new knowledge about women could then be used to allay rapidly escalating fears about allegedly rampant "feminism" at Smith and elsewhere. Furthermore, she stated, the history of women should be infused as quickly as possible into the history of *people.* As Mrs. Grierson saw it, for Smith College to encourage such research would be a most valuable undertaking—"a genuine service to scholarship."[8] Finally, to assuage President Davis' justifiable fears about continuing what could become a costly, unproductive competition and duplication of effort with Radcliffe, she proposed that, in addition to collecting the papers of United States women, Smith, unlike Radcliffe, should also collect resources of and about *international* women thus recognizing women's status and roles in the "farther reaches of time and space."[9]

While President Davis continued to harbor reservations about the wisdom of encouraging the Smith project further, he did permit the "Women's Collection" to continue and its holdings expanded significantly throughout the 1950's. By 1965, the national and international holdings of The Sophia Smith Collection included many thousands of manuscripts in impressive collections of family papers, those of individual women, a wide range of subject collections, retrospective and contemporary pamphlets, periodicals and tracts, iconographical resources, ephemera, memorabilia and nearly 80,000 books.[10] Margaret Grierson could savor many victories when she retired in 1965.

Her successors, Marcia Williams Bradley '43 (1965-1970) and Mary-Elizabeth Murdock, Ph.D., Brown University (1970-), while continuing to build on these foundations, have developed additional policies and ventures as well. In June 1983, approximately 1,960 linear feet of processed and catalogued resources of The Sophia Smith Collection share a closed stack, temperature and humidity controlled, halon protected vault with College Archives' files. All new collections as well as additions to existing holdings are preserved there as well. Present objectives are to locate and acquire primary resources by or about the world's women. Primary resources are collections of manuscript or typescript letters, diaries and journals of families and individual women as well as drawings and photographs portraying women, and materials by or about women such as manuscript addresses, oral history tapes and transcripts, ephemera and memorabilia, tracts and periodicals. In especial demand are sources that document clearly the multicultural aspects of the history of women. The subject collection priorities of The Sophia Smith Collection include women in the arts and humanities, education, the health care system, industry, peace, the professions, psychology of women, women's rights, science, sex roles, past and present activists in social reform and sports; there are also substantial iconographical resources, national and international periodicals by or about women and finally, various types of statistical analyses and reports.[1]

Although slightly over 800 individuals used the resources of The Sophia Smith Collection either by mail inquiries or in person during 1982-83, continuing efforts to publicize the facility should encourage even more individuals to visit Smith College. Several current projects are accomplishing this objective. For example, information regarding a series of eight subject bibliographies is available, free, upon request. Second, occasional major conferences such as the "Margaret Sanger Centennial Symposium" (1979-80) as well as "Women and Work" (1981-82) bring expert lecturers to Smith to analyze and evaluate the importance of outstanding individuals or significant subject areas to our perception and comprehension of the status and the roles of women. Third, major exhibitions such as "Three New England Families—Ames, Garrison and Hale," and "The Fight for Birth Control" demonstrate to visitors the quality and scope of The Sophia Smith Collection's resources and stimulate interest in the dimensions of women's experience as well. Fourth, an annual series of Interterm Symposia feature distinguished lecturers who examine critically a variety of "Historical and Contemporary Perspectives on Women." Twenty-two lectures and an equal number of films since the inception of this program in 1976 explain this project's evident success.[12] Fifth, the hundreds of photographs that publishers purchase annually from The Sophia Smith Collection as well as the College Archives attract numerous scholars to Smith. Such photographs enable individuals to study precisely how women looked, worked and lived in various historical periods. Sixth, information regarding the prices of three comprehensive catalogs containing detailed descriptions of selected sources in The Sophia Smith

Collection and a monograph commemorating Margaret Sanger is available from the Director. Finally, computers will come to the College Archives and The Sophia Smith Collection in the near future. This technology promises to revolutionize internal record keeping and to facilitate information sharing between individuals and institutions on a scale previously unimagined. Taken together, these outreach projects, as well as those to emerge in the future, will acquaint interested individuals anywhere with the abundant, unique resources of the College Archives and The Sophia Smith Collection.

Like the College Archives, the Reading Room of The Sophia Smith Collection is located on Level A, Alumnae Gymnasium at Smith College. All interested persons of at least junior high school age are welcome, on a first come, first served basis. Excepting certain holidays, the hours of The Sophia Smith Collection (Women's History Archive) are Monday through Friday *only,* 9:00-5:00, September through May; 8:00-4:00, June through August. A microfilm-microfiche reader and a photocopying machine are available. The staff responds to reasonable mail inquiries and photoduplication requests as time permits.

NOTES

1. Nina E. Browne, "The History of the Collection." n.d., 1 p.; Thomas Wentworth Higginson to Nina E. Browne, ALS dated December 2, 1903. 1 p.

2. Massachusetts Library Association *Bulletin.* Vol. 36, No. 3 June, 1946, p. 51.

3. Herbert J. Davis, *Memorandum:* "To the heads of departments and administrative offices." September 24, 1940. 1 p. While the intent of the Davis *Memorandum* was clear, his suggestion to the heads of academic departments and administrative offices never received an official approval, or mandate, from the Board of Trustees of Smith College. The Archives' three directors have been unable, therefore, to enforce policies that would guarantee the systematic transferral and deposit of priority non-current official College records in the College Archives.

4. Margaret Storrs Grierson, "An Historical Collection Of Books By Women And On Women." Essay enclosed in Friends of the Smith College Library *Annual Report,* March 1944, p. 1.

5. Grierson, Friends of the Smith College Library *Annual Report,* 1946, p. 15.

6. Grierson, "The Women's Collection." The Friends of the Smith College Library. N.D., 9 pp. p. 1.

7. Grierson, op. cit., p. 5.

8. Grierson, *Ibid.*, pp. 2-4. Grierson's concept that research in women's history would be a "genuine service to scholarship" sparked a lively debate in the Smith College community. Some faculty colleagues and top-level administrators were unpersuaded that studying women had any scholarly merit at all. Furthermore, what present and future demands would such an enterprise make on the College budget? At this juncture in the mid 1940's, the Friends of the Smith College Library provided Mrs. Grierson and the Historical Collection with its most visible and enduring emotional as well as financial support.

9. *Ibid.*, pp. 11-13. The decision to collect international resources remains today one major distinction in the acquisitions policies of The Sophia Smith Collection and The Schlesinger Library.

10. In 1983, The Sophia Smith Collection has two separate book collections. The larger of the two contains nearly 100,000 books, many acquired decades ago. This collection is shelved in William Allan Neilson Library stacks because of space considerations and because Neilson's much longer open hours make the resources more readily available to scholars. The second collection is a ''Browsing Collection'' maintained in open stacks in the Level A Reading Room. This collection contains essential reference sources and contemporary publications on a wide variety of issues of interest to women's history scholars today.

11. Examples of especially prestigious and much-used manuscript holdings presently preserved in The Sophia Smith Collection are some letters and Civil War diaries of Clara Barton, many letters of Communist and Socialist organizer Ella Reeve Bloor, selected suffrage and peace materials of Carrie Chapman Catt, papers of American Indian education specialist, Elaine Goodale Eastman, the social reform activities of the Garrison Family (1773 to the present) as well as the professional papers of two lawyers—civil rights, women's advocates Dorothy Kenyon and former congresswoman, Patsy Mink. Available also are the papers of the first American female journalist, Sara Parton (''Fanny Fern''), the founder of the 20th c. birth control movement, Margaret H. Sanger, Ellen Gates Starr, co-founder of Hull House (with Jane Addams) and industrial researcher and sociologist, Mary Van Kleeck. Detailed analyses of subject holdings, periodical titles and photograph resources are given in the Catalogs cited in this essay.

12. A full listing of guest lecturers as well as the titles of symposia film series and accompanying lectures is available upon request.

Forty Years of Collecting on Women: The Arthur and Elizabeth Schlesinger Library on the History of Women in America, Radcliffe College

Patricia Miller King

> The purposes of this organization are: To make a systematic search for undeposited source materials dealing with women's lives and activities, interests and ideas, as members of society everywhere.[1]

In the late 1930s, Mary Ritter Beard and her colleagues thus began the statement of purpose of the World Center for Women's Archives. The women recognized that it was not entirely the fault of a male-dominated profession that the roles of women were under-represented in historical works. Source materials documenting the lives of women, excepting those few who were related by blood or marriage to prominent men, had seldom been deposited in research libraries or archives. Beard and her associates set out to remedy this omission by establishing the World Center to collect appropriate materials and to encourage the study and writing of women's history. The World Center was incorporated and a small office was established in New York City, but not all prominent women were supporters. Dr. Alice Hamilton (1869-1970), retired from Harvard Medical School, but still active as a consultant for the U.S. Department of Labor, wrote:

> I am enclosing a check for your cause but I am not ready to become a sponsor. . . .Perhaps I am all wrong, but I have never seen the value of publicizing the work of women in men's fields. That always seems to me a revelation of our

> weakness rather than our strength because what we achieve is always so little compared to the record of men. Our contribution to life is different and although quite as important is so much more intangible. As I said, this may be old fashioned and absurd but it is still my feeling and keeps me from joining wholeheartedly in your enterprise.[2]

Apparently Hamilton later changed her opinion about the value of such an enterprise, for in 1953 she donated her papers to Radcliffe's Women's Archives. However, in the 1930s, although gifts and promises of papers were ample, adequate funding proved elusive. In 1940 Beard reluctantly informed her supporters that the World Center was being disbanded.

Within a few years, circumstances for the systematic collection and preservation of women's papers were more auspicious. In 1942, the Sophia Smith Collection was established at Smith College and in the following year the Woman's Rights Collection, the foundation for the Women's Archives, was donated to Radcliffe College. Both Smith and Radcliffe were to benefit from Beard's earlier efforts and her advice; both also eventually received materials earlier promised or donated to the World Center.

HISTORY OF THE SCHLESINGER LIBRARY

At Radcliffe College, the collection on the history of women, known until 1965 as the Women's Archives, began with a gift from an alumna, Maud Wood Park '98 (1871-1955).[3] A suffrage supporter even during her college years, Park, with her fellow alumna Inez Haynes Gillmore [Irwin] (1873-1970), founded the College Equal Suffrage League in 1900. She later chaired the Congressional Committee of the National American Woman Suffrage Association, the group that lobbied the 19th Amendment through Congress, and subsequently became the first president of the League of Women Voters of the United States. During a lifetime of work for woman's rights, Park saved her papers and collected other published and unpublished documents relating to the woman's rights movement from the 17th century to the 1940s.[4] In 1943, in anticipation of her 45th reunion, she offered these materials to President Ada Comstock as a memorial to the courage and achievements of the suffragists and as the beginning of a research library on women.

Initial discussions with President Comstock were favorable and on August 26, 1943, Radcliffe simultaneously announced the acquisition of the Woman's Rights Collection (WRC), as Park's gift was to be known, and the appointment of a new president, the historian Wilbur K. Jordan. Negotiations with Park and her associate Edna Stantial, a former secretary of the Boston Equal Suffrage Association for Good Government, were completed by President Jordan.[5] Park and Stantial undertook to supplement Park's personal collection with records of other suffrage leaders and prominent women and to arrange and catalog the materials. As Park and Stantial solicited additions, it became apparent that the rivalry between moderate and radical suffragists had not abated, even after the passage of 25 years. The offer of Doris Stevens' *Jailed for Freedom* was refused because the author had been a leader in Alice Paul's National Woman's Party (NWP).

At the same time that work proceeded on the WRC, President Jordan and his colleague in Harvard's History Department and Radcliffe Trustee, Arthur M. Schlesinger, sought to enlarge the scope of the undertaking. Schlesinger, who as early as 1922 in *New Viewpoints in American History,* had chastized his fellow historians for ignoring half the population in their writing of history, suggested to Jordan that he enlist the support of Mary Beard. Jordan's letter in December 1943 elicited a prompt and enthusiastic reply. Beard wrote that she would be "honored by the chance to participate in any way in the promotion of this vital educational movement at Cambridge." She informed Jordan that, on the basis of her investigation of existing collections, there was "not yet available in any library a 'wholly satisfactory collection' of materials dealing with the 'historical status and cultural contributions of women in this country and England'," and she offered to make available to him documents from her files.[6] Beard further advised Jordan to make the scope of Radcliffe's collecting as broad as possible and not to concentrate only on the "equal rights movement." Jordan in fact steered a middle course between the opinions of his various advisors, envisioning a collection going beyond Park's woman's rights and suffrage focus, but stopping far short of Beard's hope to encompass the deeds of all women in all cultures at all times.

The association with Beard provided more than helpful counsel. In 1945 she sent to the Women's Archives files of the abortive attempt to establish the World Center for Women's Archives and directed to Radcliffe the records of Leonora O'Reilly (1870-1927), a fiery organizer of women in the garment industry; those records had earlier been promised to the World Center by Mary Dreier, O'Reilly's colleague in the Women's Trade Union League of New York. Beard was also instrumental in Radcliffe's acquisition of 44 volumes of the *Woman's Journal* given to the World Center, the papers of Beard's associate (and Park's former colleague), Inez Haynes Irwin, scrapbooks of the National Consumer's League kept by Maud Nathan (1862-1946), and the extensive papers of Fannie Fern Andrews (1867-1950), the World Center's advisor on women and international law.

Despite friction occasioned by the parallel, but disparate collecting efforts of the Radcliffe Administration and Mrs. Park, and Radcliffe's ignoring the subtleties of suffrage and post-suffrage politics as they consulted with Beard and other NWP-affiliated feminists, the Women's Archives opened to the public in 1949. The WRC with its 1,156 folders of manuscript and ephemeral material, arranged in 16 file drawers and supplemented by a library of 300 volumes, numerous photographic portraits of suffrage leaders, and assorted memorabilia was housed in a separate room in Longfellow Hall.[7] The Women's Archives next door in Byerly Hall held the first fruits of Jordan's and Schlesinger's broader vision of a general collection on American women were available: the papers of Dr. Mary Putnam Jacobi (1843-1906), whose formal medical training, publications, and clinical skills had won her recognition as the leading woman physician in the United States; files of the Bureau of Vocational Information of New York (1919-26, 1928-32) and of the Association of Collegiate Alumnae and the American Association of University Women; and a collection of 119 etiquette books contributed by Schlesinger from his personal library.

In 1950 the Women's Archives became a separate department of Radcliffe College with its own director, Elizabeth B. Borden, archivist, Mary E. Howard, and a secretary. To aid Borden in establishing procedures and policies and in identifying and acquiring additional manuscript collections, Jordan appointed an Advisory Board of individuals interested in women's history, headed by Schlesinger. During the ten years of Borden's administration, many significant collections were acquired, including papers of penologists Jessie Hodder (1870-1931) and Miriam Van Waters (1887-1974), Democratic National Committeewoman Emma Guffey Miller (1874-1970), Women's Bureau chief Mary Anderson (1872-1964), and pioneer in workers' education Hilda Worthington

Smith. The largest existing collection of the letters of Harriet Beecher Stowe (1811-96) came to the Archives as part of one large family collection; the records of Nellie Nugent Somerville (1863-1952), the first woman in the Mississippi Legislature, arrived as part of another, the Somerville-Howorth Collection, which documents six generations of Mississippi women active in church, temperance, suffrage, and politics; and the first major acquisition of Blackwell family papers was made. Also acquired during the 1950s were files of the National Women's Trade Union League of New York, the Women's Educational and Industrial Union of Boston, and the Dillon Collection, which includes, the papers of several prominent Illinois and national suffragists, this collection had been assembled by Dr. Mary Earhart Dillon and had been refused by the Northwestern University Library, the Newberry Library, the New York Public Library, and the Library of Congress before finding refuge at Radcliffe.[8]

Succeeding directors built on these strong foundations. Barbara Miller Solomon (1960-65) traveled widely, speaking about the Women's Archives and women's history to alumnae and professional groups throughout the country. Her addresses included one in 1964 at the second of Lady Bird Johnson's luncheons for ''Lady Doers'' at the White House. Her years also brought a significant strengthening of informal ties between the Women's Archives and the Harvard University Library.[9] Janet Wilson James (1965-68) included in her tenure the renaming of the Library to memorialize Professor Schlesinger, who died on October 30, 1965. The new name also honored Elizabeth Bancroft Schlesinger, who shared her husband's interest in the history of women's achievements and who herself had published several articles on American women in historical journals and magazines. The change of name coincided with planning for a move from the crowded quarters in Byerly Hall to new and more adequate space in the former college library building, which had been vacated with the completion of Radcliffe's Hilles Library. The move to the extensively renovated building, which the Schlesinger Library shared with the Radcliffe Institute for Independent Study (since renamed the Mary I. Bunting Institute), took place in the summer of 1967. At that time, the director optimistically stated that the generous reading rooms and climate-controlled vaults would be adequate for the next 25 to 30 years.[10]

The rapidly changing intellectual and political climate was soon to render this prediction obsolete. By the early 1970s, the impact of the women's movement was being felt in academic circles, as activists sought to recover the heritage of their foremothers and growing numbers of practitioners of social history ignored the study of the lives of great men to investigate the history of formerly neglected groups, including women. During Jeannette Bailey Cheek's directorship (1969-1973), the numbers of users increased dramatically as undergraduate, graduate student, post-doctoral, and independent researchers sought source materials to write the history of women. Daily research visits had been seven in all of 1949 and had risen only to 247 in 1969-70. In the early 1970s, staff were overwhelmed with the flood of enthusiastic new researchers and kept no user statistics. By the time record-keeping was resumed in 1976, 3,200 daily research visits were noted in the year's register.

Other important developments during Cheek's administration were the establishment of the Friends of the Schlesinger Library, whose annual gifts support acquisitions and preservation work; the endorsement by the Advisory Board of work in oral history and its beginnings with the assistance of Katie Louchheim; the development and submission of the first proposals for foundation support, in part the result of the request of the National Historical Publications Commission; the decision to document, as completely as possible, the rapidly expanding women's movement, including the acquisition of the papers of Betty Friedan and of the National Organization for Women; and the signing of a contract with G.K. Hall and Company for the publication of the Library's catalogs. All of these initiatives have been actively pursued in the decade following Cheek's retirement in 1973: the Schlesinger Library has grown in its holdings and numbers of users, twice expanded into additional space, and undertaken a variety of special projects.

THE MANUSCRIPT HOLDINGS OF THE SCHLESINGER LIBRARY[11]

In the early years there were no written collecting guidelines; indeed, they would have seemed superfluous when many doubted the existence of sufficient material to justify a separate library on women. Some early directions and interests, in addition to woman's rights and suffrage, however, are evident in correspondence among Park, Jordan, Schlesinger, and other early supporters. The papers of prominent women were to be collected as were the records of women's organizations. Family papers and other materials illustrating women's domestic roles were sought, and for a time there seemed to be an understanding, never fully implemented, that Radcliffe would concern itself with women in politics and reform, leaving women in the arts and literature to the Sophia Smith Collection.

By the early 1960s, when the stacks and other storerooms appropriated in Byerly Hall were bulging with more than 150 ''large'' manuscript collections, that is, collections filling one or more ''Hollinger'' boxes, it seemed time to review the strengths of the holdings and to establish policies to guide future collecting. Director Barbara Solomon, in consultation with the Advisory Board, drafted guidelines in 1962. These emphasized that manuscript collecting was to be directed toward those areas where a firm basis had already been established:[12]

1. collections reflecting movements in which the impetus of women has been predominant, such as suffrage and peace, and organizations for social, educational, and political purposes,
2. collections of individuals whose work opened the way to women in particular professions and occupations,
3. collections of organizations concerned with women's employment in various occupations,
4. collections of family papers providing valuable commentary on the domestic role of women and career patterns, seen through diaries and correspondence of several generations of men as well as women, and
5. collections relating to the historical role of women in American education.

At that time it was stated that ''manuscripts of women writers would not be collected because Houghton 'covers the literary field,' except when authors were also involved in other activities appropriate to the Library's holdings.''

The guidelines were reviewed in 1971 by a subcommittee of the Advisory Board, and again in 1979-80 when the Advisory Committee (the name was changed in the mid 1970s) approved a more explicit policy statement drafted by director Patricia Miller King and members of the Library staff.[13] While the research value of each potential acquisition is always individually assessed, the Collection Development Policies provide a framework within which staff seek and appraise possible new acquisitions. Over recent years, with increasing pressure on available space and staff time, more and more marginally appropriate collections have been referred to other more suitable repositories.

A description of holdings for which the catalog cards and manuscript inventories filled three large volumes when published in 1973, and which will, it is estimated, require eleven volumes for a revised edition, can be but a summary. Thus, the following is offered with the caveat that it only touches on major subject areas and collections with a few illustrative examples.

Woman's Rights, Suffrage, Feminism, and the Women's Movement

In addition to the WRC, and the Dillon and Somerville-Howorth collections mentioned above, significant holdings include diaries, speeches, and letters of Susan B. Anthony (1820-1906), many bought at auction at Park-Bernet in December 1964. This material is especially significant for the light it throws on Anthony's early and formative years. Some letters cover her first extended stay away from home in 1837 when she attended Deborah Moulson's Quaker school near Philadelphia; others date from her years as a teacher in several upstate New York towns and record the development of her concern with the evils of drink, racial discrimination, and the status of women. Later letters describe suffrage conventions and speaking engagements as well as her family interests.

Extensive holdings of Blackwell family papers, including those donated in 1959 and others currently being acquired, are supplemented by Lucy Stone letters given by Alma Lutz. These show the involvement of members of this extraordinary family, especially Dr. Elizabeth Blackwell (1821-1910) and Antoinette Brown Blackwell (1825-1921), in a variety of 19th-century reform causes in addition to suffrage. Despite shared reform tendencies, however, family members did not agree on every issue. Lucy Stone (1818-93) insisted on retaining her own name when she married, but her sister-in-law Antoinette Brown Blackwell, the first ordained woman minister of a recognized denomination, wrote in her typescript autobiography:

> In marrying I had no hesitation in adopting my husband's name. . .I felt entirely certain of rctaining my own individual-

> ity and reasoned 'what's in a name?' I was content to make my protests against more vital issues.[14]

Antoinette Blackwell provided inspiration for Olympia Brown (1835-1926), who heard her preach while a student at Antioch. Brown was ordained as a Universalist minister in 1863 and became a vigorous spokesperson for suffrage. Her extensive papers show a reformer with a less all-embracing concern for reform than the Blackwells. At first a member of the National Woman Suffrage Association, in her later years she joined the NWP and in her 80s was distributing suffrage literature denouncing President Wilson in front of the White House. Still another 19th-century advocate of woman's rights was Boston author Caroline Wells Healey Dall (1822-1912). A participant in Margaret Fuller's conversations, Dall wrote and lectured extensively on woman's rights in the 1850s and 1860s before turning her attention to other causes.

Other collections document a younger generation of suffragists organizing in the states. Helen Brewster Owens first worked in the campaign in Kansas and then, starting in 1913, organized a district in upstate New York under the direction of Carrie Chapman Catt. Alde L. T. Blake worked in the 1912 campaign in Michigan and Mary Jane Whitely Coggeshall (1836-1911), in Iowa.

The leading intellectual of the woman's rights movement in the United States, Charlotte Perkins Gilman (1860-1935), believed that economic independence was the foremost need for women. Neglected and almost forgotten after her death, Gilman is being again appreciated as a profound and original thinker. Dozens of researchers are examining the full corpus of her publications, speeches, and correspondence, kept virtually intact by her daughter Katherine Stetson Chamberlin until its acquisition by the Schlesinger Library in 1971.

Despite the intentions of Park and Stantial to establish a doctrinally pure historical record, the radical suffragists who joined Alice Paul in the Congressional Union and the NWP have in recent years found their way into the Library's stacks in large numbers. Notable among them are Inez Milholland (1886-1916), a zealous advocate of all reform causes who undertook a speaking tour in the West for the NWP in 1916. At the time she was suffering from pernicious anemia; she collapsed in Los Angeles and died there ten weeks later.

The Library's record of the activities of NWP members continues into the post-suffrage period. In 1923, this single-minded band of feminists initiated the long struggle for the passage of an Equal Rights Amendment and in succeeding years occasionally vented their frustration in internecine battles for control of the organization. Collections that are informative on NWP affairs from the 1920s through the 1950s include the papers of Caroline Lexow Babcock, Laura M. Berrien, Florence Ledyard Kitchelt (1874-1961), Alma Lutz (1890-1973), Jeannette A. Marks (1875-1964), and Anna Kelton Wiley (1893-1962). Documentation of the women leaders (few of whom would have acknowledged the appelation feminist) who followed Park and Catt into the League of Women Voters and continued their moderate tradition on both the local and national level is equally ample. It can be found in such papers as those of Dorothy Kirchwey Brown (1888-1981), Sara Emelie Rosenfeld Ehrmann, Edna Gellhorn (1878-1970), Lucile Heming Koshland, Percy Maxim Lee, Eunice Mannheim (1907-60), Catherine Gougar Waugh McCulloch (1862-1945), Belle Sherwin (1868-1955), Anna Lord Strauss (1899-1979), and Marguerite Milton Wells (1872-1959).

By the late 1960s and early 1970s the agitation of a new generation of feminists was garnering daily headlines. It rapidly became apparent that the Women's Movement was not a passing phenomenon, but a major social movement whose impact would profoundly, radically, and permanently alter American society. In 1962, the Library had begun acquiring files of President Kennedy's Commission on the Status of Women, a group whose discussions signaled what was to come. In 1971, with the acquisition of the papers of Betty Freidan, author of *The Feminine Mystique* (1963), and designation as the official repository for the papers of the National Organization for Women (NOW), it made a wholehearted commitment to collect in-depth documentation of the campaign to end discrimination on the basis of sex in every aspect of life.

Currently the official repository for the files of such national organizations as the National Association of Commissions for Women and the Women's Equity Action League (WEAL) as well as NOW, the Library is also receiving the records of a limited number of more specialized professional or local feminist organizations. These include the Coordinating Committee on Women in the Historical Profession, Boston's 9 to 5, COYOTE (a group seeking to decriminalize prostitution), the Project on the Status and Education of Women, Sociologists for Women in Society, and the Women's Action Organization (a group of women in the U.S. foreign service agencies).

Papers of individual activists, including Elinor Guggenheimer, Wilma Scott Heide, Eve Merriam, Marguerite Rawalt, Bernice Sandler, and Barbara Seaman, are rapidly filling the shelves of the expanded manuscript vault space acquired in 1981. There are also letters to the editor of *Ms.* Magazine and records of a small number of especially significant sex discrimination suits, such as the successful class action suit initiated by the Women's Caucus against *The New York Times* on behalf of 560 women employees. Many of these contemporary collections are temporarily partially or completely restricted, as are a few holdings discussed elsewhere.

Government, Politics, and the Law

Another strong area is in the records of women who have held appointed, civil service, or elected office in the local, state, or national government. Among elected officials who have gained national prominence and whose papers are at the Library are Jeannette Rankin (1880-1973), the first woman in Congress and the only member to vote against United States participation in both World Wars; Edith Nourse Rogers (1881-1960), Republican Representative from Massachusetts for 35 years and chairman of the Veterans Affairs Committee; and Democratic Congresswoman Elizabeth Holtzman, who served in the House of Representatives from 1973 to 1980 and is now District Attorney in Brooklyn, New York. The contemporary explosion of paper and the problem it poses for research libraries is illustrated by the relative sizes of these three Congressional collections. Rankin's papers fill fewer than six shelf feet; Roger's papers have expanded to a still-manageable 25-30 feet; the papers of Holtzman, still early in her public service career, occupy more than 300 feet of shelf space.

To supplement its holdings on women in government, the Library in 1981 began an oral history project to interview more than 30 women who have made substantial contributions in appointed or civil service positions on the federal level. Supported by a grant from the National Endowment for the Humanities (NEH) and by matching funds contributed by Friends of the Library, the project includes among its interviewees: Lucy Benson, Catherine East, Kathryn Heath, Captain Grace Hopper, Mary Dublin Keyserling, Virginia McLaughlin, Katherine Oettinger, Wilma Victor, Caroline Ware, Bennetta Washington, and Aryness Joy Wickens.

Among the many lawyers and judges whose papers are at the Library are: Florence Ellinwood Allen (1884-1966), a U.S. Circuit Court of Appeals judge in Ohio; Jennie Loitman Barron (1891-1969), who became an associate justice of the Boston Municipal Court in 1937; Sarah T. Hughes, since 1961 judge of the U.S. District Court of the Northern District of Texas; Angela Parisi (1914-61), assistant corporation counsel of the City of New York; Lena Madesin Phillips (ca.1881-1955), the Kentucky lawyer who founded The International Federation of Business and Professional Women; and Harriet Pilpel, New York lawyer who defends women's freedom of choice in reproductive issues; and Justine Wise Polier, judge from 1935 to 1973 of the Domestic Relations Court of New York City.

Employment and Trade Union Activities

The conditions of women's employment and their participation in labor unions are topics of continuing research interest. The correspondence, diaries, and scrapbooks of Harriet Jane Hanson Robinson (1825-1911) and her daughter Harriette Lucy Robinson Shattuck (1850-1937) include letters from Lucy Larcom (1824-93) and other Lowell mill girls and are rich in information on working conditions for women in the 19th century. Material on early 20th-century factory work and union organizing is found in the extensive personal correspondence of Mary Dreier (1875-1963); and the previously mentioned papers of Leonora O'Reilly.

A small but significant labor dispute between President Lowell of Harvard and the scrubwomen who cleaned Widener Library is chronicled in papers of Corliss Lamont. Lowell fired the scrubwomen just before Christmas rather than pay them the minimum wage of 37 cents per hour. Lamont raised funds to recompense the 19 women for the unjustly withheld back wages and eventually pushed the University into reviewing its wage scales for all employees.

The voluminous files of worker educator Hilda Worthington Smith are supplemented by a smaller collection recording efforts of Margaret Earhart Smith (1902-60) in the same field, especially in the 1940s. Still restricted, but promising to provide insights into the women's labor movement in the 20th century, are the papers of Pauline Newman, a labor organizer from 1909 to 1917. International Ladies' Garment Workers' Union organizer, Maida Springer Kemp, is sending her papers documenting victories won over nearly five decades for women workers in this country and in various African nations. Kemp's papers accompany her oral history, recorded as part of the Library's Black Women Oral History Project and in cooperation with the "Twentieth-Century Trade Union Woman" Project. Copies of the 42 transcripts produced by that project, sponsored by the Institute of Labor and Industrial Relations of the University of Michigan and Wayne State University, are also at the Schlesinger Library.

Education

The education of women, formal and informal, at all levels from preschool through graduate programs, and women as educators, are within the scope of the Library's collecting. Holdings include such diverse items as correspondence of kindergarten educator Elizabeth Palmer Peabody (1804-94) and papers of Abigail Eliot, cofounder of the Eliot-Pearson School of Child Study at Tufts University; and records of Katharine Taylor (1888-1979), a progressive educator who directed the Shady Hill School in Cambridge, Mass., from 1921 to 1949; correspondence of university professors, including historian Helen Maud Cam (1885-1968), the first woman on the Faculty of Arts and Sciences at Harvard University; papers of college presidents Elizabeth Cary Agassiz (1822-1907) and Ada Louise Comstock (1876-1973) of Radcliffe and Sarah Gibson Blanding of Vassar College; and transcripts of the oral histories of lawyer Sadie Alexander and educator Eva Dykes, two of the three black women who in 1921 were the first women of their race to earn Ph.D.s.

Diaries and letters written by school girls and by school teachers abound. Some authors, like Frances Merritt Quick (1833-1924), related experiences as a student and later as a teacher. Vocational education for older women seeking to rejoin the labor force in the 1950s, particularly in clerical positions, is the subject of the records of the New York House and School of Industry. In-depth documentation of the development of women's studies in the 1970s will soon be acquired in materials promised by Florence Howe, president of The Feminist Press.

Holdings on education, as in other areas, reflect change in organizations over time. Fannie Fern Andrews launched the Boston Home and School Association in 1907 in a progressive effort to bring parents into more active participation in the public schools. The Intercollegiate Association of Women Students was founded in 1923 primarily to recommend social policies and regulations for the conduct of women students; its emphasis more recently has been on the elimination of differential student conduct regulations based on sex.

Religion and the Missions

Religious belief and participation in worship services and other church activities played significant roles in the lives of most women of the 19th century and have remained central concerns in the lives of many of the 20th-century descendants. Some, like suffrage leaders Antoinette Brown Blackwell, Olympia Brown, and Anna Howard Shaw, defied social conventions by seeking ordination. Others devoted lives to religion through more conventional routes, as lay missionaries or clergy wives, or by volunteering their services to church organizations.

Among the holdings of the Library are the papers of Grace Morrison Boynton (1890-1961?), a missionary educator in China; Victoria Booth Demarest (ca.1890-1982), granddaughter of the founder of The Salvation Army and itinerant evangelist, minister, musician, and author; Margaret Cook Thomson (1889-1975), a teacher and missionary for the United Presbyterian Church for more than 30 years until expelled from China in 1949 and Frances Davidson Tuttle (1876-1946) who, with her husband, served the Baptist Church as a missionary in Assam, India.

Medicine, Public Health, and Reproductive Issues

To the papers of physicians Elizabeth Blackwell, Alice Hamilton, and Mary Putnam Jacobi, have been added the extensive files of Martha May Eliot, M.D. (1891-1978), head of the U.S. Children's Bureau and national and world leader in the field of maternal and child health; papers of other physicians including Connie M. Guion (1882-1971), Harriet Hardy, and Edith Banfield Jackson (1895-1977), and files of Anna Wessel Williams (1863-1954), a research bacteriologist who was the first woman elected to office in the laboratory section of the American Public Health Association.

Other health professions are represented by Lini Moerkerk de Vries (d.1982), heroic public health nurse in the mountains of Mexico; Mary Sewall Gardner (1871-1961), a national leader in public health nursing; Carrie May Hall (1874-1963), a nursing educator who served in World War I; and Maida Herman Solomon, psychiatric social worker and educator.

Researchers interested in various aspects of sex, reproduction, and marriage will find data in the files of the Birth Control League of Massachusetts, the Massachusetts Society for Social Health, and the extensive files of Mary S. Calderone, M.D., founder and leader of the Sex Education and Information Council of the United States (SIECUS). Other sources are the papers of birth control activist Lucile Lord-Heinstein, M.D., and pioneering marriage counselor, Emily Mudd, Ph.D. The archives of the National Abortion Rights Action League (NARAL) are temporarily restricted, but researchers may have access to some of the files of the now defunct Society for Humane Abortion.

These manuscript collections are supplemented by the tapes, transcripts, and supporting materials from a series of oral history interviews sponsored by the Library from 1974 to 1976 with support from The Rockefeller Foundation. Interviewees include Drs. Calderone, Eliot, and Mudd, whose papers are also at the Library; leaders in the birth control movement such as Loraine Leeson Campbell (1905-82) deliverers of family planning services including Elizabeth Arnold, R.N., and Louise Hutchins, M.D.; and crusaders for women's right to access to medically safe, legal abortion, including Patricia Maginnis and Lana Clarke Phelan.

Social Welfare and Reform

Reform causes of every description have captured the imagination and harnessed the talents and energies of American women throughout the 19th and 20th centuries. Abolition is one of the early causes chronicled in holdings at the Library, especially in the papers of those well-known reforming families the Beechers and Stowes and the Blackwells, and in the correspondence of Lydia Maria Child (1802-80), the papers of Ellis Gray Loring (1803-58), and in the miscellaneous collection of correspondence of leading women abolitionists and suffragists assembled by Alma Lutz and bearing her name. Contemporary reformers include Virginia Foster Durr, whose concern for Civil Rights is recorded in her papers; the work of other Civil Rights activists is documented at the Library in transcripts of the Black Women Oral History Project. The anti-Vietnam War protest is represented by the files of Helen Lamb Lamont (1906-75).

In the late 19th century, much of the reforming zeal of college-educated women was directed toward settlement houses that provided a variety of services to neighborhood residents. Records at the Library include those of Denison House, founded in 1892 in Boston's South End by a small group which included Emily Balch, Helen Cheever, Vida Scudder, and Helene Dudley, who was head worker between 1893 and 1912; and papers of Mary Kingsbury Simkhovitch (1867-1951), founder of Greenwich House in New York's Greenwich Village in 1902.

In the 20th century, social work became professionalized. Eva Whiting White (1885-1974) received the first B.S. in Social Work awarded by Simmons College in 1907. She was head worker at Elizabeth Peabody House from 1909 to 1944, professor at Simmons College, 1922-50, and among her other activities was president of the Women's Educational and Industrial Union from 1929 to 1952.

The Family and Domesticity

Family collections are among the richest of the holdings, offering varied information to an endless stream of researchers investigating social customs, household arrangements, child rearing practices, and relationships between husband and wives, siblings, and mothers and daughters, and among others related by blood or marriage or connected by ties of friendship or common interests. Many prominent Boston and New England families are represented, including the Algers, Almys, Bradleys and Hydes, Cabots, Danas, Eliots, Emersons and Nichols, Gardiners, Howes, Mays and Goddards, Nichols and Shurtleffs, and Poors.

The Chamberlain-Adams family papers, 1832-1926, are but one of many family collections including a lengthy courtship correspondence. The Albert Gallatin Browne family papers include his informative letters to his wife written from Beaufort, S.C., and Savannah, Ga., during and immediately after the Civil War. The letters of Sarah Ripley (1793-1867) reveal the intellectual concerns of a 19th-century New England woman. Hamilton family papers include lengthy exchanges of letters between Dr. Alice Hamilton and her cousin Agnes (1869-1961), between classicist Edith Hamilton (1867-1963) and another cousin, Jessie, and among other siblings and cousins; they illuminate close and enduring friendships between many female relations and the choices of occupation of women born in the latter half of the 19th century.

Driggs-Rust and Huntting-Rudd family papers chronicle life in New York State, Somerville-Howorth family papers represent life in Mississippi, and the Adams family papers, available on microfilm, are a source for Massachusetts, national, and international history. The Bledsoe-Herrick family papers received from Springfield, Ohio, include writings of Sophia M'Ilvaine Bledsoe Herrick (1837-1919), who supported her three children, after separating from her husband, by serving as head of a girls' school in Baltimore, assisting her father in editing *The Southern Review,* 1874-78, and then becoming an assistant editor for *Scribner's Monthly.* Hollingsworth-Kirk papers include material on Wallis Warfield Simpson.

Insight into domestic and family life and into the endlessly varied activities of family members is also furnished in single diaries or journals that recount only a fragment of a life. Also useful are artificially created collections such as the Hooker Collection, which includes correspondence by housewives and women schoolteachers on such subjects as education, politics, marriage, and social life and customs in the period between 1788 and 1890. Only family life in the very recent past still escapes the scrutiny of the social historian roaming through these varied private writings.

Black Women Oral History Project

Aware that its resources and those available elsewhere inadequately represented the lives and achievements of black women, the Library in 1976, at the suggestion of Letitia Woods Brown, initiated a project to record the autobiographical memoirs of a group of distinguished older black women. These women, through their contributions to their communities and to their professions, have improved the quality of life in 20th-century America for black people and all citizens. The 71 interviewees, most of whom were 70 years of age or older at the time of their interviews, were selected by an advisory committee of black women scholars and community leaders. All except one of the oral histories have been transcribed, and processing has been completed on 56. The completed transcripts, except for a few that are temporarily restricted, are available for use at the Library and at more than a dozen other repositories throughout the United States and also in Germany.

A few of the interviewees in this project are: Christia Adair of Houston, a community organizer, civic worker, and teacher, who worked for equal rights for blacks and women; Margaret Walker Alexander, author, poet, and teacher; Alice Dunnigan, the first black woman journalist to be admitted to the Congressional Press galleries; Dorothy Height, President of the National Council of Negro Women; Lois Jones, an artist who was professor of design and watercolor at Howard University; Hattie Kelley, dean of women at Tuskegee Institute, 1945-62; Mary Thompson, a dentist who organized a group of dentists to provide care for the needy in Mound Bayou, La.; the Rev. Charleszetta Waddles, a social welfare and spiritual leader in Detroit; Dorothy West, one of the last living writers of the Harlem Renaissance; and Deborah Partridge Wolfe, an educator, organizational leader, and Baptist minister in Cranford, N.J.

Visual Holdings

Visual documentation of the lives of American women was at first seldom actively sought and was received mostly in conjunction with accessions of family and personal papers. More recently, photographic evidence of women's movement events and of women in previously male-dominated occupations and activities has been consciously solicited. The Library has become the repository for prints of contemporary photographers Diana Mara Henry, Bettye Lane, Freda Leinwand, and Marjorie Nichols; and to supplement the Black Women Oral History Project, the Library secured funding from Warner Communications to send Judith Sedwick around the country to take magnificent color portraits of many of the interviewees.

The concern with images by and of women had also led to the acceptance of approximately 10,000 prints and negatives of the pioneering photojournalist Jessie Tarbox Beals (1870-1942) along with related personal and family papers. A rare group of visual documents, 45 British suffrage posters, many created by members of the Artists' Suffrage League, was restored with the assistance of a grant from the Massachusetts Council on the Arts and Humanities. Perhaps most helpful to photo researchers at the Library is a project that, with the assistance of Research Publications, Inc., has microfilmed nearly 17,000 photographs in the processed holdings, and is cataloging these images.

Organizations and Their Leaders

Dozens of diverse organizations through which women worked for common purposes as diverse as radical reform and social pleasure have placed their archives at the Library. Many have been mentioned above; a few additional examples include: The Ladies' Physiological Institute of Boston and Vicinity, founded in 1848 to promote among women "a knowledge of the human system and the laws of life, and the means of relieving sickness and suffering"; the New England Women's Club, one of the oldest women's clubs in the country, which began in 1868 to provide a meeting place for women outside their homes where they could obtain knowledge and inspiration; the Saturday Morning Club of Boston, established in 1871 by Julia Ward Howe to promote "culture and social intercourse" for her daughter Maud and other young women.

"Prominent" and Not-So-Prominent Women

A few holdings defy easy categorization, except perhaps as being among those "prominent women" whose papers were to be sought. The Library has been the repository for papers of aviator Amelia Earhart (1897-1937) since 1962; in 1983 it received those of her mother, Amy Otis Earhart, including approximately 100 Amelia Earhart notes and letters dating from childhood to a few hours before she took off on her final flight. A very different life story is revealed in nearly 450 letters of anarchist Emma Goldman (1869-1940). A prolific writer, Goldman lost many of her papers when she was arrested and exiled.

Yet another celebrity is Helen Keller (1880-1968), the blind deaf-mute who overcame monumental difficulties to earn a A.B. from Radcliffe College and to become an internationally known supporter of numerous humanitarian causes. A sampling of her letters is at the Library; most of her papers are at the American Federation for the Blind. A woman who overcame obstacles of a very different nature was Maimie, a reformed prostitute from Philadelphia. In a lengthy series of letters to Fannie Quincy Howe of Boston, mostly written between 1911 and 1918. Maimie related her efforts to become "respectably" self-supporting.

"The History of Women's History"

Aware of the significance of the recent development of women's history and women's studies and their impact on scholarship and teaching, the Library has begun to acquire the records of the field of endeavor in which it participates. Before her death, Mary Beard destroyed most of her papers, but the early period of women's history is represented by the small collection of the World Center for Women's Archives which she donated and by the extensive files of Marjorie White (1894-1972). White's scrapbooks and notes were used by Beard as she wrote *Woman As Force in History* and include correspondence with Beard as well as with Mary Milbank Brown, who inspired White's interest in prehistoric woman.

Files of the Berkshire Conference of Women Historians provide a transition to the contemporary period. These women, who were historians working in all fields, in 1972 began to sponsor the Berkshire Conferences on the History of Women. Copies of unpublished papers presented at successive Berkshire Conferences on Women are at the Library. Another part of the recent past is represented by the office files of the Women's History Research Center of Berkeley, Cal. Here Laura X made a valiant effort to collect everything about and by women in the late 1960s and early 1970s until she was overwhelmed by masses of paper. Also at the Library, although still restricted, are papers of Eleanor Flexner, who was a lonely pioneer when she researched and wrote *Century of Struggle* (1951), and files of scholar and teacher Gerda Lerner, whose leadership has resulted in the introduction of women's history courses and women's studies programs into undergraduate and graduate curricula throughout the nation.

BOOKS AND PERIODICALS

In the Library's early years, books and periodicals, like manuscripts, were acquired primarily by gift. When a specific collecting policy was articulated in 1962, it stated that books were to be collected because of their functional connection with manuscript collections and to provide a working body of reference works for the convenience of researchers and staff. The 1962 collecting guidelines also allowed that historic cookery and etiquette books were to be accepted "with discrimination" as sources illuminating domestic patterns, family mores, and social thought and customs. Following this policy, by the late 1960s, the collection of printed materials had grown to approximately 8,000 volumes.

Thereafter, the growth of research demand and the availability of increased funds for acquisitions made it possible to begin the gradual transformation of the book collection from an adjunct to the manuscript holdings to a significant special collection of intrinsic worth as a resource for research. At first, buying was nearly equally divided between out-of-print and newly published volumes. The concern was not with rare and valuable volumes, but with information on the history of women. Now that major gaps in the holdings have been filled, by purchase and by the acquisition of the complete microfilms of the *History of Women,* a project in which the Library participated, most of the 1,000 or more volumes purchased annually are new publications. The Library also continues to receive several hundred additional volumes by gift each year.

The subject area of the book collection parallels the manuscript holdings in its focus on United States women in the 19th and 20th centuries. The book holdings, however, also include numerous titles in the social sciences, some comparative material about women in other cultures, books on women in the arts and in music, feminist literary criticism, and selected works of contemporary fiction. The holdings in 1983 exceed 23,000 volumes, and an additional 8,000-10,000 titles are held in microform.

Periodical subscriptions were similarly limited in the early decades, numbering approximately 20. Again a dramatic change came in the late 1960s as efforts began to acquire the rapidly proliferating and sporadically produced newsletters, journals, and other serial publications spawned by the women's movement. Subscriptions were also entered to a broader range of the popular magazines for women. Currently periodical subscriptions number nearly 300 and include the full range of U.S. popular, scholarly, and specialized publications about and for women, and a few Canadian or international titles. Some missing periodical titles and others that are deteriorating from age or frequent use are being acquired in microform.

Other printed materials include approximately 40 file drawers of ephemera: newspaper clippings, pamphlets, flyers, brochures, etc. These are arranged in subject, biography, and organization files, and provide researchers with information on topics of current concern and, from time to time, with data on women and organizations not otherwise represented in the holdings.

THE CULINARY CONNECTION

Although a few works on food and domestic economy were among the early books donated to the Women's Archives, it was not until 1961, when Harvard's Widener Library transferred to the

Women's Archives more than 1,500 volumes on American, English, and continental cookery, that cookbooks became a special focus for collecting. Since that time, the culinary collection has more than doubled in size. A large and valuable group of approximately 800 French, English, Italian, and other volumes, dating from the 17th to the 20th century, was donated by Samuel and Narcissa Chamberlain. Hundreds of other volumes have been received from Julia Child, from the library of Wilma Lord Perkins (1898-1977), a successor "Fannie Farmer," and from many other donors. In addition to social historians investigating domestic customs, the culinary collection now attracts its own coterie of devoted users, many of whom participate in the monthly meetings of a culinary history research group.

The Library's cookbooks may claim indirect responsibility for the establishment of the Women's Culinary Guild, an organization of nearly 140 professional women in the food field in the Boston area. They also have been the impetus for a series of benefit cooking demonstrations by such well-known chefs as Julia Child, Craig Claiborne, Pierre Franey, Madeleine Kammen, and Jacques Pepin. These events have added more than $50,000 to the Library's endowment.

Limited collecting of manuscript materials relating to culinary history has also been undertaken. The Library is the repository for the papers of "French Chef" Julia Child and author M. F. K. Fisher; both of these collections are temporarily restricted.

SPECIAL PROJECTS

Since 1973, with support from the National Endowment for the Humanities, the National Historical Publications and Records Commission, the William Bingham Foundation of Cleveland, Ohio, and gifts and grants to Radcliffe College for the Schlesinger Library from other private foundations, government funding agencies, and individuals, a series of special projects have been sponsored.[16] These projects have had as their objectives:

—the processing of manuscript holdings to make them accessible for research use

—the microfilming of rare, fragile, and frequently used mate-

rials, to preserve them and make it possible to loan them through interlibrary loan
—the letterpress and microfilm publication of research materials of special interest
—the conducting of oral histories with selected groups of women to improve or create documentation on their lives and accomplishments
—the support of researchers who wish to use the Library's holdings
—the sponsorship of outreach programs to increase public awareness and understanding of women's history and women's studies
—the expansion and improvement of the Library's facilities, the increase of its endowment, and the broadening of the base of financial support for its activities

As a result of these grant-funded projects, numerous manuscript collections relating to women's education, careers, family lives, and health have been processed, and improved control has been established over many collections of records of contemporary organizations and the voluminous papers of Elizabeth Holtzman. More than a dozen manuscript collections are available on microfilm or microfiche through interlibrary loan; these include the papers of the Beecher-Stowe and Blackwell families, Charlotte Perkins Gilman, the Hamilton family, Harriet Hosmer, Jeannette Rankin, and Harriet Hanson Robinson and Harriette Robinson Shattuck. The microfilming of the papers of Emma Goldman is also nearing completion. *The Maimie Papers,* a volume including nearly two-thirds of the collection of that name, has been edited and published in cooperation with The Feminist Press (1977), and a project to edit and microfilm *The Papers of the Women's Trade Union League and its Principal Leaders* (including four collections at the Schlesinger Library and holdings of six cooperating libraries) has been completed and is being distributed by Research Publications, Inc.

Three sizable oral history projects, as well as a few individual interviews have been sponsored. The first project, which focused on women who had been active in the birth control movement, the campaign to repeal the abortion laws, and in related areas, interviewed 24 women. The Black Women Oral History Project, which has been under the day-to-day oversight of project coordinator Ruth Hill, has interviewed 71 women, distributed many transcripts to other repositories, especially at institutions with strong interests in black and women's history. The current project, "Women in the Federal Government: Documentation of Their Contributions through Oral History," is interviewing more than 30 women who have served in a variety of federal departments, agencies, and offices. Except for a limited number that are temporarily restricted, copies of completed transcripts can be borrowed through interlibrary loan or purchased by other libraries. In the oral history area, in addition to sponsoring its own projects, the Library has a continuing exchange program to trade transcripts with the Columbia University Oral History Research Office and regularly acquires copies of the transcripts of appropriate interviews or series sponsored by other institutions and projects.

Two grants from the Andrew W. Mellon Foundation to encourage the research use of the holdings of the Schlesinger Library and the Henry A. Murray Center, Radcliffe College's social science research center, have supported stipends for two or more Research Scholars using the Library each year since 1978-79. In addition, the Mellon grants fund the Radcliffe Research Support Program, which gives awards of up to $1,500 for travel and other research expenses of those using the Library. A dozen or more awards are made annually under this program which will continue through 1984-85. There are four annual deadlines for the Radcliffe Research Support Program: the 15th of February, April, September, and December.

During the past decade, the Library has sponsored colloquia, conferences, programs, and presentations relating to its holdings; most have been in Cambridge and have attracted audiences of students, scholars, and Friends of the Library. In 1981, a more ambitious outreach effort was initiated, a project supported by the National Endowment for the Humanities and entitled: "Women in the Community: Who Are They? Where Where They? Where Are They Going?" Under the direction of the Curator of Printed Books, Barbara Haber, and project coordinator Joy Christi Przestwor, ten community teams were selected from 94 applicant groups from all over the United States. They were brought to Cambridge for a one-week training session, then returned to their communities where they planned and implemented programs with a humanities focus on women's issues. The final product of the project is *Connecting Women in the Community. . .a Handbook for Programs,* based on the experiences of the project staff.

THE FORTIETH ANNIVERSARY

During 1983-84, a series of special events will mark 40 years of collecting, preserving, and making available for research use unpublished and published materials documenting the lives of American women and their families. Lifetime Achievement Awards will be presented to ten distinguished women who have made important contributions in varying fields of endeavor; a scholarly conference will assess the progress made in women's history and look toward future directions; and a meeting of archivists, librarians, historians, and others will be co-sponsored with the Sophia Smith Collection to encourage the exchange of information and cooperation among institutions and individuals collecting and using research materials on the history of women. Although much of the history of women yet remains to be investigated, written, and made part of the common understanding of our heritage, surely great progress has been made in that search for "source materials dealing with women's lives and activities" that Mary Beard sought to initiate nearly a half century ago.

FOOTNOTES

1. "World Center for Women's Archives," unsigned, undated, 4 p. pamphlet, in the Mary Ritter Beard papers, Schlesinger Library, Radcliffe College (hereafter SL).

2. Beard papers, folder 17, SL. Beard's note on this letter is also of interest: "I returned Dr. Hamilton's check for five dollars until I can talk with her and make her really want to give it. When I explain to her that I too am deeply interested in women's feminine contributions and not primarily in their imitative work, I may be able to win her genuine support. But I do think it immature for her to talk about "men's fields" for that shows such a lack of historical perspective. Maybe I shall fail to win Dr. Hamilton." M.R.B.

3. Information on the history of the SL can be found in the office files of the Women's Archives (hereafter WA) and the SL in the Radcliffe College Archives (hereafter RCA). See also an unpublished masters thesis by Madeleine Bagwell Perez, " 'Remember the Ladies. . . ' The Arthur and Elizabeth Schlesinger Library on the History of Women in America: Its Role in the Collection and Preservation of Women's History Source Materials," (Wake Forest University, May 1982), at the SL. Published sources include two articles by Janet Wilson James, "The Schlesinger Library at Radcliffe College," *The Bay State Librarian,* v. 56, n. 3 (July 1966), 9-16; and "History and Women at Harvard: The Schlesinger Library," *Harvard Library Bulletin,* v. 41, n. 4 (October 1968), 385-99; Eva Moseley, "Women's Archives: Documenting the History of Women in America," *American Archivist,* v. 36 (April 1973), 215-22; Renee Gold, "A Room of One's Own: Radcliffe's Schlesinger Library," *Wilson Library Bulletin,* v. 55 (June 1981), 750-55; and reports of the Library, issued annually, 1953-64, and biennially or triennially thereafter.

4. Some of Maud Wood Park's papers are part of the WRC, SL.

5. Some correspondence of Park and Wilbur K. Jordan can be found in the office files of the WA, RCA; other papers were placed by Edna Stantial, after Park's death, in the Manuscript Division of the Library of Congress.

6. Beard papers, folder 29, SL.

7. This arrangement, demanded by Park and Stantial, lasted into the 1960s when Longfellow Hall was sold by Radcliffe and the WRC was consolidated with the WA.

8. Mary Earhard Dillon to The Women's Library, Radcliffe College, June 15, 1948; Dillon to Patricia Miller King, January 8, 1975; Dillon to Frank McCulloch, June 13, 1975, all in the office files of the SL.

9. Barbara Miller Solomon initiated the inclusion of copies of catalog cards for the WA's published holdings in Harvard's Union Catalog and Harvard's sending to the WA copies of catalog cards for books subject cataloged under ''Woman'' or ''Women.'' This arrangement terminated in 1977 when Harvard began machine-readable cataloging. Since September 1981, when the SL became a member of OCLC, Inc., through the Harvard University Library, SL cataloging information has been included in Harvard's Distributable Union Catalog (DUC). A complete copy of the microfiche DUC is available to users of theSL.

10. Unpublished annual report submitted by Janet Wilson James to the president of Radcliffe, in the office files of the SL.

11. Information on the manuscript holdings is published in Arthur and Elizabeth Schlesinger Library on the History of Women in America: *The Manuscript Inventories, Catalogs of Manuscripts, Books, and Pictures* (Boston, G.K. Hall & Co., 1973), 3 vols. (Vol. 3: *Manuscript Catalog, Manuscript Inventories, Picture Catalog); National Union Catalog of Manuscript Collections, passim.;* Andrea Hinding et al., eds., *Women's History Sources: A Guide to Archives and Manuscript Collections in the United States* (New York, Bowker, 1979). The Library staff are discussing with G.K. Hall & Co. the possibility of a complete, revised edition of the catalogs in eleven volumes.

12. Unpublished guidelines in the office files of the SL.

13. Photocopies of the Collection Development Policies of the SL are available upon request.

14. ''Antoinette Brown Blackwell, The First Woman Minister,'' a manuscript autobiography dictated to Mrs. Claude U. Gilson, Blackwell Family Collection (A-77), folder 14, p. 181, SL.

15. A micropublication of books on women published prior to 1920, also including periodicals, manuscripts, and photographs, published by Research Publications, Inc., Woodbridge, Conn.

16. Additional information on many of the SL's special projects is available on request, including a list of the manuscript holdings in microform that may be borrowed through interlibrary loan, lists of oral history transcripts available for borrowing and purchase, application information for the Radcliffe Research Scholar and Radcliffe Research Support Programs, and order forms for *Connecting Women in the Community.*

The Woman's Collection, The Texas Woman's University Library

Elizabeth Snapp

From the creation of the University in 1901, the library's collection policy involved assembling both the works of such standard women authors as Jane Austen, Elizabeth Barrett Browning, and Charlotte Brontë and the works of such recent or contemporary women authors as Charlotte Mary Yonge, Kate Douglas Wiggin, George Sand, Margaret Elizabeth Sangster, George Eliot, Mary Raymond Andrews, Elizabeth Cleghorn Gaskell, and Mary Antin. It also involved the collection of works either by or about women who were receiving recognition for contributions in their field including *Democracy and Social Ethics* and *The Spirit of Youth and the City Streets* by Jane Addams, *Introduction to Psychology* and *A First Book in Psychology* by Mary Whiton Calkins, *The Life of Alice Freeman Palmer* by G. H. Palmer, *Women in Industry* by Edith Abbott, and *Woman and Labor* by Olive Schreiner. Not unexpectedly the early collection included a varied number of works in the category of manners and morals including *Woman's Share in Primitive Culture* by O. T. Mason, *Beauty in the Household* by T. W. Deuring, *The Business Girl* by R. Ashmore, *What Dress Makes of Us* by D. Quigley, *A New Era for Woman, Health Without Drugs* by E. Dewey, and *What a Young Woman Ought to Know* and *Almost a Man* by Mary Wood-Allen. The place of women was depicted in such works as *The Subjection of Women* by John Stuart Mill, *Anti-Suffrage, Ten Good Reasons* by Grace D. Goodioni, *Woman Suffrage* published by the National American Woman's Suffrage Association, and *The Four Epoch's of Woman's Life* by Anna M. Galbraith. Biographical or autobiographical examinations of women of greater or lesser influence were illustrated in the early collection by *Mary Queen of Scots* by Jacob Abbot; *Age of Elizabeth* by Mandell Crieghton, first editor of the *English Historical Review; Margaret Fuller Ossoli* by T. W. Higginson; and *The Story of My Life* by Helen Keller.[1]

Early in 1932 Dr. Louis H. Hubbard, president of the College, recommended to Miss Mary S. Buffum, director of the library from 1928 to 1946, the creation of an officially titled "Woman's Collection." The initial guidelines focused the collection on the lives, autobiographies, letters, and memoirs of prominent women of both earlier periods and of the contemporary generation. The guidelines particularly noted the appropriateness of including women whose lives pictured either early pioneer conditions or sociological conditions.[2]

Approximately sixty works were selected from the general collection to start the Woman's Collection.[3] As a result of a concerted effort over 400 additional volumes were added to the new Collection during 1932. A large number of the new works were secured from either Blackwells or Parker.[4] During the summer and fall of 1932 President Hubbard gave a number of volumes to the Collection including works about Emma Willard, Mary Lyon, Elizabeth Cady Stanton, Susan B. Anthony, and George Sand.[5] The Woman's Collection was separately cataloged and shelved together as an entity.[6] Within two years of its establishment the new Collection contained 700 volumes.[7]

Though not, as stated in the 1932 *Lass-O* article, "the only one known of its kind in any library,"[8] it was one of the very earliest Woman's Collections to be formed in the United States.[9] It was certainly unique to Texas and there was not in 1932[10] nor is there today another separate collection of comparable contemporary quality in the South or Southwest.

The Woman's Collection followed by only one year the development of a Texas Collection, also begun at the suggestion of Dr. Hubbard.[11] This Collection has become increasingly important as a source of background material for the study of Texas women.

Dr. Ivan Schulze, director of the library from 1946 to 1969, had served on the Library Committee during the formation of the Woman's Collection as a member of the Department of English faculty. During his tenure as director he sought to narrow the Woman's Collection by placing substantially greater emphasis on works by and about American women,[12] but the collection practice never adhered completely to this theoretical mold. Benjamin Richards, director from 1969 to 1972, added a number of volumes to the Collection from book dealer offerings.

Dr. Samuel Marino, director from 1973 to 1979, moved the Woman's Collection first from an open stack area to the cage area and subsequently in 1975, as part of a rearrangement of the general collection, to a room in the basement once used as the Reserve Reading Room. As a concomitant of the rearrangement, the collection of books by and about women was transformed into a broad-based research library on women. Marino established a larger and more regular allocation for the Woman's Collection, incorporated some of the women's periodicals and women's reference books into the Woman's Collection, originated the policy of procuring the great microform collections on women, brought together an important cookbook collection as a subsection of the Woman's Collection, added a number of cassettes and phonograph records, and secured the first large manuscript collection. In 1977 a full-time librarian and clerical staff were hired to provide full service for the collection.

Elizabeth Snapp, the current director, relocated the Woman's Collection in 1981 from its outgrown quarters to the redecorated and refurbished West Reading Room with its two story domed ceiling, established an adjacent manuscript and rare book storage area, established a manuscript processing unit, substantially accelerated incorporating the works of women writers and women's periodicals into the Woman's Collection, adopted the policy of securing all of the major women's microform collections, and placed a high priority on adding manuscripts of women active in politics, in literature, and in the arts and of women illustrative of their era and the records of women's groups and organizations.

The dramatic growth of both the size and the research potential of the Woman's Collection during the past several years is due to a number of related factors. In addition to the strong commitment of the present administration of the library to according a central role to the Woman's Collection, the Collection has also received the strong and continuing support of Dr. Mary Evelyn Blagg Huey, the first woman president of the University who by making available over $90,000 in special funds made possible the rearranging and the refurbishing of the Library that enabled the Woman's Collection to be moved to the grand room of the Library, and Dr. Phyllis Bridges, Vice President for Academic Affairs and sometime chairman of the Women's Studies Committee. The Woman's Collection has not only received effective support from the University Library Committee under the chairmanship in recent years of Dr. Paul Thetford and Dr. Nancy Griffin but has also benefited greatly from the very active interest, advice, and activities of a core of dedicated women's scholars on the faculty including particularly Dr. A. Elizabeth Taylor, long one of the leading women historians in the South; Dr. Martha Swain and Dr. Ingrid Scobie of the Department of History, currently writing biographies of prominent women; and Dr. Joyce Thompson of the English faculty, recent author of *Marking a Trail: A History of the Texas Woman's University.* In 1979, in recognition of the resources about the history of Texas women available at TWU, the Texas State Legislature established the History of Texas Women Historical Collection at the Texas Woman's University. During the past year, in working with the architectural firm for the new University Library scheduled for completion in 1985 both the central administration of the University and the library administration have placed a high priority on providing outstanding reader facilities and manuscript and book storage facilities for the Woman's Collection. Attention was drawn to the architectural firm of Hendricks and Walls of Dallas, which had, among other projects, recently restored the Texas Governor's Mansion and which was ultimately selected by the Board of Regents, because of the firm's reputation for designing structures with significant aesthetic aspects as well as works of outstanding quality. Ms. Sarah Weddington, former Texas legislator, Special Assistant to President Jimmy Carter for women's issues, director of the Texas Office of State-Federal Relations in Washington, and a leading member of women's groups, has also assisted in the development of the Woman's Collection as a center for the preservation of materials of special interest to women.

The Woman's Collection currently contains in excess of 24,000 volumes of bound books. Included among the 2,500 rare books on or by women are 349 volumes by women writers listed in *American Fiction: A Contribution Toward a Bibliography, 1774-1900* by Lyle H. Wright. Although rarities have not been of primary concern, some unique and beautiful books have been included in the Collection because they deal with women. One valued possession is Anais Nin's *Nuances,* number seventy-one of ninety-nine numbered and signed copies in the first edition of the work. The beautiful book is hand-bound in Indian raw silk. Edith Wharton's *Quartet,* a collection of four short stories designed, illustrated, printed, and bound by Lewis and Dorothy Allen is also highly prized. The Collection holds one of only 140 copies printed damp on an 1846 Columbian handpress on all-rag paper. The Collection also holds copy twenty-two of an edition of seventy-five copies of *Willa Cather's Red Cloud,* a literary photographic portfolio.

In addition to the monographic volumes, the Woman's Collection currently holds over 2,350 bound periodical volumes and carries 129 current subscriptions. The periodical holdings include complete runs of several earlier women's periodicals such as *The Ladies Repository,* 1841-1876, and *The New Freewoman,* June 15, 1913, to December 15, 1913. Extensive runs, for example, are also available for *Godey's Lady's Book,* 1848-1873, and *Independent Woman,* 1932-1953, succeeded by *National Business Woman,* 1953 to date. Relatively short runs are available for such nineteenth-century titles as *Peterson's Magazine, Ladies' Companion,* and *Ladies' Treasury.*

The manuscript collections of the Woman's Collection contain research material relative to the political, social, literary, artistic, professional, and educational pursuits of women. A relatively brief introduction to a number of these collections follows.

In 1978 members of the Texas Foundation for Women's Resources began a project under the direction of Mary Beth Rogers to locate the historical source material to document the contributions of Texas women to the history of their state. Donations and grants in excess of $300,000 financed this project. In March, 1983, the files of this mammoth effort, which include more than 600 biographical files and 400 subject files as well as the files of the *Texas Women's History Project Bibliography* were donated to TWU along with the visual presentation that had been developed into an exhibit that traveled throughout the state for two years entitled "Texas Women: A Celebration of History." The research files and the exhibit present women "who shaped Texas schools, government, business and economy" as well as Texas women who "built communities, enriched life, survived hardship, worked at home and for pay, took care of children and made their presence felt in city, county and state government."[13]

The Hermine Tobolowsky Collection documents the work of the attorney who is known as the mother of the Equal Legal Rights Amendment in Texas. It includes to date approximately 1,200 letters, a clipping file of 433 articles on women and education, employment, legal status, marriage and family, religious life, the Texas legislature and leaders, and the Texas ERA. The collection also contains bills and resolutions; ERA booklets (state and national); buttons and stickers; business cards; postcards; lists of committees; contribution lists; court cases; flyers; House and Senate journal excerpts; journals, newsletters, and bulletins; legislative skits;

legislative reports; musical scores; news releases; pamphlets; pledges for ELR amendment; speeches; campaign platforms; testimonies and voting records.

The Claire Myers Owens Collection contains an extensive file of correspondence which includes letters from James Branch Cabell, Aldous Huxley, Henry Margenau, Abraham Maslow, H. L. Mencken, Edgar D. Mitchell, Kenneth Ring, Bertrand Russell, Albert Schweitzer, Paul Tillich, Carl Van Doren, and John White. It also includes copies in both manuscript and published form of her books *The Unpredictable Adventure, Awakening to the Good, Discovery of the Self,* and *Zen and the Lady* as well as the manuscript of her final book "Meditation and the Lady." The collection contains published articles from numerous journals, reviews of her books, newsclippings, interviews, speeches, photographs, unpublished writings, seminal books and journals from her personal library, and cassettes and videotapes.

The Mary Evelyn Blagg Huey Collection includes correspondence, speeches, newspaper clippings, and other papers of a university president, international educational consultant, and chairman of the United States Defense Advisory Committee on Women in the Services.

The Sarah Weddington Collection includes correspondence, journal articles, books, newspaper clippings, materials on women and leadership, and other papers of a state and national political leader and women's leader.

The Cathy Bonner Collection is principally concerned with the Texas Rape Prevention and Control Project. The Collection includes approximately 750 letters plus a large number of clippings and various speeches, reports, examination procedures, programs, and financial records. Some geographical and statistical information is included. Most of the material is from the period 1975 to 1978.

The Martha Smiley Collection of 600 items including personal correspondence, speeches, pamphlets, reports, minutes, and clippings from the period 1975 to 1979 is particularly strong in material relative to a proposed Austin area women's credit union, the Texas Women's Political Caucus, the Texas Commission on the Status of Women, the National Women's Agenda Coalition, and "200 Texas Women on the Hill Side." The Collection also contains information on the ERA, leadership training for women in public service, professional life and work force data, and various material related to women's organizations.

The Ruth Winegarten Collection contains sources and notes relative to the history of black women in Texas between 1835 and 1983. It includes correspondence, copies of materials in other archives, interviews, clippings, photographs, periodical articles, book excerpts, and a cassette tape.

The Barbara Vacker Collection contains material from the 1975 Conference on Women in Public Life: An International Women's Year Symposium held in Austin, a 1976 Retreat to discuss women's political issues, the 1977 National Women's Conference held in Houston, the Texas Women's Political Caucus conventions and committee reports, women's newsletters and newsclippings, and a *Women's Rights Handbook.*

The Madeleine Henrey Collection contains 142 unpublished letters to her husband written between 1959 and 1962, a map of her farm in Normandy, and a correspondence over a period of years with Elizabeth Snapp. One of her latter letters entitled *magnificently mistress of her trade* was published by the Texas Woman's University Press as part of the University's Diamond Jubilee celebration. The Collection also includes manuscript pages from *She Who Pays,* the typescript and galley proofs of *A Girl at Twenty,* copies of all of her works including Paris and Kobenhavn as well as London editions (mainly first editions), and water color paintings by Phyllis Ginger, her illustrator.

The LaVerne Harrell Clark Collection, containing over 3,000 items, documents her professional career as a writer and photographer from 1952 to the present. In addition to including her books *They Sang for Horses, The Face of Poetry, Revisiting the Plains Indian Country of Mari Sandoz,* and *Focus 101,* the Collection includes copies of her short stories and photographs published in numerous journals and anthologies, newsclippings, interviews, and selected issues of approximately 60 literary newsletters and journals. The correspondence files contain letters and notes to and from more than 100 poets and novelists including George Bowering; Jeremy Ingalls; Elizabeth Kray, a director of the Academy of American Poets; William Meredith; Ruth Stephan; Marguerite Young; John R. Humphreys, and May Swenson as well as letters to and from Carlos Montoya, flamenco guitarist, and his wife. The Collection also includes the works of her husband L. D. Clark, a D. H. Lawrence scholar, novelist, and short story writer.

The Willa Cather Collection includes letters to her sister and mother, family photographs, her father's diary dated 1865, newsclippings, a biographical sketch by her sister, and copies of the newsletter of the Willa Cather Pioneer Memorial and Educational Foundation, 1974.

The Nell Morris Collection documents the career of a professional home economist who was Chief Dietitian and Associate Professor of Foods and Nutrition of TWU and later director of the Consumer Services Department of Frito-Lay, Inc. The Collection consists of letters, photographs, magazine and newspaper clippings, scrapbooks, awards, cookbooks, recipe booklets, and recipes created or collected by Nell Morris. More than 750 recipes in the Collection were developed by Miss Morris and printed on bags of fritos or in frito recipe booklets. She was responsible for the company's development of the large frito for use with dips. The correspondence in the Collection spans the years 1930 to 1978. The photographs add a visual dimension to the career of this food service professional.

The Julie Benell Collection includes more than 2,000 cookbooks plus recipe booklets, personal recipes, photographs, scrapbooks, newsletters, clippings, and the manuscript of *Let's Eat At Home* of the foods editor for 25 years of the *Dallas Morning News.* The Collection also contains numerous awards that she received.

The Viola Hamilton Collection includes many of the research records of the life of a Texas Woman's University biology faculty member who was a lover of birds and wildflowers. The larger part of the Collection consists of notebooks and calendars recording the migration of various birds through Texas. There are also drawings in color of parts of various wildflowers, her correspondence, faculty contracts, membership records of the Biology Club, and brochures from special campus programs.

The Mary Eustice Collection includes the papers of a young playwright. Author of "Reunion," "Single," "The Tracks Stop Here," and "Visited on the Children," the Collection includes, in addition to her plays, her correspondence, newsclippings, scrapbooks from schooldays, and photographs.

The Winifred Wilhite Earnhart Collection includes the correspondence of this Texas poet between 1964-1980 and typescripts of her poems.

The Kate Alma Orgain Collection contains a 14 page manuscript from the very early twentieth century on the early women of Texas.

The Belle Rogers Collection contains a xerox copy of a 140 page typescript of her memoirs which provide an account of rural life in Cooke County, Texas, between 1850 and 1937.

"Today's Woman," a weekly radio program that is broadcast on the Texas State Network, is produced on cassette tape and a copy of the tape is deposited in the Woman's Collection. The program is prepared by Audrey Silvernale, News Director in the TWU Office of Information, and usually takes the form of an interview with a prominent Texas woman. The library staff began last fall to prepare transcripts of the several hundred tapes now on file in the Woman's Collection.

The American Association of University Women, Texas State Division Archives, 1926 to date, contain the following types of material although all categories are not available for each administration: annual reports of the presidents, treasurer's reports, membership reports and records from the branches, correspondence, agendas for and minutes of state board meetings and state conventions, newsletters, clippings, information on program topics and national issues, copies of branch by-laws, handbooks, petitions, resolutions, campaign platforms, brochures, flyers, survey and questionnaire results, scrapbooks and photographs. In 1981 the State Division adopted the preservation of the records of the branches as the state historical project with these records being deposited in the TWU Woman's Collection. Many branches across the state are beginning to gather their records together for the first time. These files are usually small but include yearbooks, scrapbooks, minutes of meetings, treasurer's reports, and a limited amount of correspondence.

The Texas Association for Intercollegiate Athletics for women deposited its archives in the Woman's Collection in 1982. The records cover the work of the Association from 1968 to 1979 and include copies of the constitution, handbooks, newsletters, correspondence, reports on tournaments divided by sport, reports on district meetings including agendas and minutes, reports of district commissioners, budget information, financial reports, vitas on each president, and awards.

The Ariel Club, a charter member in 1897 of the Texas Federation of Women's Clubs, was organized in 1891 in Denton, Texas. The Collection consists of yearbooks dating from the first in 1898, minutes from 1891 to 1981, correspondence, clippings from 1904 to 1978, treasurer's reports, programs of individual meetings and conventions, awards, photographs, books, booklets, and scrapbooks. The Collection also includes published histories of the club from 1891 to 1941 and from 1891 to 1960.

The Woman's Shakespeare Club, a member of the Texas Federation of Women's Clubs, was organized in 1899 in Denton, Texas. The Collection includes letters, minute books, yearbooks,treasurer's reports, clippings, scrapbooks, newsletters, annual reports, speeches, awards, ribbons, and certificates.

The Denton Business and Professional Women's Club has deposited their by-laws, yearbooks, newsletters, program material, clippings, and information about projects such as IDP. Following the completion later this year of their history, additional historical files will be added to the Collection.

The Denton League of Women Voters Collection contains the League archives from 1961 to date. Included are the publications of the local, state, and national League in the form of newsletters, workbooks, booklets, flyers, voter studies, printed material on various League issues, minutes, financial reports, correspondence, clippings, and scrapbooks.

The Texas Woman's University Archives are rich in resources for the study of the education of women in the twentieth century. The Archives include admission records; college bulletins; the student newspaper; student yearbooks; campus newsletters; literary publications; scrapbooks, minutes, treasurer's reports, membership lists, and correspondence from a variety of student organizations both professional and social; scrapbooks of individual students; departmental bulletins, brochures, and flyers; programs from special events; over 10,000 photographs and negatives; posters; biographical news files on faculty members, lecturers, and students; and subject files on campus events, departments, and buildings. The Collection is enriched with a large variety of artifacts and memorabilia displayed in the library and in other campus locations. Exhibit space is provided in Old Main, the University's first building, and displays arranged by members of the TWU National Alumnae Association, consist of such items as early school uniforms, student designs for the stained glass windows of the Little Chapel in the Woods, photographs, University tableware, the cornerstone from the first dormitory, banners, awards, portraits of the presidents of the University, and art work by students and former students. Display items also include items from early Texas homes such as one of the first Elias Howe sewing machines and a chair designed to accommodate a lady's bustle. Another exhibit, located in the Nutrition, Textiles, and Human Development Building, displays the historical gowns worn by the first ladies of the Republic of Texas and of the State of Texas. Additionally, the TWU College of Nursing has established a Nursing Archive which deals predominantly with women and includes books, scrapbooks, oral histories, posters, and nursing uniforms.

During 1982 the director of libraries was the project director for a National Endowment for the Humanities grant that enabled her and other members of the faculty to visit and study the work and the collections of several women's research centers. Preliminary work is underway to bring together for preservation in the Woman's Collection a higher percentage of the data files of statistical and other studies on or related to women that have longitudinal value by the graduate students and faculty members of the University. A valuable and interesting study that is the first in the new prospective series is the Virginia Jones Collection, which provides to date information on more than 100 contemporary American women sculptors. Although the total information available on each woman varies from file to file, the files generally include biographical sketches, professional resumes, photographs, slides, gallery listings, exhibit brochures, and correspondence between Miss Jones and the sculptors. This collection is being jointly developed by the library and Miss Jones and in its current developmental stage is closed to other researchers.

Although the unique research quality of this Woman's Collection must rest primarily upon its manuscript and book collections, the large number of microform collections not only serve to place the manuscripts and books in a broader context, but the policy of bringing together in one location the major women's microform collections and supplementing them with additional microform holdings such as the complete run of the *Union Signal* from the Ohio Historical Society and the archives of the Women's Joint Congressional Committee from the Library of Congress adds a unique research quality and character of its own. The major microform collections in the Woman's Collection, discussed very briefly below, represent approximately 22,000 volumes and consist of 14,870 monographic titles and 850 periodical titles.

American Association of University Women's Archives 1881-1976 document the origin, development, and activities of the AAUW and its predecessor organization, The Association of Collegiate Alumnae.

Bibliofem, an ongoing publication of the Fawcett Library in London, provides a current listing by author/title, subject, and classification to works about women published in the English language.

Bibliography of American Women lists 50,000 titles written by and about women during the period 1600-1900.

The Collected Correspondence of Lydia Marie Child 1817-1880 contains more than 2,600 letters of the nineteenth-century historian, novelist, biographer, editor, essayist, journalist, and pamphleteer.

The Columbia University Oral History Collection: Women Pioneers and Professionals provides transcripts of the oral histories of twenty-nine women from the 1950s to the 1970s.

Cornell University Women Rights Pamphlets trace the history of the women's rights movement from 1814 to 1912.

Gerritsen Collection of Women's History focuses on the woman's movement, women's rights, education, and employment as found in books, pamphlets, and periodicals published from 1534 to 1945.

Herstory provides access to ephemeral serial literature recording the influence of the feminist movement on women's personal and political life between 1956 and 1974.

History of Women provides copies of works in the Schlesinger Library at Radcliffe College and in the Sophia Smith Collection at Smith College covering works between the mid-seventeenth century and the early twentieth century.

The National Woman's Party Papers: The Suffrage Years: 1913-1920 record the activities surrounding the passage of the 19th Amendment.

The National Woman's Party Papers: 1913-1974 make available 450,000 pages of primary sources documenting the NWP's support of the Equal Rights Amendment.

Papers of the Women's Trade Union League and Its Principle Leaders cover the period 1903-1974.

Union Signal, 1883-1933, the organ of The Women's Christian Temperance Union.

U. S. Woman's Bureau. *Bulletin* covers information relative to working conditions such as health and safety, hours and wages, and employment trends and opportunities between 1918 and 1963.

Women and Health/Mental Health contains clippings, articles, pamphlets, essays and papers collected between 1968 and 1974 on some 150 subjects.

Women and the Law provides information on de facto sex discrimination in education, employment, divorce, housing, union activities, and social security found in essays, position papers, leaflets, pamphlets, and poetry collected between 1968 and 1974.

The Women's International League for Peace and Freedom Papers, 1915-1978, contain the archives and publications of the League.

The Women's Joint Congressional Committee covers the correspondence, information forms, minutes of meetings, treasurer's reports, membership lists, printed matter, clippings, and bills and receipts collected between 1921 and 1962.

The Women's Rights Collection contains 79 titles covering suffrage, marriage, education, employment, and social status by well-known authors such as E. Sylvia Pankhurst and Mary Wollstonecraft published from the 17th through the 20th centuries.

Researchers are welcome to use materials in the Woman's Collection during regular library hours: Monday-Thursday, 7:30 a.m. to 10:00 p.m., Friday, 7:30 a.m. to 9:00 p.m., Saturday, 9:00 a.m. to 5:00 p.m., and Sunday, 2:00 p.m. to 10:00 p.m. except for rare books and manuscripts which are available, unless restricted for some reason, Monday-Friday, 8:00 a.m. to 5:00 p.m. Most of the book collection, the reference collection, and the extensive microform collections are open and available to researchers during all hours the library is open. The Collection has its own author, title, and subject card catalog with additional entries to the clipping and pamphlet files. At this writing complete inventories are available for only about one-third of the manuscript collections. Scholars desiring to consult one or more of the manuscript collections should correspond with the director of libraries in respect to possible restrictions or availability for research of a given collection. A scholar desiring to publish quotations from manuscripts or to reproduce original art work will be required to present the written permission of the author/artist or other legal owner of the Collection to the director.

Inquiries are welcomed and encouraged. The staff is small but with adequate lead time can be extremely helpful. Visiting scholars will ordinarily be able to secure reasonable overnight accommodations on campus in the Guinn Conference Center, and meals may be taken in the faculty/staff dining room or student dining rooms of Hubbard Hall.

The Woman's Collection of the Texas Woman's University Library stands poised as a natural depository and as a strong research center for those records that reveal the life, the thought, and the contributions of women acting both singly and in groups through successive eras.

NOTES

1. "Library Accession Record," (Denton: College of Industrial Arts: State College for Women), volume 1.

2. "New Group of Books Added to Library: 'Woman's Collection' Suggested by Hubbard—To Include Notes of Prominent Women," *The Lass-O* (March 31, 1932), p. 3.

3. Ibid.

4. "Library Accession Record," volume 8.

5. Ibid.

6. *College Bulletin: The Graduate School* (Denton: Texas State College for Women, 1934), p. 66.

7. "50,000 Books Now In S.C.W. Library: Goal Aspired to Several Years Ago Reached—Boasts Two Special Collections," *The Lass-O* (March 27, 1934), p. 3.

8. "New Group of Books Added to Library," p. 3.

9. Martha S. Bell, "Special Women's Collections in United States Libraries," *College and Research Libraries* (May 1959), pp. 235-242.

10. "Women From All Walks of Life Form Subject For Unique S.C.W. Library Collection," *The Lass-O* (December 15, 1932), p. 5.

11. "New Group of Books Added to Library," p. 3.

12. "Annual Report, T.S.C.W. Library, Fiscal Year, 1951-52," p. 3. See also, "Women's Books Assembled," *The Lass-O* (April 22, 1966), p. 2.

13. Mary Beth Rogers, *Texas Women: A Celebration of History* (Austin: Texas Foundation For Women's Resources, 1981), p. 5.

Women's Studies Collections in the University of Waterloo Library

Susan Bellingham

The University of Waterloo Library, although relatively new in the Ontario system having celebrated its twenty-fifth anniversary in 1982, has amassed a large book and archive collection of research materials relating to the history of women. Supplemented by the Library's general collection of some 1.7 million volumes, the bulk of the primary source materials for women's studies is housed in the Doris Lewis Rare Book Room. This repository contains over 18,000 rare books and about 125 archive collections and by far the longest established and most active of the many subject collections currently being developed is that relating to the history of women. The major focus of the collecting activity has been to acquire materials of Canadian interest in women's studies, and this national and Canadian strength is supported by materials published from the sixteenth through to the twentieth century from an international range of sources. While all materials in the Rare Book Room are in their original format, some items in the Library's general collection are of necessity in reprint or micro format. The purpose of this paper is to detail the history and describe the contents of the Library's resources relating to women's studies with the major emphasis being placed on those items housed in the Doris Lewis Rare Book Room.

The history of the University's interest in women's studies is an important factor as it explains in part the presence of both a rare books collection and a general stacks collection relating to the study of almost all disciplines from a woman's perspective. The beginnings of the collection can be traced back to 1965 and a happy coincidence—the interest in women's studies shown by the first University Librarian, Mrs. Doris Lewis, and the unique centennial project being planned for 1967 by the National Council of Women of Canada. From 1954 to 1965 that group, as a project of their Arts and Letters Committee, had been amassing a collection of books by and about women in order to provide a Canadian counterpart to such collections as England's Fawcett Library on the History of Women and the Arthur and Elizabeth Schlesinger Library on the History of Women in America at Radcliffe College. The National Council eventually named the collection the "Lady Aberdeen Library on the History of Women" in honour of Lady Ishbel Aberdeen, the wife of one of Canada's Governors-General and the founder and first president of the National Council, who had also served as the President of the International Council of Women for nearly twenty years. In 1965, the National Council decided to seek a permanent home for their collection which by then numbered some 2000 items. After considering several Canadian repositories they visited Mrs. Lewis at the 8 year-old University of Waterloo and "liked tremendously what they saw and what they heard."[1] It was decided that the collection should come to Waterloo and with the collection came the sum of two thousand dollars to cover the costs of processing and integrating the collection into the Library's system.

The story of those collecting years and the enthusiasm and involvement of National Council members across Canada, as well as the contributions made by various other National Councils, has been told in a 1967 pamphlet published jointly by the Canadian National Council and the University of Waterloo Library. This pamphlet has recently been reprinted in the catalogue of the Lady Aberdeen Library, compiled by Jane Britton and published by the Library as No. 7 in its Bibliography Series.[2]

Paralleling the growth of the Library's collections were the teaching and publishing activities of a number of University of Waterloo faculty members in the 1970's. Since 1971 the University had been offering courses designed to approach the study of women from various pespectives and in 1972 one of these faculty members, Margrit Eichler, along with Marylee Stephenson from the University of Windsor [Ontario], founded the journal *Canadian Newsletter of Research on Women,* with a grant from the University of Waterloo.[3] Eichler and Stephenson have been called "scholars who pioneered the field of Women's Studies in Canada"[4] and Eichler along with Linda Fischer, Dr. Rota Lister and numerous other faculty members taught many courses relating to women at the University of Waterloo in the 1970's. Most recently, the University has formalized its programme of courses relating to this relatively new focus in research under a "Women's Studies Programme," offered jointly by the University of Waterloo and a neighbouring institution, Wilfrid Laurier University. Throughout the past decade, the Library has been acquiring material to support the teaching and research of the students and faculty members of the University of Waterloo, and thus the general stacks collection of monographs, periodicals, government documents and micro-materials provides contemporary resources for such study. A brief description of this general collection will appear later in this paper.

In addition to acquiring materials to support course work, the Library experienced a phenomenon common to institutions receiving such large gifts as the Lady Aberdeen Library. Following the publicity and scholarly activity surrounding the 1967 gift, many valuable donations of books and archives relating to women were made to the Library. Most notable among these gifts were two important donations, the first being the 200 volume library of books formed by the Canadian Women's Press Club (Toronto Branch) and the second a cheque, to be used to acquire additional materials, from the Canadian Federation of University Women representing the profits from the sale of their Centennial volume *The Clear Spirit: Twenty Canadian Women and their Times* (Toronto, University of Toronto Press, 1966) edited by Mary Quayle Innis. Donations of books to complement the Lady Aberdeen Library have continued with the most recent gift being one received from the National Council of Women—the second volume of *''We Twa''* (London: Collins, 1925), the reminiscences of Lord and Laby Aberdeen, which has always been an important desiderata item in the collection. Other large and important grants came from various Ontario government agencies and these grants were consolidated into what the Library termed ''Project HERS.'' This project analyzed and prepared indexing systems for various portions of the women's studies collection with the most visible result being the publication of the *Catalogue of the Lady Aberdeen Library*. Large archive collections were also donated and many of these book and archival resources will be described herein.

The collection of rare books of interest to women's studies researchers covers a range of some four hundred years with the earliest item in the collection bearing the imprint 1545. This book by Frederico Luigini is entitled *Il libro della bella donna* (Venetia: Pietrasanta, 1545) which has been roughly translated as ''The book of fair women.'' Next in chronological order is a small 31-page pamphlet by German theologian Simon Gedik. Entitled *Defensio sexus muliebris, opposita futilissimae dispvtationi recens editae, qva surppresso authoris & typographi nomine, blaspheme contenditur, mulierres homines non esse* (Lipsiae: Michael Lantzenberger, 1595) its author addresses the question of the degree of humanity possessed by women and men and attempts to answer the critics of his day who felt women's humanity was less than that of men. Containing many marginal annotations and notes in a contemporary hand, this sixteenth-century title represents the earliest item in the collection that is totally devoted to the question of women's role and place in society.

The seventeenth century, an era only recently being studied in depth from the women's perspective, is represented by several titles in the collection. Included here are such biographical works as *The exemplary lives and memorable acts of nine of the most worthy women of the world* (London: Cotes for Royston, 1640) and commentaries including Thomas Comber's *Occasional Offices of matrimony* (London: M.C. for Brome and Clavel, 1679). The difficulties of assessing women's place in society in an earlier era have been discussed by many historians and two seventeenth-century works giving views of this place are important documents of that era. The legal status of women in England in the seventeenth century is outlined in T.E.'s *The lavves [sic] resolutions of womens rights* (London, 1632) although it is now felt that the facts of law given and reality of the times often differed. A more philosophical view is expressed in William Austin's essay defending women in the "woman question"— *Haec homo, wherein the excellency of the creation of woman is described, by way of an essay* (London, by Richard Olton for Ralph Mabb, 1637). The history of the education of women in this century and earlier is revealed by writings published in later centuries by such humanists as Sir Thomas More whose *The Life of Sir Thomas More,* (London: For James Woodman and David Lyon, 1726) speaks of educating his three daughters. Another eighteenth-century treatise, Roger Ascham's "The Scholemaster" was included as a part of *The English works of Roger Ascham* edited by James Bennet (London: For R. and J. Dodsley, 1746) and relates some of Ascham's theories and practices while employed as tutor to Queen Elizabeth I.

The eighteenth century was an era in which European women, as well as men, experienced vast social, political and economic changes. The published output of this century reflects these ongoing changes and continues some of the debates of an earlier century. An example of this continuing debate is the positive view of women of Agrippa von Nettesheim, which first appeared in Latin in 1529 and was translated into French and appeared in the eighteenth century as *Sur la noblesse & excellence du sexe feminin* (Leiden: Haak, 1726). Other statements on women's role include Feijoo y Montenegro's "Defensio de las mugeres" included in his *Teatro critico universal* (Madrid: 1765) and *The female aegis: or, the duties of women* (London: Low, 1798). Traditionalist views of women and their role in society are expressed by Thomas Gisborne in *An inquiry into the duties of the female sex* (London: Cadell and Davies, 1797) and *The ladies calling* (London: J. Johnson, 1797) by Richard Allestree.

Writings from the feminist viewpoint in the eighteenth century culminated in Mary Wollstonecraft's *A Vindication of the rights of women, with strictures on political and moral subjects,* which is available in the collection in the second London edition of 1792. Wollstonecraft, the first to write specifically about the political rights of women, has become the symbol of eighteenth-century feminism and an account of her life can be found in the first American edition of her biography, written by her husband William Godwin entitled *Memoirs of Mary Wollstonecraft Godwin* (Philadelphia: Carey 1799). Other titles by Wollstonecraft in the collection include her *Original stories from real life* (London: J. Johnson, 1798) and her *Memoirs and posthumous works* (Dublin: Burnside, 1798) which contains her famed "The wrongs of woman; or Maria, a Fragment" which was also edited by her husband.

Women's equal rights to education in this century, one of the cornerstones of Wollstonecraft's theories, are discussed in a variety of sources representing a range of educational theories including Hannah More's *Strictures of the modern system of female education* (3rd ed. London: Cadell and Davies 1799) and Hester Chapone's *Letters on the improvement of the mind* (London: Hughs, 1764). Well-educated women were not common at the time but two of the women who did receive recognition for their education and scholarship in this era are Elizabeth Elstob and Caroline Herschel. Elstob, an Anglo-Saxon scholar, in the Preface to her *An English-Saxon homily on the birthday of St. Gregory* (London: Bowyer, 1709) asks and answers the question "What has a woman to do with learning?". Astronomer Caroline Herschel published *Catalogue of stars* (Londres, 1798) in conjunction with her brother William in which she reveals her own astronomical discoveries.

Biographical sketches of the era such as Ballard's *Memoirs of British ladies* (London: Evan, 1775), Mary Matilda Betham's *A bio-*

graphical dictionary of the celebrated women of every age and country (London: Crosby, 1804) and William Alexander's two volume set *The history of women from the earliest antiquity, to the present time* (London: Strahan and Cadell, 1770) are important sources of information.

One of the strengths of the collection of early printed books lies in the collection of French imprints written either by or about women. Acquired to support courses being given on French women writers as a part of the Women's Studies Programme, this collection contains first or early editions of the complete works of Madame de Genlis including her most noted work *Mademoiselle de Clermont* (Londres: 1802) and her three-volume *Les petites émigrés* (Hambourg: 1798) which express in part her theories of education. Also included are works by other eighteenth-century writers such as Mademoiselle Francoise de Graffigny whose *Lettres d'un peruviane* (Paris: Briasson, 1759) appear in French with most uniquely, an Italian translation on facing pages published in 1749; the memoirs of Madame de Motteville detailing her life as lady-in-waiting to Anne of Austria and the memoirs of Madame Leprince de Beaumont, the author of over seventy moral and instructive tales for children.

The Rare Book Room's collection of domestic manuals such as cookbooks, household instructors and gardening books have a popular as well as a research value. Giving as they do glimpses into everyday life of another era, the several dozen items in this subject area range from Gervase Markham's *The English house-wife* (London: George Sawbridge, 1675) and his *A new orchard and garden. . .with the country house-wifes garden for herbs of common use* (London: George Sawbridge, 1676) to such locally produced items as Edna Staebler's *Food that really schmecks* (Toronto: Ryerson, 1968) which contains information on the life and culture of the Mennonites of Waterloo County. In the absence of original papers to reveal what daily life was like for most eighteenth-century women, the lengthy title-page and illustrations in *The universal cook, and city and country housekeeper* (London; Noble, 1797) and the relatively rare tenth edition of *The housekeeper's instructor; or universal family cook* (London: J. Stratford [1800]) reveal all too clearly how a woman would occupy her day. The presentation inscriptions, often one can assume, from mother to daughter, first aid recipes noted in the margins and scribbled recipes on fly-leaves and endpapers all help to bring to life the domestic routine of an earlier era and add to the charm of these seemingly ordinary volumes. Representing as they do the conventions and standards of their day, items in this group give a realistic view of the domestic routines of earlier years.

Nineteenth century printed works in the collection are dominated by the topic of suffrage, ranging from a play—*A suffragette town meeting: an entertainment in one act* (Boston: Baker, 1872) by Lilian Bridgham to Carrie S. Burnham's *Woman suffrage: the argu ment of Carrie S. Burnham before Chief Justice Reed* (Philadelphia Citizen Suffrage Association, 1873), to a large series of publications by the National American Suffrage Association. Equally as important as suffrage in the nineteenth century materials are the many examples of the literary output of women including a wide range of periodicals.

In writing on the periodical collection at the Schlesinger Library, Janet Wilson James of that library, has stated that "probably no single source tells so much about the interests, values and aspirations of. . .women as the magazines published for their consumption."[5] The University of Waterloo has recently acquired a large collection of periodicals which will undoubtedly confirm this. The collection was acquired with the assistance of a grant from the programme operated by the Social Sciences and Humanities Research Council of Canada to strengthen collections of national significance in Canadian university libraries. The collection itself consists of 35,000 issues of women's periodicals published in England from 1893 to 1977. These issues have been uniformly bound by their publisher Amalgamated Press in 1842 separate volumes and represent the complete runs of most of Amalgamated's publications. Formed in 1891 by Alfred Harmsworth, Amalgamated's sole purpose was to publish women's magazines and included in the collection is the complete run of its first publication *Forget-Me-Not: A Pictorial Journal for Ladies* and its successor *Forget-Me-Not Novels* which is present in all 369 numbers published from 1919 to 1926. One of the longest runs in the collection is represented by *Women's World: A Home Journal for Every Lady* which was published from 1903/4 to 1958. Also included are many titles which were published serially and as separate novels and were works of popular fiction at that time.

The richest area in the Library's rare book collections relating to women is the section devoted to Canadian themes and writers. Foremost among this group is an item referred to as the "first English novel in a Canadian setting"—the four-volume *History of Emily*

Montague (London: Dodsley, 1769) written by Mrs. Frances (Moore) Brooke. Brooke had accompanied her husband, the first Church of England clergyman in Quebec, to Canada in 1763 and it is believed that this novel, or at least the notes for its creation, were begun by Brooke while in Quebec. Dedicated to Guy Carleton, the Governor of Quebec, the novel describes in detail both the scenery and the social life of the Quebec and Sillery regions. Another important early work relating to women is the collection's earliest Canadian imprint and an item said to be the first printed Canadian biography, *La vie de la venerable soeur Marguerite de Bourgeois* (Ville-Marie [i.e., Montreal]: Gray, 1818), detailing the life of a notable seventeenth century Canadian woman who was beatified in 1950.

Nineteenth century Canadiana is highlighted by pioneer literature and tales of the difficulties encountered while settling a land with a harsh and often inhospitable climate. The cheerfulness and fortitude with which most women faced this challenge make these items among the most fascinating in the collection. The earliest of this genre is the output of two of the three Strickland sisters who had emigrated to Canada from England, namely Susanna Moodie and Catherine Parr Traill. First or early editions of many of their works are available and include the first British and first American editions of two of Moodie's most famous works, *Roughing it in the bush; or life in Canada* (London: Bentley, 1852 and New York: George Putnan, 1852) and *Life in the clearings versus the bush* (London: Bentley 1853 and New York: DeWitt and Davenport [1854]). Traill's early literary output is represented by the first British edition of *The backwoods of Canada: being letters from the wife of an emigrant officer* (London: Knight, 1836) and the first American editions of *The Canadian crusoes* (New York: C.S. Francis, 1858) and *Stories of the Canadian forest* (New York: C.S. Francis, 1857).

The collection contains a variety of later works in this genre, many of which reflect Canada's geographical diversity. These include Sir Wilfrid Grenfell's autographed copy of his wife's book *Le petit nord; or annals of a Labrador harbour* (London: Hodder and Stoughton, n.d.) which she, Anne Grenfell wrote in conjunction with Katie Spalding; *I lived in paradise* (Winnipeg, Bluman Bros, 1942), Margaret Galloway's autographed copy of her early life in Brandon, Manitoba which includes numerous turn of the century photographs and *The new north: being some account of a woman's journey through Canada to the Arctic* (New York: Appleton, 1912) by Agnes Deans Cameron. Also included are *Five years in western Canada: a Paisley lady's letters,* 1909 to 1914 (Paisley[?] 1914) which was published anonymously by Molly Collinge, and Martha Louise Black's autographed copy of her *My ninety years* (London, Nelson, 1938) which complements her collection of papers housed in the Doris Lewis Rare Book Room. Other earlier accounts of Canadian women settlers include *The Christian heroine of Canada, or, life of Miss Le Ber* by Abbe Faillon (Montreal: J. Lovell, 1861) and *La premiere Canadienne du nord-ouest, ou biographie de Marie-Anne Gaboury* (Montreal: Cadieux & Derome, 1833) by George Dugas.

Diaries kept by Canadian women have been found to be enlightening not only for women's history but quite naturally for the larger history of the period in which they were being written. First among these diarists was Mrs. John Graves Simcoe, wife of the first Lieutenant-Governor of Upper-Canada, who came to the Canada in 1791. Her entertaining diaries, along with her many sketches, were first published in 1911 under the title *The diary of Mrs. Simcoe, with notes and biography by John Ross Robertson* (Toronto: Briggs, 1911) and have remained an invaluable historical source. The next outstanding diary writer in chronological order was Mrs. Anna Jameson, and the 1852 second edition of her diaries published under the titled *Sketches in Canada, and rambles among the red men* (London, Longman Brown Green, 1852), although less lively than the original 1838 edition, does provide an interesting account of her journeys. A last very important chronicle is that of Matilda Edgar, later Lady Edgar, whose family letters were published under the title *Ten years of Upper Canada in peace and war 1805-1815* (Toronto: Briggs, 1895).

Books by lesser and often almost unknown Canadian women writers are also available. Many of these are of local interest and include a novel entitled *The Cromaboo mail carrier* (Guelph: [Ontario], 1878) written by Miss Mary Leslie under the pseudonym James Thomas Jones. Copies of this murder mystery story were immediately withdrawn by Miss Leslie due to the uproar caused by its publication. Based on thinly disguised names and places in the vicinity of Drumbo, Ontario, the novel caused such distress among local citizens that its distribution was stopped by Miss Leslie and few copies have come to light in the last one hundred years. Narratives of Indian captivities are relatively infrequent occurrences in Canadian literature and one of the most interesting was written by two women in 1885. A brief and authentic account by Theresa Gowanlock and Theresa Delaney, *Two months in the camp of Big Bear,* published in 1885 contains the very rare "Parkdale, Ontario" imprint. This slim volume illustrated with many drawings contains the story of two women who accompanied their husbands to Frog Lake just as the North West Rebellion of 1885 broke out. Both women describe in the narrative the murder of their husbands before their eyes and their subsequent wanderings on the prairies until they were rescued by the Mounted Police.

Other collections in the Rare Books Room, although not acquired with women's studies in mind, have been found to have a rich research potential. Largest of these is the Henry H. Crapo Dance Collection, described as "the only sizeable special collection of rare materials relating to the history of dance and ballet found in any collection in Canada"[6] which contains a number of items useful for women's studies. These items range from Raoul Feuillet's landmark treatise of 1704 *Recueil de dances* (Paris: Chez Feuiller, 1704) containing as it does dances recommended "tant pour homme que pour femmes" to the very fine library of a Belgian dancer who danced under the stage name of "Isa Belli." Isa Belli's library contains some of the most important treatises on dance and was collected by her from 1945 to 1966. In 1967 Dr. Crapo, a former University of Waterloo faculty member and donor of the nucleus collection, purchased many of the books in her collection and in 1979 the University of Waterloo was able to purchase a further portion of the personal library of this ballerina, most noted for her work in keeping dance alive in Belgium during the period of the Second World War. The library has recently acquired, with the assistance of a grant from the Social Sciences and Humanities Research Council of Canada, a second library of books formed by a woman dancer, Hilda Butsova who was for many years understudy to Anna Pavlova. Butsova's great personal interest in publications on Pavlova as well as on other significant ballerinas make this collection a rich resource for dance as well as for biography. Biographies and detailed information on both Isa Belli and Butsova are sadly lacking and certainly a study of their personal libraries, as represented in their collections in the Doris Lewis Rare Book Room, and of their collecting experiences would shed light on their philosophy and theory of dance. Personal libraries provide a tantalizing glimpse into the lives of the famous and present excellent research potential to the scholar.

Another very large collection, which is made up of writings, engravings and critical works of the English sculptor and author Eric Gill, provides researchers with a unique and individual view of many aspects of social and family history in England from 1916 to 1940. Gill's philosophy and writings on such topics as birth control, dress, costume and beauty, as well as his relationship with several important English contemporaries, such as Beatrice Warde, Faith Ashford and Eleanor Farjeon, provide interesting research opportunities among the over six hundred items in this collection.

An archive collection, and one most illustrative of the latent potential of many collections, is the manuscript diaries of fur trader Donald McKay from 1799-1806. These diaries, the originals of which are housed in the Doris Lewis Rare Book Room, were used by Jennifer Brown in her recent study of the Canadian fur trade entitled *Strangers in blood: fur trade company families in Indian country* (Vancouver: University of British Columbia Press, 1980) and a detailed analysis of these diaries revealed that McKay's life was made somewhat easier by the presence of his "girl" who figured frequently in his entries.[7]

Another very large group of collections—the private press collections—are a rich resource for material, particularly literary, of early and often ephemeral writings by women. Included here are a large group of items from the Hogarth Press including a first edition of Virginia Woolf's *A room of one's own* (London: Hogarth Press, 1929) as well as a large number of other titles by her. Recent additions to this collection include first editions of three of Woolf's first four publications. In chronological order these include *The voyage out* (London: Duckworth, 1915) in its original green cloth boards; *The mark on the wall* (Richmond: Hogarth, 1919) which is imprinted "second edition" but which is, in fact, the first separate appearance of Woolf's story; and *Night and day* (London: Duckworth, [1919]). The first American and first trade editions of *Orlando* (New York: Crosby Gaige, 1928 and London: Hogarth, 1928), a work which links the life and work of Virginia Woolf with that of Vita Sackville-West, have also been acquired. *Orlando,* which Woolf dedicated to "V. Sackville-West", was published in a trade edition by Woolf and her husband at their Hogarth Press and the recently-acquired copy contains the white dust-jacket printed in black with illustrations.

Private press editions of other women writers are also available and, in the Canadian context, the almost complete set of "Ryerson Poetry Chapbooks" contains a large number of titles by lesser-known Canadian writers. Works of Victoria Sackville-West, Edith Sitwell, and others are frequently found in these collections.

It is, however, in the area of archives that the University of Waterloo collections are strongest, and it is in using such primary resources that the most significant and exciting research on the history of Canadian women is being done, both at the University of Waterloo and elsewhere. In contrast to most Canadian institutions, the University of Waterloo's collections of women's papers were developed from the first as resources for the study of the history of women and thus do not suffer from the problems of other institutions in which women's papers are often buried in the papers of their more well-known and usually more powerful male relatives. The difficulties experienced by such institutions and by their researchers in identifying, recovering and assessing such hidden records have been commented on by a number of Canadian writers and most eloquently by Dr. Veronica Strong-Boag.[8] Strong-Boag's analysis of existing resources and her recommendations to the Canadian archival community are important comments on the need for a systematic and complete retrieval of documentation essential to a comprehensive view of Canadian history from a woman's perspective.

The University of Waterloo archive collections, acquired as they were as a direct result and in many cases as a part of the gift of the Lady Aberdeen Library present a wide range of original resources. Foremost among these collections is the collection of papers of Dr. Elizabeth Smith Shortt, one of the first three women to graduate in medicine in Canada. Covering some twenty-one feet of shelf space this collection was donated by Dr. Shortt's daughters, Miss Lorraine Shortt and Mrs. Muriel Clarke. A member of the National Council of Women of Canada, Mrs. Clarke was inspired by the 1967 donation of the Lady Aberdeen Library to donate her mother's papers to the University of Waterloo where they have received considerable research attention. Born to a prosperous Ontario farming family in Winona, Ontario in 1859, Elizabeth Smith first sought a career as a teacher but left teaching to attend Medical School at Queen's University in Kingston, Ontario. Graduating in 1884 after a sometimes stormy student career, Dr. Shortt entered general practice in Hamilton, Ontario. In 1886, she married Dr. Adam Shortt, at that time a faculty member of Queen's University, and took up a teaching position there which she held until 1893. An ardent diarist and letter-writer, Dr. Shortt's papers amply document her life from her first diary entry in 1872 until her death in 1949. Her diaries, outlining as they do her difficult life at Queen's Medical College are perhaps the most important part of the collection, and portions of the diaries have been edited for publication by Dr. Veronica Strong-Boag.[9] Supplemented as they are by original materials from Elizabeth's sister, Mauritania, her mother Damaris Isabella (McGee) and her daughter, Mrs. Muriel Clarke, this collection covers a broad range of Canadian women's educational, medical and rural experience.

To turn from this, the largest collection in the Doris Lewis Rare Book Room, to a collection which numbers among the smallest, takes the researcher to a very important judicial and legal decision affecting Canadian women. This collection is made up of the papers of Judge Emily Murphy and the decision referred to is the so-called "Persons Case" of 1929. Emily Murphy had been appointed in 1916 as the first woman Magistrate in the British Empire and it was she who inaugurated and brought to a successful issue the movement that resulted in the British Privy Council decision of 1929 declaring that women were to be considered "persons" under the terms of what was then Canada's constitution, the British North America Act. As a result of this constitutional ruling, women were given the right to be appointed to the Senate of Canada. Although the bulk of Murphy's papers are housed in the City of Edmonton (Alberta) Archives,[10] the University of Waterloo does have a small collection of material relating to the "Person's Case." The library's collection contains the printed government documents both Canadian and British relating to the case, a small amount of correspondence including a letter from Prime Minister William Lyon Mackenzie King, a number of photographs and newspaper clippings as well as two notebooks compiled by Judge Murphy during her term as police magistrate in Edmonton. Also included are several reviews of books written by Judge Murphy under her pen name of "Janey Canuck." The rare book collection holds several first editions of books written under this name including *The impressions of Janey Canuck abroad* (Toronto: 1902), *Janey Canuck in the west* (London: Cassell, 1910), *Open trails* (London: Cassell, 1912), with a dedication inscription from Murphy to her brother Bill, and *Our little Canadian cousins of the great northwest* (Boston: L.C. Page, 1923), which contains a presentation inscription from Murphy to her sister, Annie J. Ferguson. Received from the Emily Murphy Estate are two additional volumes of interest—one which relates to Murphy's work as a Police Court Magistrate entitled *The black candle* (London: Hurst &

Blackwell 1926), on the narcotics habit, and a presentation copy of the 1945 biography of Murphy entitled *Emily Murphy, crusader* (Toronto: MacMillan, 1945) written by her daughter Byrne Hope Sanders.

Legal decisions relating to the status and interests of Canadian women are the focus of another collection housed in the Doris Lewis Rare Book Room—the Dorothea Palmer Papers. Miss Palmer, an employee of the Parents' Information Bureau of Kitchener, Ontario, was arrested in 1937 near Ottawa on a charge of distributing birth control information, at that time an offence under Section 207 Subsection 2 of the Criminal Code of Canada. Described as having 'established a record for cases heard in Magistrate's Court in Canada,' Miss Palmer's trial occupied twenty full days, the verbatim record of the proceedings extending beyond 750,000 words, the argument a further 120,000 words and the magistrate's written verdict some nineteen folio pages. Among the forty witnesses called at this landmark trial was Kitchener industrialist A. R. Kaufman, the founder of the Parents' Information Bureau, sponsor of Palmer's defense and the donor of the collection. Following Miss Palmer's acquittal on March 17, 1937, the Crown appealed the case and the appeal was dismissed on June 2, 1937. Included in the collection are a series of correspondence between lawyers involved in the case, some of the exhibits entered as evidence in the trial, and a large series of mounted newsclippings which reported the trial in newspapers across Canada. A comparison of these news stories is most revealing of the various attitudes towards birth control as expressed in the smaller weekly papers and those in the large dailies.

Following the death of Kaufman in 1979, his Estate donated the remaining files of the Parents' Information Bureau, and these two collections present a wide range of material for documenting Canadian attitudes towards birth control from 1930 to World War II. Kaufman had established the Parents' Information Bureau in Kitchener, Ontario following his discovery of high fertility among the poor and unskilled workers whom he had been forced to lay off in 1929. These files reveal the growth of the Bureau during the 1930's and detail Kaufman's attitudes to birth control as they were revealed in his printed statements. Most recently, the transcript of a 1977 interview with Kaufman has been donated by a researcher and although the transcript and Kaufman's comments on it are restricted, access may be had by applying to the interviewer.

Two other collections, both relating to Canadian medical matters, will be found in the collection. The first of these is the collection of correspondence and clippings of Canadian nurse Catherine Taylor (1874-1967). Born in Clinton (Ontario) Taylor was graduated from St. Luke's Hospital, New York and in 1917 went to England where she worked for the American Red Cross in various hospitals during World War I. The collection contains letters to friends from 1917 to 1967 concerning her work. A second medical collection, in this case centering on World War II, will be found in the papers of Dr. Olive Russell, the bulk of whose papers are housed in the Public Archives of Canada. Dr. Russell, a graduate of the University of Toronto, first served as a personnel selection officer for the Canadian Women's Army Corps during World War II. Following this she went to the United States where she was well-known for her work as psychologist, educator and proponent of legalizing euthanasia. Included in the collection are clippings, a small amount of correspondence and a proof copy of Dr. Russell's best-known work *Freedom to die* (New York: Human Sciences Press, 1975).

Papers of several Canadian women writers are also available in the collection and present the researcher with ample resources to study the creative process. The largest of these collections is the papers of Isabel Ecclestone Mackay. Surely one of the most neglected of Canadian writers, Mackay published an enormous quantity of material from 1909 to 1928 and yet has received almost no critical attention. The University of Waterloo collection contains copies of Mackay's eighteen separately published works as well as two scrapbooks compiled by Mackay made up of her periodical publications in the form of essays, poems and short stories. In addition to printed works, the collection, which was donated by Mackay's daughters, contains manuscript material in the form of correspondence with such figures as Pauline Johnson and Bliss Carman, unpublished poems, and short pieces. Ephemeral material also present includes photographs and reviews of Mackay's works clipped from a wide variety of North American sources. Mackay's fictional work included *The House of Windows* (London: Cassell, 1912) "one of the first works of Canadian fiction to attack low wages and bad working conditions for women"[11] and *Blencarrow,* (Toronto: T. Allen, 1926) her best-known work which documents life in a Canadian small town. Mackay's work as seen through her papers presents the output of a prolific author about whom little biographical, critical or bibliographical work has been done.

Equally as neglected as Mackay is fellow Western-Canadian writer Elaine M. Catley. Born in Bath, England, Catley emigrated to Calgary, Alberta in 1915 after her marriage. From 1921 to 1942 she had many poems and feature articles accepted for publication in the *Calgary Herald* and in about forty smaller periodicals; she has also had six small books of verse published. A member of the Canadian Authors Association for 25 years, she served in all offices up to President. She was also a member of the Canadian Women's Press Club for three years and won a number of prizes for her poems. Her papers contain six manuscript notebooks of poems covering the period 1912 to 1963. Of particular interest are those poems written shortly after Mrs. Catley's arrival in Canada in 1915 giving her impressions of her new homeland. Also included are typescripts and later published versions of these poems, many in the *Calgary Herald* and others in Catley's six published books. Catley's correspondence with Canadian notables such as Nellie McClung, Charles G.D. Roberts, and Laura Goodman Salverson is also available. Among Catley's unpublished manuscripts in the collection is one written in 1971 entitled "Reminiscences of early Canadian writers I have known."

Papers and materials of other Canadian writers included in the collection are those of journalist E. Cora Hind. These consist of two audio tapes, printed biographical and photographic material prepared by the Canadian Broadcasting Corporation documenting her life, and a scrapbook of articles published by Annie Elizabeth May Hewlett. This scrapbook details life on "Cannington Manor," a community established by a group of Englishmen in the 1880's in southeastern Saskatchewan.

Also included are writers who were non-Canadian but who, in many cases, had connections with other National Councils of Women and thus decided to have their papers included as a part of the Lady Aberdeen Library on the History of Women. In other cases, small collections were acquired by purchase or donation. Collections received under the former category—as a part of an at times tenuous connection with various Councils of Women—include some pieces of correspondence of Emily Bax, the second woman to be employed as secretary at the American Embassy in London and author of *Miss Bax of the Embassy* (Boston: Houghton Mifflin, 1939). A collection of one linear foot of materials of Alice Riggs Hunt (1884-1974), journalist and suffrage worker, contains papers made up of correspondence with such figures as E. Sylvia Pankhurst, Carrie Chapman Catt and Jane Addams, as well as manuscripts of her unpublished reports of the Paris Peace Conference of 1918. Included in this collection are memorabilia of the type which, although they add little to the scholarly research value of the collection, do wonders to bring to life a particular period. Included in Hunt's papers are souvenirs and realia of various suffrage conferences and meetings of the Votes for Women Party, which include a linen breast banner and a flag in purple and gold imprinted with the slogan "Votes for Women," an accordian style photograph album opening to six feet in length entitled "Parade of Suffragists on Fifth Avenue, New York City, May 6, 1911," in which many of the participants have been identified in manuscript notes on each photograph, and a small china statue of three squawking geese with the phrase "We want our votes" printed on its base.

Another important item, in this case donated by its British author to the National Council of Women of Canada in honour of the death of a Canadian friend, is an 141-page unpublished typescript bound in blue boards with the title in gilt on the upper cover "History of the Canadian Hut." Written by Gladys Lillian King and dated September 1919, the manuscript outlines the work of the Canadian Y.M.C.A. in establishing a "hut" or hostel in London for Canadian soldiers on leave during World War I. King, a member of the Military Women Police, details her experiences under such headings as "Weakness Personified: Showing how men under the influence of alcohol were assisted and cared for, with anecdotes"; "The Greatest Social Problem—being a straightforward talk—from a woman's point of view—on a subject that should concern all thinking people" and "Peace-Victory Marches-Farewell."

Included among non-Canadian papers acquired by purchase or gift is a letter written by Victoria Sackville-West dated March 9, 1944 in which she discusses the effects of the war on South-West England; an apparently unpublished play by Naomi Gwladys Royde-Smith entitled "Mafro"; two letters written by American suffragette Lucy Stone, founder of the *Woman's journal* and a letter dated 1838 written by Amelia Opie inserted in her 1937 biography written by Jacobine Menzies-Wilson and Helen Lloyd.

Papers of two women actively involved in Canadian radio broadcasting are also available in the collection, both having been acquired in conjunction with the gift of the Lady Aberdeen Library. Elizabeth Long's connections with the National Council of Women were very close as she had served as Vice-President of that group as well as Vice-President of the International Council of Women. Long was also the convenor of the project to put together the Lady Aberdeen Library and her papers contain a great deal of information on the formation of that collection. In her professional life, Long worked for the Canadian Broadcasting Corporation and was the first woman in that organization to hold an important executive position, that of Supervisor of Women's Interests. In this capacity Miss Long prepared a series of radio broadcasts on women which were said to be the most comprehensive plan of international broadcasts for women of any radio system in the world. The research notes for these broadcasts and the resulting radio scripts all form a part of Long's three foot archive.

The papers of a second broadcaster, Ms. Claire Wallace, also contain both the research notes and finished scripts of various radio shows directed towards women beginning in 1935. An index to all persons mentioned in Wallace's major shows "Teatime Topics" and "They Tell Me" has been prepared and provides access to material in the over fourteen feet of radio script scrapbooks compiled by Wallace. In 1942 Wallace had the distinction of being the first woman to broadcast nationally over the CBC network and in 1946 received the Beaver Award as Canada's top woman commentator.

Papers and manuscripts related to several other careers and areas of interest are also represented in the archives. The role of the politician's wife is reflected in the collection of Martha Louise Black who was the wife of Yukon Governor George Black, and who was elected in 1935 to the Canadian House of Commons. The experience of modern Canadian missionaries is contained in the letters of Beulah Misener Alloway, who died in Kenya in 1954. Nor are contributions of women to Canadian art neglected—some of the papers of potter Alice Mary Hagen and material relating to the sculptors Florence Wyle and Frances Loring are available to users of the Doris Lewis Rare Book Room.

A last collection which has been found most useful is the collection of copies of the four hundred and sixty-nine briefs presented to the federal government's "Royal Commission on the Status of Women." Although many of these briefs are classed as "Confidential" the several hundred which are available provide expressions of opinions ranging from those of "A Group of Women, St. Catharines, Ontario" to the "Women of the Saskatchewan Farmers Union." A subject index to these briefs is available for use by researchers.

As stated earlier, a brief section of this paper will be devoted to describing the Library's general collections of material useful and necessary for those researchers in the area of women's studies. The formulation of collections development policies which are responsive to women's studies remains a problem due to the interdisciplinary, often controversial, and when connected to the women's movement, political nature of the field. However, the University of Waterloo has attempted to acquire through its collection development policies for each discipline, those materials which are required to provide a large body of primary and secondary source materials for the study of women. In providing these materials the Library has attempted to acquire materials listed in standard bibliographies in the field although most of these bibliographies are related particularly to American sources, viewpoints and needs. However, the collection does contain a good basic collection and a comparison of holdings to the Stineman's *Women's Studies: A Recommended Core Bibliography* reveals that the Library holds 70% of items listed in that publication.

Canadian counterparts to Stineman's are lacking although there are some for certain selected areas such as history. In analyzing the Library's holding in this particular area, a comparison against the items listed in Light and Strong-Boag's *True daughter's of the north: Canadian women's history, a bibliography* (Toronto: Ontario Institute for Studies for Education, 1980) it was found that the collection contained 80% of the items listed. Canadian bibliographical and review publications such as the journal *Resources for feminist research* are searched against the Library's holdings on a regular basis for information of newly printed materials while other compilations such as Light and Strong-Boag's *True Daughters of the north: Canadian women's history: an annotated bibliography* (Toronto: Ontario Institute for Studies in Education, 1980) are used to compile desiderata and want lists.

Older publications, when not acquired specifically for the Rare Books Room collection have been acquired in micro or reprint format. Included here is the large 10,097 item *History of women collection* (Research Publications, Inc.) and the periodical collection entitled *Herstory* representing serial publications from 1956 to 1974 from the International Women's History Periodical Archive prepared by Women's History Research Center at Berkeley, California. Other collections currently available include the following: *Bibliofem,* an ongoing publication of the Fawcett Library in London, which provides a current listing by author, title, subject, and classification to works about women published in the English language; *Women and Health* (Women's History Research Center) which contains clippings, articles, pamphlets, essays and papers collected between 1968 and 1974 on some 150 subjects; *Les Femmes* a collection of 192 titles on microfiche based on the collection from the Bibliotheque National in France; *Sex Research: Early literature from statistics to erotica, 1700-1860* (Research Publications Inc.) which contains 1000 titles on microfilm and *Marriage, Sex and the Family in England, 1660-1800* (Garland Reprint Series) which is a 69 title facsimile series bound in 44 volumes which documents the origins of the modern family.

Cataloguing and organizing such a collection as that found in the Doris Lewis Rare Book Room is not an easy task. Traditional subject headings and methods of access have long been found inadequate and the cataloguing staff have attempted, while staying within the confines of the Library's general cataloguing scheme, to provide additional points of entry into the collection. To this end a separate card file, very broadly based in scope, of items relating to women has been kept by the staff and contains references and notes directing researchers to particular books or parts of books which might be of relevance to their particular research interests. Other special files maintained in the Rare Books Room have also been found of value and include the provenance and bookplate files, the chronological file arranged by imprint date and the subscription list file. This latter file continues a project on women appearing in eighteenth century subscription lists begun by staff member Jane Britton in conjunction with work being done by the Project for historical bio-bibliography at Newcastle upon Tyne, England.[12] The Department maintains a reference collection containing annotated copies of many of the standard bibliographies previously mentioned.

The resources of the Doris Lewis Rare Book Room are available to all researchers during the Room's hours of opening (Monday to Friday, 9 a.m. to 4 p.m.) and additional hours of access can usually be arranged by prior appointment. New additions to the collection are detailed in the Department's quarterly *Newsletter* and catalogues and bibliographies describing the collections in greater depth appear at irregular intervals as numbers in the Library's "Bibliography Series."

NOTES

1. National Council of Women of Canada. *The Lady Aberdeen Library on the History of Women.* (Waterloo: University of Waterloo Library, 1967) p. xiv.
2. University of Waterloo. Library. Lady Aberdeen Collection. *A catalogue of the Lady Aberdeen Library on the History of women in the University of Waterloo Library.*

University of Waterloo Library bibliography; no. 7. Compiled by Jane Britton. The Catalogue is available for $10.00 from Jorn Jorgensen, University of Waterloo Library.

3. *Canadian Newsletter of Research of Women.* Vol (1), May 1972, p. 1. This journal is now called *Resources for Feminist Research* and is published with the assistance of the Women's Programmes of the Department of the Secretary of State and the Ontario Institute for Studies in Education.

4. Conrad, Margaret R. "Women's Studies in Canada" *Dalhousie Review* Vol 60 (3), Autumn 1980, p.5.

5. James, Janet Wilson. "History and women at Harvard." *Harvard Library Bulletin,* XVI (October, 1968): 385-399.

6. Collier, Clifford. *Dance resources in Canadian libraries.* Ottawa: National Library. Research collections in Canadian libraries. Special studies; 8. 1982, p.73.

7. Brown, Jennifer. *Strangers in blood: fur trade families in Indian country* (Vancouver: University of British Columbia Press, 1980).

8. Strong-Boag, Veronica. "Raising Clio's consciousness: women's history and archives in Canada." *Archivaria,* 6 (Summer 1978) p. 70-82.

9. Shortt, Elizabeth Smith *'A Woman with a purpose—The Diaries of Elizabeth Smith 1872-1884.* (Toronto: University of Toronto, 1980).

10. Edmonton (Alta.) Archives. *Emily Murphy collection M.S.2.* Prepared by Mary W. Campbell. Edmonton: City of Edmonton Parks and Recreation, 1983.

11. Story, Norah. *The Oxford Companion to Canadian History* (Toronto: Oxford University Press, 1967) p. 490.

12. Wallis, P.J. and R.V. *Women Filter* (Newcastle: Project for Historical Biobibliography, 1984).

From Tradition to Trend: Small but Noteworthy Collections

Suzanne Hildenbrand

Traditional women's collections are concerned with woman's past, but in recent years there has been a trend toward collections that focus on woman's present. While traditional collections provide the sources for historical scholarship, representatives of the newer trend provide the documentation for social change. Even when research oriented, these collections support change in laws, hiring practices, admissions procedures and so on. Nurtured by a revitalized feminism they reflect the feminist agenda in their emphasis. Education, work, politics and sexuality, for example, are each the theme of one or more collections. Although generally small in size and focused on one issue they have little else in common. They may be held in university centers, non-profit organizations, or private homes. Many suffer from lack of funds, but others are generously supported by grants. Some of these collections are marginal to the library world, others are leaders in it. No overview of women's collections today would be complete without an examination of representatives of this trend.

EDUCATION

The Center for the Study, Education and Advancement of Women, University of California, Berkeley

The Center is representative of a group of centers serving the needs of campus and community women that opened in colleges and universities in the 70s. The Center serves its constitutency by promoting research on and by women, sponsoring lectures, workshops and discussion groups, conducting conferences and providing consultation on academic and career matters. A newsletter, entitled *Connections* is issued.

The library is a vital part of the Center, supporting both the research and service functions. It is the first stop for those researching women, or for women looking for funding or a career. The collection includes more than a thousand books, including some unavailable elsewhere on the campus, forty regularly received journals, theses, dissertations, newsletters, pamphlets and clippings. All materials are non-circulating. Books are accessed by author, title or subject through a catalog, with locally produced subject headings, while *Women's Studies Abstracts* is available to access material in periodicals. The main subject emphasis has been work, and there is much career or vocational counseling material. Other subjects covered are varied and include women's history, the ERA, abortion and financial aid. When information is not available in the collection itself, the reference librarian refers inquirers to an appropriate source elsewhere.

The Career Resource Room contains vertical file material, college catalogs, career-oriented journals and the *Career Opportunity Index & Update* as well as current job listings.

Three personal collections are available for use at the Center. The Elizabeth Monroe Drews Collection which focuses on the status of women in the 1950s and 1960s. Drews was a member of President Kennedy's commission on the Status of Women and a founding member of N.O.W. The collection includes her working papers and numerous articles and papers that she had collected. The Catharine Scholten Collection consists of books on women's history, with emphasis on the area of Scholten's dissertation which was entitled "Childbearing in America." Finally, the Bea Bain Collection contains many of the important early women's movement works.

The librarian assists with research strategies and the library occasionally sponsors workshops on researching women's issues. Acquisition lists and bibliographies are regularly prepared for distribution, free of charge.

The library is located in building T-9 on the Berkeley campus and is open Monday thru Friday from 9:00AM to 4:00PM, during academic sessions. During other times, it is advised to consult the staff before planning a visit. The telephone number is 642-4786. The librarian is Ms. Jane Scantlebury.

The Women's Educational Resources Centre of the Ontario Institute for the Study of Education, Affiliated with the University of Toronto

The Centre was established in 1976 with materials collected for a project on women and education. While this topic continues to be the main concern, the Centre has expanded and now has material on the Canadian women's movement, children's material and a small amount of general Canadian history. It holds, as well, the bibliographic sources used to produce the well-known *Resources for Feminist Research/Documentation sur la Recherche Feministe.* These latter include Women's Studies reading lists, course outlines and syllabi, audio-visual catalogs and catalogs or guides to original sources in Canada such as private libraries, personal papers and special collections. In addition to its holdings, the collection offers a valuable Information and Referral Service to Toronto women to "facilitate daily communication among women and women's groups." Addresses and telephone numbers, project descriptions and announcements of meetings and other events are provided.

Education holdings at the Centre include material on the status of women in public school systems, community colleges and colleges and universities. Material on vocational and academic programs conducted by community organizations such as the Young Women's Christian Association is included as well as material on women's re-entry programs. Information on sexism at all educational levels is available and non-sexist and feminist children's materials are also collected at the Centre; these include books, recordings, lesson plans and curricular materials. There is a Women's Kit, containing records, slides, pamphlets and posters, prepared by the Ontario Institute for the Study of Education, with a guide for suggestions on use.

The documents and archives of the contemporary feminist movement in Canada form a special collection, and include correspondence, pamphlets, minutes and other documentation. There is an extensive collection of feminist and women's periodicals, including full runs of those issued by Canadian women's groups in either French or English. Subject indexing is provided for these periodicals.

The Toronto Star and *The Globe and Mail* are clipped for everything relevant to women while the *New York Times* is selectively clipped. There are, in addition, unpublished papers from Canadian scholarly meetings.

The Centre is located at O.I.S.E. at 252 Bloor St. W., Toronto, Ontario, room S 630 and is open Tuesday, Wednesday and Friday from 9:15 AM to 4:30 PM, and Thursday from 10:00 AM to 8:00 PM. The telephone number is 923-6641, ext. 244. Ms. Frieda Forman is Collection Coordinator.

WORK

The Marguerite Rawalt Resource Center of the Business and Professional Women's Foundation

Dating back to an earlier period of feminist awareness, the original National Federation of Business and Professional Women's Clubs was founded in 1919 on the eve of suffrage. Reorganized in 1956 as the Business and Professional Women's Foundation it has as its goal the improvement of the economic status of working women. To assist in achieving this goal, the Foundation declared its intention to establish a "clearing house of information for and about the advancement of working women."

The Rawalt Resource Center, named in 1980 for Marguerite Rawalt, former BPW national president and women's rights activist, was a unique resource when it opened in 1957. Although other work-oriented collections have since been founded, it remains the largest and most vigorous, as evidenced by its size and its leadership role.

The collection includes more than 20,000 books and journals and a vertical file collection which contains clippings, pamphlets, brochures, conference reports and speeches. Access to these is by *Library of Congress Subject Headings,* modified to eliminate sexist language. Information is available on the following topics: jobs, careers, occupational segregation, comparable worth, sexual harassment, occupational health and safety, displaced homemakers and women's legal and economic status.

The Center prepares information packets on topics that are frequently the subject of requests. Fourteen of these are currently available. It also prepares bimonthly acquisitions lists and summaries and bibliographies on major issues of importance to working women.

The Center has launched a pacesetting automation project, entitled "Information for Working Women." A database that can be accessed by libraries across the country is being developed. The estimated completion date is 1985. A first phase in this automation project was the creation of a thesaurus to provide a uniform vocabulary to describe issues of importance to working women. The development of this vocabulary has been coordinated with the National Council for Research on Women, a group of 38 research organizations throughout the country. When completed the thesaurus should be the most comprehensive and authoritative vocabularly on women's issues to date. Specialists from various disciplines such as economics, anthropology, and science, as well as librarians from around the nation have all cooperated. A pre-publication test of the thesaurus will be held in various selected libraries and research centers.

The Rawalt Resource Center is open to the public and answers telephone and mail queries. Ms. Cheryl Sloan is the librarian and the Center is located at the Foundation at 2012 Massachusetts Avenue, NW, Washington DC, 20036.

Catalyst Library and Audiovisual Center

Catalyst is a national nonprofit organization that since its founding in 1962 has worked to foster the full participation of women in business and professional life by furthering women's upward mobility, expanding career options and helping to reconcile the needs of the workplace and the family.

The Catalyst Library is another major clearinghouse on women and work. It was originally established in 1975 with a three-year grant from the Andrew W. Mellon Foundation as a resource for in-house research. Demand for the information available at Catalyst however, was unprecedented and a second Mellon Foundation grant permitted Catalyst to expand its service beyond its own staff. A third Mellon Foundation grant provided for an Audiovisual Center and the introduction of a database service. The Library contains more than 5,000 catalogued items, 125 periodicals, 2,000 vertical file items, corporate files, statistical surveys, dissertations and conference reports, government reports from agencies such as the Women's Bureau, the Department of Labor and the Civil Rights Commission and copies of relevant legislation such as the Equal Opportunity Act. More than thirty bibliographies have been prepared on topics such as job sharing, flexitime and financial assistance for education. These are available to the public.

The Audiovisual Center contains materials selected by a Catalyst committee and an annotated bibliography entitled *Catalyst Media Review* is issued bimonthly. Screenings can be arranged through Center staff.

The library staff has developed a database containing bibliographic citations and abstracts of materials in the Library's extensive holdings. The database may be accessed via the Bibliographic Retrieval System (BRS), a database vendor. A thesaurus has been constructed to facilitate access.

The Catalyst Library and Audiovisual Center, 14 E. 60th St. NY, NY 10022, is open to the public Monday through Thursdays, 9:00AM to 5:00PM, and Monday evenings until 7:30 PM. The Director of Information Services is Ms. Gurley Turner.

POLITICS

The Center for the American Woman and Politics, Eagleton Institute, Rutgers University

Increased political participation by women citizens is the primary goal of the Center for the American Woman and Politics. Projects such as Bringing More Women into Public Office, funded by the Charles H. Revson Foundation, and production of the database entitled National Information Bank on Women Public Officials are typical Center activities.

The Reference Collection, unique in the country in its subject, consists of three sections: periodicals; papers, reports and articles; and books. The periodicals collection consists of about one hundred and twenty-two titles. A collection of working papers, newspaper clippings and published and unpublished papers, the latter numbering about eight hundred, make up the second section. Substantive papers and reports are catalogued in a 3 by 5 card file by subject and author but the more ephemeral materials such as notes, clippings and brief articles are not catalogued. The book collection consists of over six hundred titles as well as government documents and special editions of journals that focus on women's political participation. This collection is also catalogued by author and title, with title cards bearing annotations.

Although small, this collection is tailored to meet the needs of a diverse group of users, including journalists, scholars and would-be office seekers. Much of the reference work is done by mail or phone with about ten times as many phone queries answered as those from visitors. Journalists researching stories about the gender gap or the possibility of a woman vice presidential candidate are often referred to the Center and its reference collection by the National Organization for Women. A major bibliography, *Women's Political Participation in the United States, 1950-1976* (N.Y., Garland, 1977) was compiled by the Assistant Director of the Center, who is director of the Reference Collection, Ms. Kathy Stanwick.

The collection is open between 9:00AM and 4:00PM, Monday through Friday. Materials do not circulate, but photocopying facilities are available at nominal cost. A listing of periodicals held and of the subject headings, devised at the Center, used in the vertical file system are available for $2.00 each. Inquiries should be addressed to Ms. Kathy Stanwick, Assistant Director of the Center for the American Woman and Politics, Eagleton Institute, Rutgers University, New Brunswick, N.J. 08901.

SEXUALITY

The National Clearinghouse on Marital Rape Library

The library of the National Clearinghouse on Marital Rape began in 1979, when Laura X—the X stands for women's history being anonymous and replaces women's legal owners' names—became outraged at the media treatment of Greta Rideout who had charged her husband with rape. Laura is known to librarians and women's studies researchers as president of the Women's History Research Center which issues the microfilm series Herstory, Women and Health/Mental Health and Women and Law.

The mission of the Clearinghouse was, and remains, to combat marital rape. In support of this goal the Clearinghouse conducts research, public education, organizational work, and litigation advocacy. It has been difficult to develop a collection in support of this mission since many continue to deny the existence of the issue. No one kept track of information about cases in the handful of states where marital rape was a crime, and neither police nor rape crisis shelters anywhere concerned themselves with the issue. A computer search in 1979 produced only three relevant items in the literature and a search of LEXIS produced citations only to cases which had gone to appeal. Yet documentation was vitally needed if the necessary legislation was to be drafted, presented and passed.

A network of volunteer researchers was enlisted to track down elusive information and a press clipping service was employed to collect items. Collection of information was expedited by the passage of the California marital rape law in 1979. Debates in the legislature and comment in the press were gathered and added to what was found by careful scrutiny of general literature and followup of items in bibliographies and footnotes. Painstakingly the volunteers established a library of some 700 files of clippings, theses, studies, law review articles, professional papers, letters from victims, testimony at legislative hearings, bills (including both those that passed and those that failed), sections of books, interviews with victims, newsletter articles, book reviews, bibliographies, cartoons, poetry, film reviews, briefs, judges decisions, interviews with district attorneys, tapes of radio and TV programs on the topic and pamphlets and lobbying packets. This material is accessed under headings constructed at the Clearinghouse. Frequently used headings are: Statistics, Police Training Manuals, Charges, Cases, Shelters/Centers, District Attorneys Policies and Studies, Self-Defense, Trial Personnel, Conviction and After, and Other Countries Legislation.

A bibliographic guide is available from the Clearinghouse for $3 and other publications include a newsletter, a socio-legal chart of marital rape case histories and a pamphlet on marital rape victims who kill their husbands in self-defense.

Information on the collection and on the publications can be obtained by sending a request and a stamped, self-addressed envelope to Laura X at The National Clearinghouse on Marital Rape, located in Laura's home, at 2325 Oak St., Berkeley, California 94708.

The Lesbian Herstory Archives

Lesbians have been traditionally even less visible in standard history than other women. Not only were records lost, but there was a real aversion on the part of those who construct indexes, guides and subject headings to use the word "lesbian." Today the Lesbian Herstory Archives is determined to recapture as much of the past as possible and to collect the contemporary materials for a future history. The Archives is a grassroots operation, maintained by volunteers and housed in a private residence. In keeping with this character, the archives is non-elitist, collecting materials of a popular nature and papers of lesbian women, regardless of status.

Reflecting the newer trend in women's collections, however, the Lesbian Herstory Archives is concerned with much more than establishing a lesbian past. It is also actively engaged in the political struggles of the lesbian community today. Furthermore, the Archives is a force for community building among lesbians, providing a welcome, and often a meal or lodging for visitors from out of town and actively networking among lesbians nationally. Indeed, providing a better past, and political struggle, can both be seen as supportive of the larger goal of community building.

While a collective supports the LHA, three members have made a lifetime commitment to it. These are Deborah Edel, Joan Nestle and Judith Schwartz. A major goal of the collective is to train future generations of lesbians in the need for the Archives and the skills to maintain it.

Although the Archives began modestly in 1974 with one filing cabinet of materials and a complete set of the lesbian journal *The Ladder* it contains today more than three thousand books and a large collection of posters, videotapes, photographs and manuscripts including letters, diaries and so on. While no specific figures are available on holdings of this latter type, users of the Archives note that they have grown beyond the original filing cabinet and now spill out into the halls, dining room and other areas of the apartment.

The collective carries on all the traditional archival work. Access is facilitated by a catalog which employs terms developed by the Circle of Lesbian Indexers. In addition, daily tours of the Archives are given, at the rate of about five hundred a year. A newsletter is published, as well as bibliographies. Slide shows are produced and presented to various groups. Reference services are provided and study groups and regional archives are encouraged.

Inquiries concerning holdings, publications or visits should be addressed to The Lesbian Herstory Archives, P.O. Box 1258, New York, NY 10116.

Editor's Note: Largely because of space limitations, this issue of *Special Collections* does not include reference to several other collections of Lesbians. Most of these collections have been listed in other Haworth Press publications. We do plan a scheduled issue on all collections relevant to the gay/lesbian movement, however, and will thus be able to give such collections adequate space.—L.A.

ACCESS

Feminist Library Services: The Women's Studies Librarian-at-Large, University of Wisconsin System

Susan E. Searing

The position of Women's Studies Librarian-at-Large for the University of Wisconsin System embodies a philosophy of cooperative library service, melded with a vision of women's studies as an integral part of the liberal arts curriculum. As a specialized program geared to a statewide academic user group, the Office of the Librarian-at-Large is an innovative alternative to a special collection in women's studies. How do the unique services of this office compare with the services and resources that come with the establishment of a separate collection? This article will attempt to answer this question by placing the discussion of the history and services of the Office of the Women's Studies Librarian-at-Large within a broader and comparative context of library services to women's studies.

I will first briefly outline the historical development of the field of women's studies, including the explosion of feminist publishing, both mainstream and small press, over the last decade. I will then examine special collections in women's studies and the Office of the Women's Studies Librarian-at-Large as different responses to the growing need for library services in women's studies, exploring the unique value of each.

The new academic field of women's studies has established itself in remarkably short time, as evidenced by the rapid accumulation of a body of scholarship and the proliferation of courses and programs. From a handful of classes a decade ago, the field has swelled to offer an estimated 20,000 courses in the United States each year. Some 450 colleges grant degrees or certificates in women's studies.

The author gratefully acknowledges the assistance of Catherine Loeb in the research and writing of this article.

At the 26 campuses of the University of Wisconsin alone, some 250 women's studies courses are on the books. Even more significant is the phenomenal impact of feminist scholarship on the traditional disciplines. The increasing attention to women and women's issues in such areas as psychology, history, literature, sociology and anthropology cannot be ignored, nor can the spate of new research in such professional fields as medicine, law, social work, business, education, and library science.

Women's studies has from the outset reflected two goals seemingly in contradiction. On the one hand, the original impetus was to increase the number and quality of women's studies courses, to stabilize programs and course offerings by making them part of the permanent curriculum, to achieve tenured appointments for women's studies instructors, and to build the support mechanisms that characterize a mature field of study—professional associations, annual conferences and colloquia, research institutes, juried journals, and so on. On the other hand, carving out a comfortable niche in the campus hierarchy of departments and divisions was never put forth as the ultimate goal of academic feminists. Rather, they strove for legitimacy as prerequisite to a total transformation of the traditional disciplines through the incorporation of women's studies scholarship and values. Programs at different institutions at different times have given one goal or the other higher priority, but, with the advent of the eighties, the idea of "mainstreaming" has taken on new force nationwide.

In its brief history, women's studies has had an astonishing impact on scholarly publishing. As is typical of a new field, especially one so politicized, the first materials were published independently, issued by pioneering women's studies programs, and shared within professional caucuses. The perils of haphazard distribution and lack of reviews plagued librarians and researchers who tried to stay abreast of the alternative movement-oriented literature. Teachers were challenged to find (and often forced to invent) materials to support the new curriculum.

Today, by contrast, women's studies publishing is big business. Commercial publishers and university presses issue specialized catalogs of their women-related titles, and popular books geared to a feminist audience regularly grace the best seller lists. The growth of mainstream publishing on women has not meant the demise of small women's presses, however. Publishers like The Feminist Press and Persephone Press continue to issue books that represent the vanguard of women's studies scholarship. Of recent importance are several anthologies that strive to push women's studies beyond its white, middle-class, North American, heterosexual boundaries.[1]

A quick look at another category of publication, periodicals, will further illustrate the vitality of both traditional and alternative publishing in the field. Women's movement magazines, operating outside the academic mainstream, printed some of the earliest theoretical pieces about women's position in society, as well as pathbreaking historical and literary analyses. *Quest, Chrysalis,* and *off our backs* are among the important non-academic sources for thoughtful feminist writings. Today, women's studies can boast of several academic journals, the most widely recognized being *Signs: A Journal of Women in Culture and Society.* Other respected scholarly journals include *Frontiers, Women's Studies Quarterly, Feminist Studies, The International Journal of Women's Studies,* and *Women's Studies International Forum.* In addition, many new titles reflect the burgeoning research and writing in specialized areas—*Women and Politics, Tulsa Studies in Women's Literature, Psychology of Women Quarterly, Sex Roles, Women's Art Journal,* and the *Women's Rights Law Reporter,* to name just a few. The publishers of women's studies journals include university presses, women's studies programs, professional associations, feminist collectives, and profit-making companies. *Feminist Periodicals,*[2] a publication of the UW Women's Studies Librarian-at-Large, now reproduces the tables of contents of over 60 general and specialized periodicals. Further bibliographic control of the periodical literature is provided by *Women Studies Abstracts,* a long-lived small press quarterly, and *Studies on Women Abstracts,* a newer commercial venture.[3]

Together, the expansion of women's studies curricula nationwide and the blossoming of feminist publishing demand innovative and vigorous new library services. Faced with a vast array of resources in many disciplines, emanating from both familiar and alternative sources, most academic libraries either rely on subject specialists to select appropriate materials on women in their fields or identify an additional bibliographer to handle acquisitions in women's studies as a whole. To aid researchers in their use of the materials, some colleges and universities have established separate collections, and one, the University of Wisconsin, has pioneered with a librarian-at-large to serve several campuses. In the remainder of this article, we examine the specialized collection as a strategy for serving the community of women's studies scholars and handling the wealth of the new literature, and conclude by describing the different path taken by the University of Wisconsin System toward the same end.

A library contemplating a separate collection in women's studies can look to some highly successful models. Radcliffe's Schlesinger Library on the History of Women in America, for example, is a national treasurehouse of printed and manuscript materials. Ohio State University has established a women's studies library for its students; Northwestern has created a Women's Collection of primary sources and periodicals within its Special Collections department.

Within the University of Wisconsin System, there are several separate collections. College Library, the undergraduate and reserve library at UW-Madison, has a Women's Reading Area with paperback books and extensive vertical files. The Cairns Collections in the Rare Book Department of UW-Madison's Memorial Library comprehensively collects all editions of the works of nine American women writers, with accompanying primary and secondary documentation. At UW-Eau Claire, the library's Helen X. Sampson Collection was formed from the donation of a private library of books and reprints. At UW-Whitewater, UW-LaCrosse, and UW-Milwaukee, the women's studies programs make available sizeable book, periodical, and vertical file collections to students and researchers. These collections have no formal relation to the campus libraries. At UW-River Falls, the Women's Resource Center offers a small collection that supports students' curricular needs as well as their queries regarding career planning, reentering college or the workforce, coping with sexism on a personal basis, and other concerns.

Faculty often view a special collection as critical. For example, Florence Howe and Paul Lauter, in their proposal for an evaluative longitudinal data base on women's studies programs, count library resources among the items to be recorded. In asking, "Is the women's studies library collection housed in a separate place in the library? Is there an additional library in the program's offices?" they imply that separate collections are indicative of an institution's commitment to women's studies.[4]

Special collections do serve as concrete evidence of institutional support for women's studies programs. They are more visible than a mere budget line for adding materials to the general collection; if cut, they will be noticed immediately. However, there may be a price to pay for this separate budget allocation: book selectors in the traditional disciplines may assume that the existence of a special collection relieves them of any responsibility for women's studies acquisitions. A study of computerized acquisitions records at UW-Whitewater showed that—even in the absence of a special collection—funds in the traditional disciplines are rarely spent on women's studies texts.[5] The establishment of a special collection might further solidify this pattern. With the wealth of feminist scholarship in virtually every field of the humanities and social sciences, it seems only fair that departmental funds should also be used toward women's studies materials.

Without doubt, special collections facilitate the location and use of research materials. Women's studies books are scattered throughout the Library of Congress classification scheme, making browsing unproductive. The UW-Whitewater study found that only 21.5% of the titles bought on the women's studies budget line fell between HQ 1101 and HQ 2030, the "women and feminism" call number range. These works represented only the most general overviews of women's condition, anthologies addressing many issues, and books specifically about the women's liberation movement. Bringing together all the materials on women from every discipline makes life easier for students and faculty alike.

But the efficiency factor is double-edged. Facilitating retrieval of materials for researchers may handicap them in the long run, for they will not be forced to acquire library skills beyond the knack of browsing. A strong bibliographic instruction program and clearly written handouts may be more educationally empowering than a separate collection. Nor can anyone make the plea, as is often raised in defense of special libraries, that proximity to laboratories, classrooms, or faculty offices is required. Women's studies is an interdisciplinary field, and its practitioners are found in every corner of the campus.

Female students in particular may be drawn to a special women's studies collection because of its allure as "women's space"—a refuge from the sexism of the campus at large, a place to study together with other women, a comfortable but stimulating intellectual nest. This is a prime reason why collections spring up in women's studies program offices and campus women's centers, although these organizations rarely have the resources to duplicate more than a small portion of the library's holdings. In a like manner, women's centers in the community invariably establish a lending library and resource files early in their existence.

The need for women's space, where women can claim some control over the content and organization of the information housed there, is a powerful one. But is it the library's role to respond to this need, or can other agencies on campus serve better? If a women's collection offers a comfortable environment for some students, will it not also turn others away? One can imagine a pooh-pooher of "women's lib" stumbling upon an interesting feminist book while off in the stacks on another errand. If such materials are accessible only in special collections, serendipitous consciousness-raising can never occur. While an integrated collection provides no guarantee that browsers will be exposed to women's studies materials (and indeed, may place barriers in the paths of those intentionally seeking such works), at least it does not close off the avenues of chance enlightenment.

There are several practical hurdles to setting up and maintaining a special collection. The greatest of these is funding. Only a large university library, with other special collections as precedents, is likely to establish a separate library for women's studies. Money is needed to acquire materials, to furnish the space, and to staff the collection—all on an ongoing basis.

Another fundamental problem is outlining a selection policy for the collection. Freud, for example, is crucial to an understanding of popular and professional notions of women's psychology. Should his works be on the shelves of a special collection? Does *The Total Woman* belong there alongside *The Second Sex?* There are some guides to building such a collection (*Women's Studies: A Recommended Core Bibliography* is probably the best), but difficult choices will inevitably arise.[6] The library must be prepared to explain selection policy to its users.

In addition to the sticky job of delineating the subject scope of women's studies, the question of duplication must also be resolved from the outset. Should a women's studies collection duplicate materials held in other campus libraries? Based on the interdisciplinary nature of women's studies, coupled with the value of maintaining an integrated main collection to support the incorporation of knowledge about women into the general consciousness, the answer is "yes." Is such duplication affordable and wise? The answer is clearly "no," given the explosion of feminist publishing and the spiraling costs of books and periodicals in all fields. Absent significant outside funding, no academic library today could afford to build a separate women's studies collection from scratch. Rather, the core of a new collection would have to be formed by pulling relevant titles from the shelves of the general collection and recataloging them. Continuing fiscal constraints would inevitably force librarians to purchase new women-related titles only for the special collection. Thus throughout this article special collections and integrated collections are treated as either/or propositions, a dichotomy based as much on financial considerations and on philosophical ones.

From the foregoing discussion, it appears that both separate women's studies collections and integrated collections offer advantages and disadvantages to the user. Neither approach, in and of itself, is ideal. Therefore, other considerations specific to a given institution will determine the course a library takes in supplying the tools of research to its clientele in women's studies. This was true at the University of Wisconsin, as the following brief history of the position of the Women's Studies Librarian-at-Large will illustrate.

Housed in the Memorial Library of UW-Madison, the Librarian-at-Large and her staff reach out to the 13 four-year campuses, the 13 two-year campuses, and Extension, which together constitute the University of Wisconsin System. The System itself is a relatively new entity, and the story of the Librarian-at-Large is inextricably bound up with the philosophy that brought Wisconsin's system of public higher education into its present configuration.

The position of Women's Studies Librarian-at-Large was filled for the first time in 1977, but the proposal predated the position by several years. Its advocates were the faculty and librarians involved in two groups: the Association of Faculty Women on the Madison campus; and the systemwide Task Force on Women's Studies.

The Association of Faculty Women struggled throughout the early seventies to improve the status of women faculty and staff on the Madison campus. The group tackled such issues as affirmative action, grievance procedures, and women's athletics. One of the AFW's primary goals was to establish and legitimize women's studies courses. Today, due in part to the group's passionate and unflagging commitment, the Women's Studies Program at UW-Madison is among the largest and best in the country, with a renowned research center attached to it.

Keenly aware that bureaucratic knowledge is power, some members of the AFW formed a Budget Committee to educate themselves about the complex process of acquiring and spending state funds. After studying the policies under which fiscal proposals were submitted, reviewed, and eventually channeled to the state legislature, the committee decided to try its hand at the process. Members drafted a financial request and justification for an entirely new position, a Women's Studies Librarian-at-Large, with additional money requested for program support and a discretionary acquisitions budget.

The committee, which included librarians, realized that new curricular programs were typically approved without considering whether the libraries were prepared to acquire and make available the resources necessary to support the classes. If women's studies programs were to succeed on the UW campuses, the committee members believed, advance planning for library services was crucial. And if resources and services were to be available to the entire state system, a single special collection clearly would not suffice. On the other hand, a specialist librarian, working with faculty, librarians, and administrators throughout the System, could provide the guidance needed to build strong collections statewide and could offer assistance to researchers exploring this new field.

The Budget Committee's proposal was endorsed by the Task Force on Women's Studies, a multicampus group officially charged with making recommendations for the development of women's studies within the UW System. From the Task Force, the proposal traveled to the Board of Regents, where it also gained approval. However, at the next step it died, when the governor vetoed all requests for new projects during the biennial budget period.

Disappointed but hardly defeated, the UW faculty and librarians mobilized to accomplish themselves some of the goals they had formulated for the Librarian-at-Large. They convened a statewide conference on the development of library resources for women's studies; they generated lists of women-related materials held at each campus; and they compiled a core list of essential monographs in women's studies, based on faculty recommendations.[7] By 1977, however, it was clear that the limits of what could be achieved by collective action had been reached. The administrators of women's studies programs throughout the System (programs now more firmly rooted than at the time of the initial proposal) appealed to the Vice-President for Academic Affairs to fund the Women's Studies Librarian-at-Large position through an internal re-allocation. This he did, on a two-year pilot basis.

At the same time, an Advisory Panel was established, consisting of women's studies program directors, faculty, librarians, a member of System administration, and a student. The Panel assists the Librarian-at-Large in formulating and implementing policy, recommends new services and projects, and advises on the policies and personalities within the System.

It must be stressed that the development of women's studies within the University of Wisconsin had atypically strong support at the highest administrative levels. It owed much of its momentum to the sense of possibility fostered by the sweeping reorganization of the network of state-supported colleges and universities in 1971. Curriculum development remained a local concern, but new program proposals that responded to recommendations by the Task Force on Women's Studies were received favorably by the System administration.

Formal bonds of cooperation unite the women's studies programs, although each continues to reflect the unique character of its own campus in its philosophy of extracurricular service to students, community outreach, and pedagogical style. Women's Studies coordinators meet twice a year, and a state conference for faculty, students, and librarians is held every fall. A *Directory of Institution Program Administrators, Contact Persons, Committees and Programs*[8] now appears annually, and *Women's Studies Research in Wisconsin,*[9] abstracts of research in progress, is issued twice a year. In addition, the Office of the Women's Studies Librarian-at-Large has published two editions of *Women's Studies in Wisconsin: Who's Who and Where,*[10] a directory and index of nearly 700 individuals.

Into this supportive environment came Esther Stineman, the first Women's Studies Librarian-at-Large, in the fall of 1977. Although many of the networking mechanisms described above were not yet in place, the spirit of enthusiasm and cooperation was strong. In her tenure in the position, Stineman tackled several major projects. Two of these entailed unprecedented cooperation among the UW libraries. One was the creation of a union list of women's studies materials, offering main entry and, most importantly, subject access to books and other resources throughout the System. The union catalog aids the Librarian-at-Large and her staff in conducting subject searches for individuals and in compiling reading lists on current topics.

Stineman's other major coup was engineering the purchase, as a Systemwide resource, of the *History of Women* microfilm collection.[11] This very expensive set is an incredibly rich repository of primary sources for the study of women's past, including books, periodicals, manuscripts, pamphlets, and photographs drawn from several leading collections around the country. Housed in Memorial Library on the Madison campus, reels of the set are easily obtained on interlibrary loan by users elsewhere in the state.

Stineman, with the assistance of Catherine Loeb, revised and greatly expanded the existing core bibliography of women's studies books, annotating the entries in the process. Their efforts resulted in the highly acclaimed *Women's Studies: A Recommended Core Bibliography,* a guide to 1,763 books and periodicals deemed essential to undergraduate library collections supporting women's studies courses.

Last, Stineman obtained grant money to produce a series of slide-tape shows, collectively titled "Where Are the Women?", that illustrate the specific problems and the unique thrills of researching women in the social sciences, history, and the humanities. These slide-tape modules, while somewhat dated, still accurately portray the basic premises of women's studies. They are available on interlibrary loan from the library at UW-Platteville.

In addition to these large and visible projects, Stineman laid the foundation of reference service, on-demand bibliographic assistance, and library instruction that forms the core of ongoing service provided by the Librarian-at-Large and her staff. Her successor, Linda Parker, strengthened the network of women's studies scholars and librarians in Wisconsin and maintained an active program of public service, supplementing rather than duplicating reference and instruction functions at the UW libraries.

Parker took to heart the stated goal of the Librarian-at-Large that reads, "To establish the University of Wisconsin System as a national leader in the discipline on women's studies." She became an activist in women's groups in the American Library Association, and she organized librarians into a task force within the National Women's Studies Association. She spoke in a variety of forums about the office and its services and about the critical need for libraries to acquire and publicize women's materials. To many feminist librarians around the country (this writer included), who were themselves, often in isolation, attempting to furnish information about women to faculty, students, and the general public, Linda Parker and the UW office shone as beacons of inspiration.

Parker brought the office into the automated age by acquiring a microcomputer and instituting an online search service. Putting their women's studies expertise to work, the office staff was able to conduct efficient searches in bibliographic data bases available through BRS and Dialog. Parker also launched a national ad hoc group to develop an online data base in women's studies, an effort now backed by the National Council for Research on Women.

The solidification and expansion of the office's publication program, overseen by Catherine Loeb, also occurred under Parker. As the office became better known to students and researchers, regular publications proved to be an efficient means of meeting the growing demands on the office for bibliographic assistance. Librarians could rely on the publications to monitor the growing literature of women's studies and to serve as tools for collection development. The quarterly *Feminist Periodicals,* a compendium of contents pages, and the biennial *Women's Studies in Wisconsin: Who's Who & Where* have already been described. The quarterly *Feminist Collections: Women's Studies Library Resources in Wisconsin*[12] features reports from women's studies programs, substantive review essays by specialists, evaluations of new reference books, descriptions of library collections and archives in Wisconsin and elsewhere, profiles of feminist presses and bookstores, interviews with authors, and much more.

New Books on Women & Feminism[13] chronicles new monographs and periodicals in the English language of relevance to women's studies. Children's materials and nonprint items are selectively included also. Issued twice a year, *New Books on Women & Feminism* is the most comprehensive continuing bibliography in the field. Past numbers have been annotated, and it is hoped that smoother production procedures will make this service feasible again.

A series of topical reading lists, *Wisconsin Bibliographies in Women's Studies,* covers such broad topics as women and literature and such specialized subjects as assertiveness training for women in health care fields. As of this writing, 22 bibliographies are available.[14] The list has grown through the contribution of bibliographies by faculty in the UW System and through the work done by practicum students at the UW-Madison Library School. Although the subject coverage is still uneven, the Librarian-at-Large and her staff strive to respond to the latest interests of their clientele. Recent additions to the series have focused on Black women's studies, mainstreaming women's studies, women in management, and women and technology. Sourcelists on Jewish women's studies, career planning for women, and women in military, among others, are currently being developed.[15]

Now under the direction of Susan Searing, the office has entered a new stage. No longer a pilot project, the office has a six-year record of service to Wisconsin scholars and librarians and is accepted as an integral component of academic library services in the state. The highly successful publications represent the major commitment of staff time and office resources. Reference service, by telephone and letter as well as in person, continues to complement the fine efforts of librarians on the several campuses who, over the years, have eagerly learned more from the Librarian-at-Large about women's studies resources. Bibliographic instruction workshops and presentations at faculty seminars are regular duties of the Librarian-at-Large, as is maintenance of the Women's Studies Union List and files of syllabi and reading lists. The Librarian-at-Large continues to contribute to national projects such as the women's studies data base task force, and to play an active role in professional organizations.

The emphasis now lies on improving existing services and resources, rather than developing new programs. Currently, for example, attention is focused on upgrading coverage of nonprint materials in the publications and bibliographies, and on using the word processing and data management capabilities of the microcomputer to streamline the in-house production of reading lists and newsletters. Plans are underway for a supplement to *Women's Studies: A Recommended Core Bibliography,* and for revisions of the reading lists distributed by the office.

The Women's Studies Librarian-at-Large serves the needs of many different users. Librarians, for instance, consult the various publications for reviews and references useful in collection building; faculty refer to them when advising students on term paper projects and in carrying out their own research; women's studies program coordinators count on them for current awareness; conference planners use them to determine topics of current interest when scheduling panels and discussions.

The services of the Librarian-at-Large do not exist in a vacuum, but are integrated with the vital activities of teaching and research on the UW campuses. For example, a recent project involved collaboration with the staff of the UW-Madison Land Tenure Center to compile a bibliography of campus holdings relating to women in developing countries. The production of the bibliography was supported by a Ford Foundation grant to the Women's Studies Research Center as one of a number of activities focused on women in Third World countries. Cooperation is likewise evident in the instructional functions of the office. The Librarian-at-Large recently participated in curriculum development seminars at UW-Whitewater and UW-Oshkosh that brought nationally-recognized experts to the campuses to help faculty from various departments incorporate the new scholarship about women into their courses.

In the context of mainstreaming women's studies, the value of a Librarian-at-large is reaffirmed. By gathering and disseminating information about men, women, and the role of gender in our society, the office operates as a vital node in the feminist communication network. As the field has grown and changed, and as women's studies programs have matured on the UW campuses, services of the Women's Studies Librarian-at-Large have expanded and shifted emphasis. The Librarian-at-Large can respond flexibly to new demands in part because she and her staff are not tied to a collection.

Far from being an orphaned librarian without a collection to call her own, the Librarian-at-Large has an extended family of libraries across the state, and the freedom to travel and draw upon many rich resources and knowledgeable colleagues. Working with librarians, faculty, and administrators throughout the state, the Librarian-at-Large contributes to Wisconsin's reputation as a center for women's studies research and teaching.

NOTES

1. See, for example, *This Bridge Called My Back: Writings by Radical Women of Color,* edited by Cherríe Moraga and Gloria Anzaldúa (Watertown, MA: Persephone Press, 1981); *Lesbian Studies: Present and Future,* edited by Margaret Criukshank (Old Westbury, NY: The Feminist Press, 1982); *The Jewish Women's Studies Guide,* edited by Ellen Sue Levi Elwell and Edward R. Levenson (Fresh Meadows, NY: Biblio Press, 1982); and *All the Women Are White, All the Blacks Are Men, But Some of Us Are Brave: Black Women's Studies,* edited by Gloria T. Hull, Patricia Bell Scott, and Barbara Smith (Old Westbury, NY: The Feminist Press, 1982).

2. *Feminist Periodicals: A Current Listing of Contents,* vol. 1, no. 1 (March 1981)– .

3. The fullest listing of women's periodicals is *Women's Periodicals and Newspapers from the 18th Century to 1981,* edited by James P. Danky (Boston: G.K. Hall, 1982).

4. Florence Howe and Paul Lauter, *The Impact of Women's Studies on the Campus and the Disciplines* (Washington: National Institute of Education, 1980), p.73.

5. "From the Editors: Report on a Study of Women's Studies Acquisitions at UW-Whitewater," *Feminist Collections* vol. 4, no. 3 (Spring 1983), 3-5.

6. Esther Stineman, *Women's Studies: A Recommended Core Bibliography* (Littleton, Co: Libraries Unlimited, 1979). Stineman's opus, like other general bibliographies in women's studies, concentrates on materials that, if not actually espousing a feminist viewpoint, are rarely antithetical to it. In *Women's Periodicals and Newspapers from the 18th Century to 1981* (noted above), James Danky and his colleagues choose instead to document

the full range of women's experiences; right-wing and apolitical serials are listed alongside suffragist and feminist publications. These two approaches to bibliography-making have obvious parallels to collection development.

7. Dorothy Schultz and Miriam Allman, *Women's Studies Resources: A Core Collection List for Undergraduate Libraries* (Madison, WI: University of Wisconsin System, September 1977).

8. *Women's Studies: Directory of Institution Program Administrators, Contact Persons, Committees and Programs* (Madison, WI: University of Wisconsin System, Winter 1980/81—).

9. *Women's Studies Research in Wisconsin: A Report,* vol. 1, no. 1 (December 1981)— .

10. Catherine Loeb, Donna Vukelich, and Linda Shult, *Women's Studies in Wisconsin: Who's Who & Where,* 2nd ed. (Madison, WI: Women's Studies Librarian-at-Large, University of Wisconsin System, 1982).

11. *History of Women* (New Haven: Research Publications, 1975).

12. *Feminist Collections: Women's Studies Library Resources in Wisconsin,* vol. 1, no. 1 (February 1980)— .

13. *New Books on Women & Feminism,* no. 1 (June 1979)— .

14. A full list of materials distributed by the Women's Studies Librarian-at-Large may be obtained by writing to her at 112A Memorial Library, 728 State St., Madison, WI 53706.

15. The publications of the Librarian-at-Large are distributed free upon request to Wisconsin residents. Non-residents may subscribe to the full set of publications for $12 a year as individuals, or $24 a year as organizations.

Issues of Access to Information About Women

Ellen Gay Detlefsen

Five important points need to be made when considering issues of access to information for, by, and about women. The *first* is that information about women is one problem, but feminist or women's studies information is another problem. The *second* point is that interdisciplinary approaches to women's information and feminist information are necessary. A *third* point is that massive terminology and vocabulary problems are present when working with either women's or feminist information sources. A *fourth* point is that the greater proportion of services and indexes of choice for women's or feminist information are not machine-accessible, but—the *fifth* point—a few projects have surfaced recently which hint at progress in the area of machine-accessible women's and feminist information.[1]

Point 1: Material about women is not necessarily the same as feminist material or women's studies material. Information simply about women or females can be, and often is, totally reflective of male bias and traditional sex role socialization and not at all feminist, regardless of the gender of the author. Feminism, a newer concept, asserts a point of view that has been lacking in traditional scholarship, one that affirms the equality of all humans without regard to gender. It recognizes no discrimination based on sex or sexual preference. Women's Studies material is somewhere in the middle; women's studies scholars and bibliographers often try to work with scholarship from both traditional and feminist viewpoints.

It is important to recognize the first major study on women's studies bibliography, done as a dissertation at Rutgers University in 1980. In her study entitled *Communication and Information Patterns in the Emerging Interdisciplinary Area of Women's Studies,* Elizabeth Futas applied bibliometric techniques and citation pattern studies to women's studies materials (not just feminist materials), and she concluded that:

> Women's Studies most closely resembles the social science disciplines of economics, political science, sociology, and education. . .(and that) is least like art, music, and religion . . .

She went on to assert that "the literature of the field of women's studies is predominantly (to be found) in journal articles in English and by single authors." This kind of literature—from journals, with only one name, and in English—is ideally suited for machine-based access. Futas also stated that "Women's Studies journals carry only a fraction of the total literature (of the field), noting that women's studies materials already appear in many journals already accessible with machine-based techniques." Futas also showed that the "predominant topic in the literature of women's studies is psychology, with medicine second," and that "the few highly-cited individuals teaching in the field of women's studies are from psychology and education."[2] Hers is ground-breaking work, providing for the first time scientific and quantified evidence of the manner in which women's studies scholarship is produced, published, and made accessible.

Point 2: The interdisciplinarity that Futas suggests is both an advantage and a handicap for those using the literature and scholarship on women and their concerns. A broad range of disciplines requires an interdisciplinary approach to retrieval and access. Again, interdisciplinary searches are often best handled with machine-accessible techniques, particularly when the searcher can employ cross-database or multi-file searching. For example, recent searches on topics in women's studies involved anywhere from eight to eleven files for the most useful coverage. For good information on the topic of *abortion as a political issue,* one might profitably search the following files: *Population Bibliography, United States Political Science Documents,* the *Magazine Index,* both *ERIC* files, *Social Science Citation Index, Sociological Abstracts, Psychological Abstracts,* the *Public Affairs Information Service,* the *National Criminal Justice Reference Service,* and the *MEDLINE* file. When reviewing the results, however, much winnowing of the output was necessary, but key material was found in each file.

Similarly, a search on the issue of *pay equity or comparable worth theory* might easily entail the use of eight or more files: both

ERIC files and the *Social Science Citation Index*, the *Public Affairs Information Service, Management Contents, Predicasts, LEXIS*, the *GPO Monthly Catalog*, and the *Catalyst Resources for Women* file. Again, kernels of information surfaced in each file, but much review was necessary.

Point 3: One of the reasons for the noise and winnowing of output in search of the kernel of information is the problem of vocabulary. Vocabulary issues are complex, and plague both print and database tools for access. Four specific problems are apparent. First, terminology is fluid, and different terms mean different things to different people at different times. For example, the terms "comparable worth for comparable work," "equal pay for work of equal value," "comparable pay for comparable worth," and "pay equity" mean the same thing, but they do not mean the same thing as "equal pay." When one wants to refer to a profession whose practitioners are primarily women—librarianship, nursing, teaching, social work, clinical dietetics—one may refer to a "feminized profession," or a "female-dominant profession," or a "traditionally female profession," even a "semi-profession," but these terms rarely appear in a thesaurus or posting dictionary. One must attempt to locate information about them through the use of much larger terms such as "job segregation," "salary and wage differentials," and "occupational stratification."

A second vocabulary problem results from the fact that the standard terminologies and thesauri are frequently sexist or gender-stereotyped, and lack feminist terms altogether. The "woman as" syndrome still appears in many places, with references to "women as lawyers," and "women as criminals" instead of "lawyers" or "criminals." Similarly, the use of "wife" or "husband" to refer to a marital partner, instead of "spouse," still appears frequently. Only the latest *Thesaurus of ERIC Descriptors* claim to be non-sexist and to have eliminated sexist terminology and added feminist terminology. The term "battered women" has been added as an ERIC descriptor, for instance.

As the use of sexist language in thesauri and terminology is the most persistent vocabulary problem, one might turn to the latest *Thesaurus of ERIC Descriptors* to locate more useful or current terms, but a second source is of greater value. When searching for alternative or contemporary or gender-free headings, one should consult Joan K. Marshall's *On Equal Terms: A Thesaurus for Nonsexist Indexing and Cataloguing.*[3] This tool, which won the Ralph

R. Shaw Award from the American Library Association as the best piece of library literature in its year of publication, can be used effectively to generate terms for free-text searching and role-free indexing. It ought to be used by database producers and vendors as a guide for the revision and construction of stereotype-free thesauri.

A second project to develop a stereotype-free thesaurus has been undertaken by a group sponsored by the National Council for Research on Women—a consortium of women's research centers and programs, largely affiliated with academic institutions or women's professional organizations. The Thesaurus Task Force anticipates the publication of a "common set of index categories and descriptors" for women's concerns and issues in 1985. This thesaurus is to be the centerpiece of a large national effort to make research collections and library holdings about women's issues accessible by computer. Individuals and women's research centers across America have supplied working lists of subject headings and index terms, which are to be merged into a working document to be reviewed by professionals in a variety of information and lexicographical fields, with a final publication due out in January, 1985.[4]

A third vocabulary problem is that many terms understood in common parlance and used by indexers and searchers are still too broad and imprecise to allow for targetted searching by machine or by hand. For example, the term "abortion" is almost never subdivided to indicate a difference in use or application as a gynecological issue on the one hand, and as a political issue on the other. Similarly, it is not subdivided to indicate a pro-choice or anti-choice point of view, leaving the user to wrestle with technical literature from OB-GYN journals, propaganda from both sides, and attitudinal scholarship encountered almost by chance. In a more general way, the very term "women's studies" is often expressed by proponents as "woman studies," "women studies," "feminist studies," "gender studies," and "the study of women and men in society." Remembering to search under all these possibilities is sometimes difficult, and always time-consuming.

A fourth vocabulary issue, specific to machine-based searching, is that terminology in common use when dealing with women's issues or concerns is not easily amenable to truncation. For example, truncating "woman" and "women" to "wom*" or "wom$" will indeed bring up "woman" and "women" but also "wombat." To truncate and use "fem*" brings out "femur." Shortening "sexuality" and "sexual" to "sex*" or "sex$" will bring out the first two, but it will also yield uses of "sexy" and "sextet" and "sexuagesima." One must be precise and careful when seeking to save time by truncation with the broad terms in women's studies.

Point 4: The fourth general point is that coverage of women's studies journals and feminist periodicals is sparse at best, and non-existent in most traditional indexing and abstracting services. In fact, the greatest number of feminist journals are indexed only in two services which are *not* machine-based—*Women's Studies Abstracts* and *Social Sciences Index.* Even coverage in non-scholarly and traditional women's magazines is scarce; the best access for materials from journals like *Good Housekeeping, Ladies Home Journal, Women's Day,* etc.—which do carry information regularly on topics such as the ERA, comparable worth, women entrepreneurs, job-sharing and women's health—is in the *Magazine Index* (in either microform or database formats).

Six scholarly indexing and abstracting services stand out by reason of their coverage of both feminist and women's studies journals and because they also index the mainstream scholarly journals in which materials of interest also appear; four of the six are fully machine-accessible: *Social Science Citation Index* (and to a lesser extent, *Arts and Humanities Citation Index), Psychological Abstracts, Sociological Abstracts,* and the *Current Index to Journals in Education.* The two that are only manually searchable are *Women's Studies Abstracts* and *Social Sciences Index.* Each of these six services indexes from three to six of the major women's studies or feminist journals; these journals are *Signs, Feminist Studies, International Journal of Women's Studies, Sex Roles, Psychology of Women Quarterly,* and *Women's Studies Quarterly.* At this writing only *Women's Studies Abstracts* covers all of these journals, but its usefulness is limited by the absence of a controlled vocabulary, by having no recent cumulations, and by its policy of indexing some articles while indexing and abstracting others. *Social Sciences Index,* which includes coverage of a majority of these titles, also has no controlled vocabulary and no abstracts, but is available to many libraries more cheaply because of the H.W. Wilson Company practice of a service basis for subscriptions. It is more amenable to adding new titles, including feminist titles, through the practice of user election of titles for inclusion.

Point 5: The last major point is that a number of new products or services have surfaced recently which hint at or promise more machine-accessibility for women's or feminist materials. In the late

1970's the Women's Educational Equity Communications Network (WEECN) with federal funding through the Women's Educational Equity Act Program, produced a series of useful tools: a booklet entitled *Computer Searching: A Resource for Women's Educational Equity,* a leaflet on *Numerical Data Tapes Relevant to Women's Educational Equity,* and a three volume set on *Resources in Women's Educational Equity-I, II, III.*[5] WEECN's best product was a tertiary data base which merged citations on women's educational equity from thirteen separate databases into one file and indexed them with one common vocabulary. These citations dealt with women and educational equity broadly construed: women; girls; Title IX; sports; higher, secondary, elementary, and preschool education; libraries; psychology; administration; economics; history; the professions, etc.—a wide social sciences approach. Alas, WEECN's federal WEEAP funding contracts expired and were not renewed in the 80's; the tertiary file, the complex program to merge citations, and the carefully-developed plan for copyright permissions are sitting quietly on magnetic tape somewhere in California, and many in the worlds of librarianship and women's studies hope that it can someday be revived, updated, and made a permanent information product.

A more widely available machine-accessible source has recently been distributed through the BRS bibliographic network/vendor. The file entitled *Catalyst Resources for Women* represents an index to the vertical file holdings of Catalyst, a national career resource center for women, with special strengths in issues involving the dual-career family, re-entry women, and women's service on and to corporate boards. This file offers access to a wide variety of material—empheral and published, private and public—otherwise difficult to find. It is, as well, an ever-growing file as new materials are added and indexed monthly.

Two other bibliographical endeavors are of interest; one is computer-produced but neither are machine-accessible. *Bibliofem,* a product of the Fawcett Library in London and the British Equal Opportunity Commission's Information Center, is a current COM (*c*omputer-*o*utput-*m*icrofiche) bibliography of materials of interest. The new *Studies on Women Abstracts,* produced by the Carfax Publishing Company, has recently begun coverage of women's studies titles, with a heavy emphasis on the social science disciplines.

Most of the other new projects which demonstrate movement towards machine-accessibility for information of concern to those in women's studies and feminist communities are not bibliographical efforts; most are either directories or professional networks. Among the important directory projects are *CWONC* and the *National Women's Mailing List. CWONC* is a computerized file of biographies of 1000 important Canadian women, produced at York University as a prototype machine-readable biographical dictionary; the acronym stands for *C*anadian *W*omen of *N*ote, *C*omputerized. The *National Women's Mailing List* is an information and referral device for women, akin to the political action networks of the radical right in the U.S.; the NWML[6] stores profiles of those who register with the organization and matches those profiles against the information suppliers who request a mailing list. The network is intended to match only those whose stated information needs match the information to be supplied. In practice, this tailored approach to information dissemination has worked very well. Four possible professional networks have appeared which hint at woman-to-woman networking in support of more access to information of concern. Two are national professional associations for women at work in non-traditional fields; the *Women in Information Processing* (WIP) group, and the *Association for Women in Computing.* Both are listed in the very valuable *Directory of Women's Organizations in Library and Information Science*—a project undertaken by the Committee on the Status of Women in Librarianship of the American Library Association. A fledgling *Feminist Computer Network* was also described in an 1980 article in *Ms* and in the *Media Report to Women,* but its present status is in doubt. The American Library Association's Association of College and Research Libraries has just launched a *Women's Studies Discussion Group,*[7] which included issues of access on its founding agenda.

Three major special collections on contemporary women's issues have each begun planning for increased accessibility to their materials through the use of machine-based techniques. They are cooperating with one another in an effort to build compatible systems that may someday be part of a national resource data-base. The obvious problem facing all three is funding, but each is persisting in planning for a more accessible future. The three collections are the Marguerite Rawalt Resource Center of the Business and Professional Women's Foundation in Washington, DC, the Information Center of Catalyst in New York, and the Library of the Women's Action Alliance, also in New York.

The two major historical collections on women and women's concerns—the *Sophia Smith Collection at Smith College* and the *Schlesinger Library at Radcliffe College*—have no present plans for machine-based access to their holdings, but each has a published catalog and is also accessible through the Library of Congress-sponsored *National Union Catalog of Manuscript Collections.*

Finally, as an illustration of how one might approach a difficult search for information on a women's studies topic or feminist issue, I (as one scholar and librarian) will share the steps that I would take:

> first, *a machine-based search* of *Sociological Abstracts, Psychological abstracts,* the *Social Science Citation Index* (using both citation and Permuter TM searching), *PAIS, ERIC* (both files), *Magazine Index,* and *Catalyst Resources for Women;*
>
> second, *a manual search of Women's Studies Abstracts* and *Social Sciences Index;*
>
> third, *five telephone calls to colleagues* in the women's information community: (1) *Adelaide Sukiennik,* Women's Studies Bibliographer, University Library System, University of Pittsburgh; (2) *Sue Searing,* Women's Studies Librarian-at-Large, University of Wisconsin System, Madison; (3) *Sarah Pritchard,* Women's Studies Specialist, General Reading Room, Library of Congress; (4) *Gurley Turner,* Director of Information Services, Catalyst Inc., New York; (5) *Cheryl Sloane,* Librarian, Business & Professional Women's Foundation, Washington, DC.

After all that, I'd quit looking. Access to information about, by, and for women is still a tremendously difficult problem, and one must necessarily exhaust print tools, machine-readable files, *and* human resources.

NOTES

1. Portions of this work have been presented at the ASIS annual conference in Washington, DC, in October 1981, and at the NWSA annual conference in Columbus, OH, in June 1983. I am indebted to a group of professional colleagues at the University of Pittsburgh whose skills and review have aided in the writing of this paper; these exceptional women are (in alphabetical order) Patti Corbett, Barbara Epstein, Ingrid Glasco, Susan Neuman, Gladys Shapera, Patti Schmid, and Adelaide Sukiennik.

2. Elizabeth Futas. *Communication and Information Patterns in the Emerging Interdisciplinary Area of Women's Studies.* New Brunswick, NJ: Graduate School of Library Science, 1980. Dissertation.

3. Joan K. Marshall. *On Equal Terms: A Thesaurus for Non-Sexist Indexing and Cataloging.* New York: Neal-Schuman, 1979.

4. For further information or to be kept informed on the progress of the thesaurus task force, contact Cheryl Sloan, Business & Professional Women's Foundation, Washington, DC.

5. Copies of this booklet, leaflet, and three volume reference set are no longer available. Academic and research libraries may at least have acquired and catalogued the multi-volume set entitled *Resources in Women's Educational Equity*-I, II, III. Further information *may* by available from the parent organization for WEECN: Far West Laboratories for Educational Research, in San Francisco, CA.

6. To request a form for individual or organizational registration, contact the National Women's Mailing List, 1195 Valencia Street, San Francisco, CA 94110.

7. For more information on the directory, the committee, or the ACRL Discussion Group contact the Committee on the Status of Women in Librarianship, American Library Association, Chicago, IL 60611.

Best Reference Works for the Study of Minority and Third World Women

Beth Stafford

INTRODUCTION

Many lose sight of the fact that women's studies has a global nature. Too frequently the common perception is that it is the reserve of a limited number of white women in North America and Western Europe. Indeed, women's studies endeavors to encompass women of all ages, classes, races, cultures, and sexual preferences, no matter where they happen to live. The existence of women's studies programs and institutes in several countries outside North America and Europe (such as India, Japan and Lebanon) attests to that fact.

The intention of this article is to provide an overview or guide to the best women's studies reference sources published within roughly the past five years. In order to provide a multinational, multicultural perspective on the field of women's studies, I have chosen to discuss very few general United States-based reference sources but to emphasize the best of those sources specific to women of color or of minority status worldwide and in the United States. This discussion incorporates only substantial, obtainable works published as monographs or available as separates and written at least in part in English. Because women's studies is a young field, many of the sources are bibliographies but of varying levels of complexity.

Clearly it is not possible to achieve total coverage of all geographic areas and cultural entities. In some cases, sources general to an area do not cover all individual countries or languages for one reason or other. This is true of the main Latin American resource, which covers only Spanish-speaking countries. In the case of sub-Saharan Africa, the best general monographic source is not easily obtainable, and it is advisable to consult sources found in Africana serials.

One of the results of the meetings and programs held in conjunction with the 1975 International Women's Year was the stimulation of greater interest in the status of females all over the world, as evidenced by the establishment of the International Women's Decade. With that interest also came a demand for information that (mostly) women scholars and librarians are seeking to meet with the publication of almost countless new sources pertaining to women. Many, if not most, of the sources have been the first of their kind. Some of the resources discussed below were inspired by the IWY directly.

AFRO-AMERICAN WOMEN IN NORTH AMERICA

A groundbreaking work for Black women's studies and Black feminism is *But Some of Us are Brave* (The Feminist Press, 1982), edited by Gloria Hull, Patricia Bell Scott, and Barbara Smith. It is both a reference source and a teaching tool, its content ranging as it does from essays by Black feminists to several different bibliographies to course syllabi. The excellent essays consider the political situation of Afro-American women on both the personal and aggregate levels. They speak to the relationship of Black women's studies to Black feminist politics and the Black feminist movement; the need for Black women's studies to be analytical, feminist, and radical; and the need for those who teach in the field to be aware of the complex political positions Afro-American women have in academe and of the potentially antagonistic conditions under which they must work.

The editors have very successfully organized a blend of essays by both scholars and those not affiliated with academe into sections on Black feminism, confronting racism, Black women in the social sciences, survival (body, mind, and spirit), Black women's literature bibliographies and bibliographic essays, and course syllabi. The text brings out the necessity for both "intellectual" and "practical" knowledge.

Several bibliographies and bibliographic essays make up a substantial portion of this unique resource. They include bibliographies and essays on Afro-American women poets, novelists, composers, and playwrights. There is also a general bibliographic essay on Afro-American women from 1800 to 1910. Perhaps most unusual is the essay and listing of non-print materials on Black women, complete with a list of distributors and addresses. Many of the sections in this part of the book include biographical information on the women being discussed. Most of the bibliographies furnish complete bibliographic information. A list of additional resources includes sections on the writings of women in prison, special periodical issues on Black women, and more.

Rounding out this invaluable anthology is a section containing syllabi for general, social science and literature courses on Black women.

An earlier compilation, Janet Sims' *The Progress of Afro-American women: a Selected Bibliography and Resource Guide* (Greenwood, 1980) accesses nearly 3,600 nineteenth- and twentieth-century resources pertaining to Black American women. This unannotated bibliography is organized into thirty-three subjects ranging from slave narratives to Black women's participation in the feminist movement, to law enforcement, to Black women's organizations and institutions. Citations are more complete than many in the Hull volume bibliographies.

Materials covered in the bibliography include books, chapters of books, journal and newspaper articles, non-print materials, and some government documents. An index affords access by author and some subjects.

The best collective biography of Black women in this country to date is Marianna W. Davis' *Contributions of Black Women to America* (Kenday, 1982). It is organized into ten different manuscripts by subject field. Volume one includes women active in the arts, business and commerce, the media, law, and sports. Volume two covers the areas of civil rights, politics and government, education, medicine, and the sciences. Each bibliographic volume has its own table of contents, introductory essay, notes, bibliography, and index.

The editor has assembled an impressive group of scholars, librarians, writers and other experts as consultants, editors and evaluators. The organization within each section is excellent—as are the introductory essays and bibliographies. These bibliographies provide ample access to further reading and do reference earlier biographies of Black American women.

The lack of a master index for the entire work is a drawback. To find information on a multi-talented woman such as Ida B. Wells Barnett or Mary Church Terrell a person must consult more than one index. Barnett, for instance, is discussed in five of the ten areas of achievement. Unfortunately, this multiplicity of indices has resulted in some predictable problems, such as the same woman being listed by different surnames in different indices (e.g., Wells in one, Barnett in another) and the applicable *see also* reference not always being complete.

One of the intended goals for this ambitious undertaking was to compile and disseminate information on the contributions of Black women to this country for the period 1776 to 1977. While the materials available did not allow coverage beginning in 1776 for each of the areas, coverage is very extensive and does include contemporary women. This work is a major contribution to Black women's studies and points the way for further research and publication.

NATIVE AMERICAN WOMEN

An interesting new bibliography on Native American women is *Native American Women: a Contextual Bibliography* (Indiana University Press, 1983) by anthropologist Rayna Green. She has annotated nearly seven hundred books, articles, theses and book chapters written between 1620 and 1980 that are specifically about Native American women as individuals or as members of groups. Materials about or by Native American women in the United States (including Alaska) and Canada are included. Except for some good bibliographies, works on Native South American women and U.S. Chicanas are not covered.

An extensive introduction provides an excellent overview and evaluation of the trends and issues reflected in the literature about and by Native North American women through the years. Green points out the biases and weaknesses of past research, such as the predilection of scholars to study only those tribes they already are interested in and which fit into scholars' own definitions. She suggests that it would be more useful and enlightening to study tribes that might offer contradictions to old ideas—such as patriarchy.

It is the goal of this bibliography to encourage scholars, both non-Indian and Indian, to change the direction and approach of their research so that they ask how they can serve Native peoples in setting their own agendas and pursuing their own definitions.

The book is arranged alphabetically by main entry, with entries being numbered consecutively. A date index, followed by a subject index, completes this volume.

A special issue of *Frontiers: a Journal of Women's Studies* (University of Colorado Women's Studies Program, 1981) has a different purpose and broader scope for the study of Native American women. Guest edited by Linda Hogan, the issue has an interesting variety of scholarly essays, interviews, poetry, and reminiscences by or about Native American women. A few sample titles of essays include "Remembering the Reindeer Queen," "Native American Women in Westerns: Reality and Myth," and "Two Cherokee Women."

An excellent extensive bibliography on Native women in North and South America (including Chicanas), compiled and introduced by Lyle Koehler, rounds out the special issue. This bibliography is not annotated, but it is much broader in scope than the Green bibliography, which stresses anthropology. The Koehler bibliography includes well over one thousand books, chapters, articles, and theses on or by Native American women. The bibliography is classified under such subjects as Bibliography; Native American Women in Traditional and Modern Societies, Religion, and Economic Life (in separate sections); Out-Breeding Across Racial Lines; and Native Women Writing, Speaking Non-Fiction, among others. The Koehler and Green bibliographies complement each other well. In keeping with *Frontiers'* editorial policy of bridging the gap between academic and community women, this special issue has a variety of material in it. The Koehler bibliography is academic and covers more discipline areas than Green's as well as more populations.

LATINAS IN THE UNITED STATES

The two most comprehensive compilations of materials on Latinas in this country this author has seen are Martha Cotera's *Latina Sourcebook: Bibliography of Mexican-American, Cuban, Puerto Rico [sic], and Other Hispanic Women Materials in the U.S.* (Information Systems Development, 1982) and a special issue of *Frontiers: a Journal of Women's Studies* (University of Colorado Women's Studies Program, 1980) called *Chicanas en el Ambiente Nacional/Chicanas in the National Landscape.*

Ms. Cotera's bibliography presents well over 200 books, articles, theses, and films in a classified format. Nearly all of the items have brief, descriptive annotations. Four major divisions of the bibliography include general references on Hispanic women and separate sections for Cuban, Puerto Rican and Mexican-American women. Coverage includes some information on women in Latin America as well as in the U.S.. Subdivisions distinguish reference materials, background readings and student materials. A lengthy directory of journals and publishers in mainly North America and Latin America rounds out this ambitious and valuable tool.

The Cotera listing is particularly strong with respect to materials from Latina/o sources. Of course, it also provides access to materials relevant to a more diverse and larger population than the *Frontiers* issue (next).

Chicanas en el Ambiente Nacional incorporates a variety of materials. Two of the essays are "Toward a Feminist Pedagogy for Chicana Self-actualization" and "Gender and Ethnic Identity Among Chicanos". There are also excerpts from some books on Chicanas and an excellent review essay on six reference works on the same women.

Among all the sections of this special issue, the broadest in scope is La Chicana: a Bibliographic Survey by Catherine Loeb. A very helpful introductory overview which provides excellent background reading prefaces the bibliography. This unclassified, unannotated survey includes over 300 recent books, articles, theses, and ERIC documents. The bibliographies by Loeb and Cotera complement each other well.

ASIAN-AMERICAN WOMEN

The journal *Bridge: Asian American Perspectives* has issued three special issues on Asian and Asian-American women in the past five years (Bridge, Winter 1978/79, Spring, 1979, and Asian Cine-Vision, Summer, 1983). Each issue contains a mixture of fiction, poetry and essays with such titles as "Feminism is Fine, But What's It Done for Asia America?" and the "History of Philipino Women in Hawaii"—along with some book reviews.

The first issue has a five-page, mostly unannotated bibliography of books, journals and articles on Asian-American women that was compiled by three women in the Asian American Librarians Association, with assistance from others. It lists readily available materials at the Asian American Studies Library at University of California, Berkeley and the Asian Community Library in Oakland, California. The second issue (Spring, 1979) consists of mainly poetry and essays.

The Summer, 1983, issue, includes an annotated Women's Resource Guide, by Elaine Fong and Stephanie Yoo. Organizations, Art and the Arts, Media and Publications are all represented in this very useful compilation. The Publications section updates the earlier bibliography.*

In all three issues the editors discuss racism and sexism as being one struggle—as they relate to Asian-American women. The latest issue centers on the strength of women, from several different aspects, and includes interviews, essays, poetry and fiction plus reviews of films, books, art, photography, and theatre.

JEWISH WOMEN

Aviva Cantor's *The Jewish Woman: 1900-1980* (Biblio, 1981) is the most convenient single guide to materials about Jewish women to date. The author's intention was to compile a bibliography of English-language materials that would be generally accessible through libraries, publishers, or organizations—Judaica specialist or not. The end product is a very useful guide organized under the rubrics History/Herstory, United States and Canada, Israel, and the Holocaust. Biographies and autobiographies are integrated into these four sections. The last rubric is Religious Life and Law.

This partially annotated bibliography provides access to books, chapters, journals and newspapers on Jewish women worldwide and in all time periods. Works by Jewish women are included selectively, according to whether or not they provide insight into the lives of and issues of concern to Jewish women today.

It is of interest to note that there are more than twice as many listings published between 1977 and 1980 as in the previous seventy-six years. Another of the author's goals is to point out gaps in authorship in the present literature and to encourage more scholarship of all forms on Jewish women. This bibliography certainly is a good start.

MUSLIM WOMEN

An example of another type of resource on women that is based along cultural lines is Inger Ruud's *Women's Status in the Muslim World* (Brill, 1981). It accesses materials of all sorts having to do

*Another useful update is the bibliography in *This Bridge Called My Back*, by Cherrie Moraga et al. (Persephone, 1981).

with women in the Muslim world from North Africa, Sub-Saharan Africa, the Middle East, through Asia, the Soviet Union, the United States, and Europe. The majority of materials covered were written in this century and the bibliography was compiled for its usefulness, not its comprehensiveness.

Over 900 unannotated citations for books, articles, and doctoral dissertations in English and Western European languages are arranged into two main sections—by main entry and by subject, including a topographical subsection. Literary works by or about women are included. Other subject rubrics include struggle for emancipation/feminist movements, women and health, and the veil (Purdah), among others.

WOMEN IN INTERNATIONAL DEVELOPMENT

An entire field of women in international development has emerged in the past five years or so, with many universities here and elsewhere establishing special units to insure that development projects originating in their institutions provide for the needs of women in the economically developing countries that their projects involve. For instance, in the past agricultural development projects have frequently been directed at men in places where the women are responsible for producing food. As a consequence, projects have failed because the people needing information and training were prevented from acquiring it. In many cases the situation of women in developing countries has actually deteriorated as a result of development projects. Much research and myriad bibliographies have been produced on the subject in recent years. Because there are so many sources, I will discuss the most comprehensive one and briefly mention two more.

An extraordinary resource guide has recently been produced by ISIS: Women's International Information and Communication Service in Geneva, Switzerland. Called *Women in Development: a Resource Guide for Organization and Action* (ISIS, 1983), it blends development thought with feminist thought into a sourcebook that directly deals with several issues of most immediate concern to women in developing countries. Specifically, they are: Women and Multinationals; Women and Rural Developments; Women and Health; Education and Communication, and Migration and Tourism—each representing a major section of the book. The introductory section of the guide is enhanced by an essay on rethinking the issues of development and women and by a survey of women and development literature.

Each section begins with an overview of how the subject under consideration affects the lives of women, followed by an exposition on how women are responding in terms of developing theories and organizing to cope with the issues and trends. Selective but substantial lists of groups and bibliographies of materials for research and organizing complete each section of this guide.

This book is intended as a guide to recent thinking and literature on women and development and to a feminist critique of them. It points out that women are speaking to the issues of food, water and economic exploitation everywhere from a feminist perspective, as the forces that marginalize women in both developed and developing countries are really the same. This is a valuable guide to a massive literature and a feminist critique. It is hoped the book will contribute to the evolution of a new theory and practice of women and development that incorporates a feminist perspective.

Many sources on women and development in particular geographic areas exist. Among the best examples are *Caribbean Resource Kit for Women* (University of the West Indies Women and Development Unit, and Women's International Tribune Centre, 1982) and *Information Kit for Women in Africa* (International Women's Tribune Centre, and African Training and Research Centre for Women, 1981). The Caribbean work includes sections on fourteen Country Profiles for the region, Activities and Resources, information on Regional Organizations, and Financial/Technical Assistance sources. It includes non-Spanish countries and resources in other languages.

The African source gives similar types of information: Funding/Technical Assistance, Women's Projects, ATRCW Publications, and ATRCW Information. Both sources are aimed at assisting women in those areas and those interested in developing projects oriented toward these women or in doing research.

SUB-SAHARAN AFRICA

As stated in the Introduction, there are complications with sources on all of sub-Saharan Africa. Best among the multitude of sources on women in individual sub-Saharan African countries is *Women in Tanzania: an Analytical Bibliography* (Scandinavian Institute of African Studies, and Swedish International Development Authority, 1983). This is an expanded edition of an earlier work produced by the same authors—Ophelia Mascarenhas and Marjorie Mbilinyi—both of whom are affiliated with the University of Dar es Salaam.

The authors' intention is to pose "the question" of women in Tanzania, to elucidate the issues being raised in research and in government and other agency programs, and to critique both the explicit and implicit positions taken by such programs and research. First of the two major divisions of the book is a collection of four essays clarifying the relationship between ideological and political struggles over the question of women and the concrete struggles that working class and peasant women face.

Part Two, entitled Writings on the Question of Women, consists of critical annotations of selected materials, along with introductory essays for each of the subsections. Subsections include, among other topics, Approaches to the Analysis of Women's Oppression, Ideology, Political Participation, Family and Domestic Labor, and Women's Projects and cooperatives. This annotated listing provides access to information on women in developing countries and on women in Africa as well as information on women in Tanzania specifically. Another valuable feature is that the listing describes the content of much unpublished and non-English-language (e.g., Swahili) material. In addition to providing essays and analytical annotations for the materials covered, the bibliography also indicates locations.

THE ARAB WORLD

Samira Rafidi Meghdessian has compiled an excellent select bibliography called *The Status of the Arab Women* (Mansell, 1980), under the auspices of the Institute for Women's Studies in the Arab World in Beirut, Lebanon. Covering mostly materials published since 1950, the book is a guide to research materials on the economic, religious, legal and social status of twentieth-century Arab women. It includes over sixteen hundred books, journal articles, conference proceedings, theses, dissertations, published and unpublished papers and bibliographies (whether published as separates or as parts of books). Materials represent all Arab countries from the Middle East and North Africa. Most materials are in English or

French, but others in German, Spanish and Italian also appear. A particularly important feature is the unpublished materials included in this work.

Three major sections access background materials for the researcher: Cultural and Social Background of the Middle East, Women in the Arab Middle East: General Works, and Women in North Africa: General Works. Meghdessian states that the section on the cultural and social background is intended only as a basic list of materials on the subject and makes suggestions for other sources the researcher must pursue for information. The other main sections are: Women in Islam and the Law, Conferences and Seminars on the Arab Woman, and Women in Individual Arab Countries.

Entries are arranged alphabetically by author as far as possible. There are an author index and an index by very broad subject.

SOUTH ASIA

Carol Sakala's *Women of South Asia: a Guide to Resources* (Kraus, 1980) accesses resources relating to a population that has in the past been largely ignored by both scholars of South Asia and scholars of women's studies. The materials this book encompasses cover both historical and contemporary India, Pakistan, Bangladesh, Sri Lanka, and Nepal.

Of the two major sections of the book, the dominant one is the bibliography. Based on, but not limited to, the holdings of the South Asian collection of the University of Chicago's Regenstein Library, it lists over 4,600 Western-language books, sections of books, articles, serials, dissertations, films and recordings. The vast majority of them are annotated. Publications include, as the compiler says, "standard, classical works and recent first-rate scholarly works on South Asian women and. . .examples of peripheral but pertinent works," published between the late eighteenth century and mid-1979.

The bibliography is particularly strong in the social sciences and humanities. Works covered are those that focus especially on women, those that relate incidentally or refer to women, and those that refer to associations with women. Works referring to associations with women include works on feminine cosmological principles or goddesses. Works relating incidentally to women are those in such fields as family planning and law.

Creative writing and literary criticism are included. Another area in the book is the activities and experiences of Western women in South Asia during the time the British were in power.

The organization of the book describes historical periods and especially cultural areas significant for South Asia and South Asians. A very detailed Outline of Headings preceding the bibliography reflects "some of the major dimensions of the lives of South Asian women." It is wise to rely heavily on it. Annotations are descriptive, and there are cross references between sections of the bibliography. There are author and subject indexes.

CHINA

Until now, the most complete single separately published resource on women in China has been Diana Martin's *Women in Chinese Society: an Annotated Bibliography* (Commonwealth Bureau of Agricultural Economics, 1974), which listed around 200 items, most of which are not annotated.

Scheduled for publication in 1984, *Women in China: an Annotated Bibliography* (Greenwood), by Karen Wei, will provide access to well over 1100 books, journals, chapters, dissertations on women in mainland China and Taiwan.

Coverage includes materials written from the late nineteenth century through 1982 in Western languages. The work is arranged under the subjects Bibliography; Legal Status, Laws, etc.; Biography, Autobiography; Women's Movement, Emancipation, Feminism, Liberation; Education, Economic Conditions, Employment, Occupation; Women in Literature and the Arts; Family, Marriage, Divorce, Position, Status, Social Conditions.

Annotations are brief and descriptive. It is anticipated that this work will be the most comprehensive of its kind.

KOREA AND JAPAN

Hesung Chun Koh, Director of Research and Development at Yale University's Human Relations Area Files, has compiled and edited an impressive, innovative guide to literature about women in Japan and Korea. It is the first English-language book-length bibliography on the subject. *Korean and Japanese Women: an Analytic Bibliographic Guide* (Greenwood, 1982) lists about 580 selective references to source documents and studies important to the understanding of Korean and Japanese women, simultaneously annotating and analyzing them on several different bases. (For example, because the roles women play vary much more widely according to women's ages in Japan and Korea and because marital status is more important in these countries historically and currently than in the West, an entire index is devoted to analyzing the resources covered in terms of roles.)

The guide was compiled out of a conviction that to understand properly the problems and concerns of Asian-American women one must study the aspects of their Asian cultural heritage as related to the problems they now face and the ways they are dealing with them. For example, Asian-American women continue to outnumber Asian-American men in a fast growing ethnic group in the United States. As a result, more and more Asian-American women are in the public domain as participants in the labor force, and this has led to many new problems that cannot be ignored. Consequently, while the goal of the guide is to facilitate understanding of Asian-American women, with a miniscule number of exceptions, all of the resources listed and analyzed are about women in Japan and Korea. Materials are in Japanese, Korean and English.

The primary aim of the bibliography is to facilitate a wide variety of descriptive or comparative research on Korean and Japanese women. Characteristics of this guide which foster such research are: wide ranging categories of analysis, many and new types of indexes, the elaborate system approach that is used to classify information in each document and the use of a computer in the production of the guide. For example, the guide provides a way to compare easily data on women from different social classes.

Ms. Koh offers her guide as a methodological model for analysis and organization of information on women in general. It incorporates features that are not present in most bibliographies on women. She would hope other guides would also provide an evaluative guide to the literature; organize information in a way that facilitates comparison of women with men or with each other in different historical eras or cultures; specify the context of sex roles (e.g., urban vs. rural) provide information on social class and life stages, and provide cross-cultural information on women and sex roles.

This guide is of value to women's studies researchers, scholars of Japanese or Korean society and culture, and to researchers in comparative studies on a worldwide or smaller scale.

SOUTHEAST ASIA

The best single guide to resources on women in Southeast Asia is *Women in Southeast Asia: a Bibliography* by Fan Kok Sim (G. K. Hall, 1982). It is an extensive listing of materials written in languages using the Roman alphabet which concern women in the region generally and in Burma, Indochina, Indonesia, Malaysia, The Philippines, Singapore and Thailand specifically. The bibliography encompasses both published and unpublished essentially twentieth-century sources such as books, articles, book chapters, theses, conference papers, pamphlets, mimeographed papers, government publications, and documents written up to 1980. Most are in English, Malay, and Indonesian, with some in French and Dutch. Many items are annotated descriptively.

This bibliography is based on the resources in the University of Malaya Library and other academic libraries in the area and is the most comprehensive source for information on its subject. It is arranged first by type of material (e.g., Biographies) and then by broad subject areas (e.g., Health and Welfare). There is an author index.

LATIN AMERICA

The major monographic source for materials on women in Latin America is Meri Knaster's *Women in Spanish America: an Annotated Bibliography from pre-Conquest to Contemporary Times* (G. K. Hall, 1977). As the title implies, only Spanish-speaking countries of Latin America are covered. In spite of this, this is still the most comprehensive monographic single source for Spanish- or English-language materials on women in that part of the world.*

In this work Ms. Knaster seeks to provide a guide to the literature on the subject of women in Spanish-speaking countries of Latin America. It is hoped that the book will stimulate and facilitate the development of scholarly research on women in the nineteen countries covered. This compilation describes over 2500 books, chapters, articles, pamphlets, dissertations, government documents and international agency publications. The documents covered include

*For resources on other Latin American countries, see the *Caribbean Resource Kit for Women*, discussed elsewhere in this article.

references to women from pre-Conquest to contemporary times. Publication dates range from the seventeenth century to 1974. Coverage is quite broad and seeks to be comprehensive rather than specialized—in terms of both subject matter and types of materials encompassed.

Organization is by fifteen broad subject areas, such as The Arts or Magic, Religion and Ritual or Law, and then by geographic area (Spanish America: General, Middle America, South America, Caribbean). Each subject section is preceded by scope notes explaining the rationale behind the choice or division of material in that section and suggesting cross-references or reference guides for additional information.

GENERAL

An extremely valuable recent contribution to the reference literature of women's studies is *Women's Periodicals and Newspapers from the 18th Century to 1981: a Union List of the Holdings of Madison, Wisconsin, Libraries* (G. K. Hall, 1982), edited by James P. Danky. This gives complete bibliographic and order information, annotations and locations for nearly 1,500 periodical and newspaper titles.

In addition to giving all this information so helpful to researchers and librarians, this work incorporates a variety of unusual, highly useful indexes. These indexes provide access by editor, subject (e.g., Afro-Americans, Asian-Americans, etc.) publisher, place of publication, catchword and subtitle, chronology, and foreign language from Arabic to Yiddish. The cutoff date for the union list is 1981.

This is the most comprehensive work on women's periodicals and newspapers, for research involving such publications in this country and many worldwide.

Women: a Bibliography of Bibliographies (G. K. Hall, 1980) by Pat Ballou is an extensive, selective, annotated bibliography of bibliographies on women-related topics published between 1970 and 1979. It includes non-English-language titles in a total compilation of well over five hundred items. Both separately published bibliographies and those issued as parts of books or as journal articles (from women's movement publications as well as scholarly works) appear here. Three divisions of citations form the basic outline of this work: a section by particular type or format (including dissertations and library catalogs); a section by geographic subjects (such as U.S. and Third World); a topical subjects section, arranged by general subject areas (e.g., Economics), which have very specific subdivisions (e.g., Employment reentry). There are cross references throughout and a personal name index.

Still one of the more useful bibliographies to date is Esther Stineman's *Women's Studies; a Recommended Core Bibliography* (Libraries Unlimited, 1979). This work indexes and annotates English-language in-print publications that support research on women. It is organized around traditional subject disciplines and autobiography, biography, diaries, memoirs and letters. Four different sub-categories of reference works are given: Audio-visual materials, Bibliographies, Biographical materials and General. There is also a separate section of basic works (classics) on the women's movement and feminist theory, plus a selective listing of periodicals. Excellent scope notes introduce each section in the book. Lucid annotations are evaluative as well as descriptive. Ms. Stineman also addresses the problem of total collection improvement.

Women's History Sources: a Guide to Archives and Manuscript Collections in the United States (Bowker, 1979), edited by Andrea Hinding, characterizes over 18,000 collections in nearly 1,600 repositories. Each characterization includes information on the title, type of record, dates, collection size, restrictions on access, repository name and description of contents.

The index volume accesses the collections by personal and corporate name, subject, geographic location. Material is also indexed by certain types such as oral histories, and there is geographic/subject access by state. This reference work also brings out materials on previously little known minority women whose attainments at state and local levels parallel those of women active on a national level. Obviously these volumes are a marked achievement for research on women.

A vital resource, *The Women's Annual: the Year in Review* (G. K. Hall, 1981-) chronicles the changes in the position of women in this country and current intellectual evolution in women's studies areas. Expanding upon the primary thrust of her now standard, highly praised *Women in America: a Guide to Books* (G. K. Hall. 1978) and its updated edition (University of Illinois Press, 1981), Barbara Haber, editor of *The Women's Annual,* saw the need for a yearly source-book of up-to-date information on women. In order to meet that need, she has assembled a group of appropriate experts whose writings and perspectives provide a structured report of current topics about women. The intention is to record accurately the progress and setbacks in the struggle to improve the position of American women and thereby to elucidate information on the *status quo* of contemporary history.

Each of the delineated subject areas (which include Third World women in the U.S.) is dealt with in two ways: describing the evolvement of social action on behalf of women and reporting the results of the latest women's studies scholarship. Each section consists of a substantial essay with a bibliography and list of further resources. An extremely important contribution to women's studies.

Representative Women's Collections*

UNITED STATES

WEST COAST LESBIAN COLLECTION
Box 23753
Oakland, CA 94623

IDA RUST MACPHERSON COLLECTION
Denison Library
Scripps College
Claremont, CA 91711

CENTER FOR THE STUDY EDUCATION AND ADVANCEMENT OF WOMEN
Univ of California
Berkeley, CA 94720

WOMEN'S RESOURCES AND RESEARCH CENTER
University of California
Davis, CA 95616

CENTER FOR WOMEN'S STUDIES AND SERVICES
San Diego, CA 92101

NATIONAL CLEARINGHOUSE ON MARITAL RAPE
Berkeley, CA 94708

HARTFORD FEMINIST LIBRARY
Hill Center
Hartford, CT 06105

MARGUERITE RAWALT RESOURCE CENTER
Business and Professional Women's Foundation
Washington, DC 20036

RESOURCE CENTER
International Center for Research on Women
Washington, DC 20036

BETHUNE MUSEUM-ARCHIVES
Washington, DC 20005

EQUITY POLICY CENTER
Washington, DC 20036

AMERICAN ASSOCIATION OF UNIVERSITY WOMEN
Washington, DC 20036

NAIAD PRESS
P.O. Box 10543
Tallahassee, FL 32302

WOMEN'S RESOURCE & RESEARCH CENTER
Spelman Coll
Atlanta, GA 30314

MIDWEST WOMEN'S HISTORICAL COLLECTION
University of Illinois
Chicago Circle, IL 60680

WOMEN'S COLLECTION
Northwestern Univ
Evanston, IL 60201

MIDWEST WOMEN'S HISTORICAL COLLECTION
Univ of Illinois
Chicago Circle, IL 60680

ALETTA JACOBS GERRITSEN COLL
Univ of Kansas
Lawrence, KA 66044

---

*See Editor's footnote, p. 145.

MAINE WOMEN WRITERS COLLECTION
Westbrook College
Portland, ME 04103

NEW ALEXANDRIA LESBIAN LIBRARY
Northampton, MA 01060

PINE MANOR JUNIOR COLL
Chestnut Hill, MA 02167

CHURCH AND WOMAN
Mugar Memorial Library
Boston Univ
Boston, MA 02215
Formed by Alma Lutz

GALATEA COLLECTION
Boston Public Library
Boston, MA 02117
Higginson Collection

ARTHUR & ELIZABETH SCHLESINGER LIBRARY ON THE HISTORY OF WOMEN IN AMERICA
Radcliffe College
Cambridge, MA 02138

UNIVERSITY OF LOWELL
Lowell, MA 01854

NURSING ARCHIVES
Mugar Memorial Library
Boston University
Boston, MA 02215

SOPHIA SMITH COLLECTION
Neilson Library
Smith College
Northampton, MA 01063

CENTER FOR CONTINUING EDUCATION OF WOMEN
University of Michigan
Ann Arbor, MI 48109
Check Jean Campbell

WOMEN'S MUSIC COLLECTION
Music Library
Univ of Michigan
Ann Arbor, MI 48109

WOMEN'S STUDIES LIBRARY
University of Michigan
Ann Arbor, MI 48109

KRESGE LIBRARY
Oakland Univ
Rochester, MI 48063

WOMEN'S MOVEMENT COLLECTION
Social Welfare Archives
Univ of Minnesota
Minneapolis, MN 55455

WOMAN COLLECTION
Coll of St. Catherine
St. Paul, MN 55116

WOMEN IN THE WEST
Univ of Nevada
Reno, NV 89507

WOMEN'S INFORMATION & REFERRAL SERVICE
Montclair Public Library
Montclair, NJ 07042

WOMEN'S ARCHIVES OF NEW JERSEY
New Jersey Historical Society
Newark, NJ 07104

HOLDEN COLLECTION
Firestone Library
Princeton Univ
Princeton, NJ 08540

REFERENCE COLL
Center for the American Woman and Politics
Eagleton Institute Rutgers Univ
New Brunswick, NJ 08901

INFORMATION SERVICES
Information Services
Women's Action Alliance
New York, NY 10017

SCHWIMMER-LLOYD COLLECTION
New York Public Library
New York, NY 10018

BIRDIE GOLDSMITH AST COLLECTION
Barnard College Women's Center
Barnard College
New York, NY 11027

NATIONAL BOARD OF THE YWCA
New York, NY 10022

OVERBURY COLLECTION
Barnard College
New York, NY 10027

LESBIAN HERSTORY ARCHIVES
New York, NY 10016

CATALYST LIBRARY
& AUDIOVISUAL CENTER
Catalyst
New York, NY 10022

INSTITUTE FOR WOMEN
AND WORK
Library
Cornell Univ/NYSSILR
New York, NY 10010
COMMENT: New Address

WOMEN'S COLLECTION
Jackson Library
Univ of North Carolina
Greensboro, NC 27412

AFRO-AMERICAN WOMEN'S
COLLECTION
Holgate Library
Bennett Coll
Greensboro, NC 27420

WOMEN'S STUDIES LIBRARY
University Libraries
Ohio State Univ
Columbus, OH 43210-1286

CENTER FOR THE STUDY OF
WOMEN IN SOCIETY
University of Oregon
Eugene, OR 97403

WOMEN IN MEDICINE
Florence A. Moore Medical Library
Medical College of Pennsylvania
Philadelphia, PA 19129

IDA JANE DACUS LIBRARY
Winthrop Coll
Rock Hill, SC 29733

THE WOMAN'S COLLECTION
Library
Texas Woman's Univ
Denton, TX 76204

WRITINGS ON VIRGINIA WOMEN
Lipscomb Library
Randolph Macon Women's Coll
Lynchburg, VA 24503

RESEARCH CENTER ON WOMEN
Alverno College
Milwaukee, WI 53215

CANADA

E.O.W. RESOURCE CENTRE
Office of Equal Opportunities
for Women
Ottawa, Ontario (Canada)

WOMEN'S MOVEMENT ARCHIVES
P.O. Box 928
Toronto, Ontario (Canada)

YORK YWCA WOMEN'S
COLLECTION
Founders College
York University
Downsview, Ontario (Canada)

LIBRARY
Univ of Waterloo
Waterloo, Ontario (Canada)

WOMEN'S EDUCATIONAL
RESOURCES
Ontario Institute for the Study
of Education
Toronto, Ontario (Canada)

WOMEN'S INFORMATION
& REFERRAL SERVICE/CENTRE
D'INFORMATION ET DE
REFERENCE POUR FEMMES
Montreal, Quebec (Canada)

CENTRE DE DOCUMENTATION
L'Institut Simone De Beauvoir De
L'Universite Concordia
Montreal, Quebec (Canada)

FOREIGN

CENTRO DE ESTUDIOS DE LA
MUJER
Buenos Aires, Argentina

IRENE GREENWOOD COLLECTION
Murdoch University Library
Murdoch University
Willeton, Australia

KVINFO
Royal Library
Copenhagen, Denmark

RESOURCE AND DOCUMENTATION CENTRE
African Training and Research Centre for Women
Addis Ababa, Ethiopia

BIBLIOTHEQUE MARGUERITE DURAND
Paris Municipal Library
Paris, France

EQUAL OPPORTUNITIES COMMISSION
Manchester, Great Britain

FAWCETT LIBRARY
City of London Polytechnic
London, Great Britain
Includes Bibliofem Project

FEMINIST ARCHIVE
Bath, Great Britain

WOMEN'S RESEARCH AND RESOURCE CENTRE
London, Great Britain

RIGHTS OF WOMEN BULLETIN
London, Great Britain
Legal Profession Women/Newsletter

KVENNASOGUSAFN ISLANDS
Library of the History of Icelandic Women
Reykjavik, Iceland

FEMINIST RESOURCE CENTRE
Bombay, India

RESEARCH UNIT ON WOMEN'S STUDIES
Women's University
Bombay, India

SAHELI
New Delhi, India

LIBRARY
Feminist Centre
Tel Aviv, Israel

WOMEN'S SUFFRAGE CENTER
Tokyo, Japan

RESEARCH & DOCUMENTATION CENTRE
Institute for Women's Studies in the Arab World (Beirut University College)
Beirut, Lebanon

CIDHAL (COMMUNICACION, INTERCAMBIA Y DESARROLLO HUMANO EN AMERICA LATINA
Cuernavaca, Mexico

INTERNATIONAL ARCHIVES FOR THE WOMEN'S MOVEMENT/ INTERNATIONAL ARCHIEF VOOR DE VROUWENBEWEGING (IAV)
Amsterdam, Netherlands

WOMEN'S HISTORY ARCHIVES
University Library
Goteborg University
Goteborg, Sweden